Seeing Light

An Enquiry into the Origins of Resurrection Faith

— PETER R. GANT —

Sacristy Press

Sacristy Press
PO Box 612, Durham, DH1 9HT

www.sacristy.co.uk

First published in 2019 by Sacristy Press, Durham

Copyright © Peter R. Gant 2019
The moral rights of the author have been asserted.

All rights reserved, no part of this publication may be reproduced or transmitted in any form or by any means, electronic, mechanical photocopying, documentary, film or in any other format without prior written permission of the publisher.

Scripture quotations, unless otherwise stated, are from the New Revised Standard Version Bible: Anglicized Edition, copyright © 1989, 1995 National Council of the Churches of Christ in the United States of America. Used by permission. All rights reserved worldwide.

Approximately 370 words are from *The Complete Dead Sea Scrolls in English* by Geza Vermes (London: Allen Lane, Penguin Press 1997) copyright © G. Vermes, 1962, 1965, 1968, 1975, 1995, 1997.

Other material is used by kind permission of the relevant copyright holders who are identified in the text or notes. Every reasonable effort has been made to trace the copyright holders of material reproduced in this book, but if any have been inadvertently overlooked the publisher would be glad to hear from them.

Sacristy Limited, registered in England & Wales, number 7565667

British Library Cataloguing-in-Publication Data
A catalogue record for the book is available from the British Library

Paperback ISBN 978-1-78959-047-0
Hardback ISBN 978-1-78959-050-0

To Robert Morgan

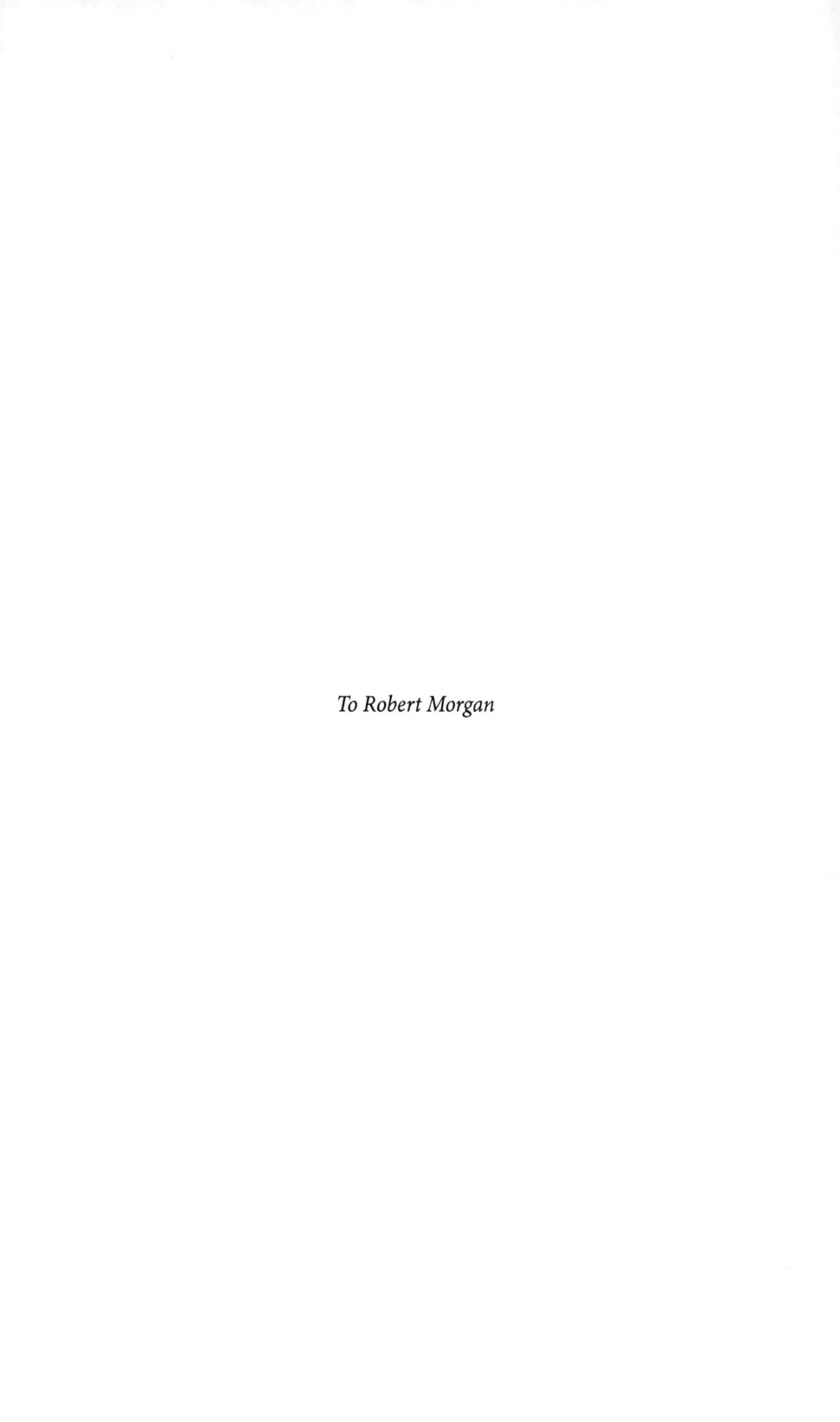

Foreword

Peter Gant, a serving priest of the Church of England in the Diocese of Guildford, returned to theological studies at Oxford after a career as a senior civil servant, hoping to answer a basic question he and some other thoughtful believers—and many half-believers—have found troubling. Granted that the truth of Jesus' resurrection was foundational for early Christian faith, and remains central to most Christian belief today, how is it to be understood? Or can what must ultimately remain (as a God-event) a mystery be understood at all? What understanding is appropriate for underpinning or elucidating Christian faith today? With a first degree in physics, Gant takes modern scientific views of the world for granted and does not expect to find divine interventions disturbing the course of nature. In particular, he considers the reversal of a decomposing corpse after death problematic, and therefore accounts of resurrection which see it as a resuscitation unpersuasive. The Fourth Evangelist tells the story of Lazarus as a sign or pointer to the resurrection of Jesus, but not as a parallel. The Lazarus of John 11 would, in due course, die again; Jesus, the revelation of God, was exalted and is now worshipped as living Lord and God. How can someone who shares this faith that "Christ is risen" make sense of that divine mystery in a different intellectual environment? Is it possible to affirm it as truth about God and about Jesus, not merely about the disciples' convictions?

In the modern world one natural way of approaching the question is by asking how the disciples came to their convictions, and what were the conditions for the possibility of any such faith. These must surely include the beliefs about God's past, present, and future interaction with the world that they, in their historical context, already accepted. Also presumably important was what drew them to Jesus in his ministry, and what they learned from him. The simple explanation of the emergence of their resurrection faith, that some of them found Jesus' tomb empty early on the Sunday morning following the crucifixion and saw visions or appearances of him which convinced them that God had vindicated his persecuted prophet can, at best, be only part of the answer. Since the eighteenth-century deists, especially Reimarus (1694–1768), it has been clear to some that the Easter narratives of the four canonical Gospels contain contradictions which make it hard for careful readers to take the reports of what followed the crucifixion of Jesus straightforwardly as reliable history. Nevertheless, the disciples were convinced that Jesus had been "resurrected" by God, and it is natural to ask about the causes or factual basis for their belief. This requires historical investigation, not only of the reports of what was experienced soon after the crucifixion, but also of the Jewish religious milieu in which their resurrection belief took shape. Peter Gant therefore offers a guide through the relevant early Jewish beliefs from the book of Daniel in the second century BC to the development of rabbinic Judaism following the destruction of Jerusalem and the Temple by the Romans in AD 70. But their beliefs must also have connected with their previous experience of the messianic prophet Jesus, whom they had followed, and their exposure to his teachings. In particular, his proclamation of God's coming "rule" or sovereignty ("kingdom") might be key to what they thought had now happened, especially if Jesus had given any clues about what he expected to happen to himself as the new age dawned.

This investigation runs deep into the territory of the critical study of the Gospels over the past 200 years, with its inevitable plethora of possible hypotheses. Because the Gospels were written in the light of subsequent resurrection faith, their accounts of Jesus' ministry and teaching can be expected to reflect something of those later beliefs, as well as some record of what Jesus said, did, and suffered. Unpicking them to determine what probably stemmed from Jesus' ministry, and what is indirect evidence for the first-generation Palestinian and Hellenistic churches, is therefore a precarious and uncertain enterprise. Gant is able to offer plausible reconstructions and so suggest possible explanations of the emergence of resurrection faith through a historical investigation which can never be demonstrated, but whose possibility does not prejudice the religious question of its theological truth. Without claiming more certainty than the fragmentary evidence will bear, and without any religious agenda beyond his own quest for a better understanding of his faith, he provides a model for other modern-minded Christians to keep the resurrection of Jesus at the centre of their faith. I hope his book will do for them what it has done for him.

Robert Morgan
Linacre College, Oxford

Acknowledgements

I would like to thank all those who have encouraged and assisted me in the researching and writing of this book, especially the late Alan Fairhurst, who read and commented on the initial drafts. It was Alan who brought about my introduction to Robert Morgan, under whose critical guidance and invaluable mentoring the text and the thinking behind it have evolved and improved out of all recognition. I must also thank my proof readers, especially eagle-eyed Dudley Green at Charterhouse and Denis Mulliner, lately of the Chapel Royal. My partner Judith Fox's input has been invaluable, not least in providing a modern Jewish perspective and in identifying passages which, without amendment, might have been unintelligible to non-Christian readers. Thanks also to Natalie Watson, my editor, and to Richard Hilton and his colleagues at Sacristy Press. Finally, much of this book was researched and written at Gladstone's Library at Hawarden, a little-known but outstanding national resource for readers and writers alike. So additional thanks to the Warden, Peter Fletcher, and his always helpful staff.

Note about quotations

Quotations from the Hebrew scriptures, the Apocrypha, and the New Testament are from the *New Revised Standard Version Bible: Anglicized Edition* (1995). Unless otherwise indicated, extracts from the *Pseudepigrapha* are from *The Old Testament Pseudepigrapha* (1983 and 1985), edited by James H. Charlesworth. Quotations from the Dead Sea Scrolls are from Geza Vermes's *The Complete Dead Sea Scrolls in English* (1997), unless otherwise attributed. Extracts from other sources are acknowledged in the endnotes.

Contents

Foreword iv
Acknowledgements vii
Note about quotations. viii

Chapter 1. The Problem Exposed 1
Pre-Enlightenment world views. 3
Enlightenment and post-Enlightenment historiography 9
The Jesus of History and the Jesus Christ of the Church 15
The way forward. 19

Chapter 2. Resurrection and Immortality 22
The Hellenization of Palestine and the Maccabean Insurgency. 23
Resurrection for reward or punishment 25
The democratization of resurrection. 27
The necessary vindication of the persecuted righteous man 31
Afterlife belief in 1 Enoch 34
Sheol as a temporary waiting place 39
Bypassing *Sheol* and going straight to heaven 41
The realized eschatology of the Qumran community. 44
The evidence of Josephus 46
Conclusion 48

Chapter 3. Angels and Angelomorphic Transformation 50
The location of heaven. 50
The angelic hierarchy. 51
The angel of Yhwh. 52
The Divine Name angel. 54
Angels with names. 56
The great angelic prince. 57

Parallel action in heaven and on earth 59
Personal angels 62
The angelomorphic transformation of humans 63
Transformation and heavenly ascent 68
Angelomorphic transformation after death 70
Dual identity: Michael–Melchizedek and Jacob–Israel 77
Dual identity: Enoch and the Son of Man 78
Conclusion 82

Chapter 4. The Heavenly Redeemer 83
One like a son of man 84
Heavenly redeemer figures in the Qumran Scrolls 87
The enthroned Son of Man in the Similitudes 89
"That man" in the Ezra Apocalypse 96
The man with a sceptre 98
The victorious warrior-messiah 99
The coming lord 101
A heavenly redeemer tradition? 102
Conclusion 103

Chapter 5. Jesus' Vision of the Future 104
The kingdom of God: traditional views 106
John the Baptist and the kingdom of God 109
John the Baptist and Jesus 112
Jesus' afterlife beliefs 115
Jesus and the kingdom of God 117
The Son of Man sayings 121
Jesus and the coming Son of Man 127
The kingdom of God and the Son of Man traditions 129
Conclusion 131

Chapter 6. Estimations of Jesus 132
Popular eschatological expectations 133
The Anointed One 135
The Son of God 137
The Lord 143

An eschatological prophet. 146
A specific person 149
The coming Son of Man 154
Partner to a heavenly being. 158
An angelomorphic being. 162
Conclusion 165

Chapter 7. The Earliest Resurrection Testimony. 167
Resurrection formulae. 167
Christological hymns. 171
The invocation or acclamation of Jesus as Lord. 178
The earliest resurrection-appearances tradition 180
Resurrection "on the third day". 183
Lack of reference to the women. 186
Paul's revelation 188
Physical or spiritual resurrection?. 191
The relationship between exaltation and resurrection 198
Conclusion 199

Chapter 8. Resurrection Belief: Twenty Years On. 201
Scriptural exegesis 202
Resurrection as the inauguration of the new age. 207
Resurrection and *parousia* 212
Resurrection and the Spirit of God 217
Resurrection and atonement. 222
Conclusion 229

Chapter 9. Resurrection Belief: Later Narratives and Stories 231
The empty tomb narratives in the Gospels. 232
The historicity of the empty-tomb tradition. 236
The appearance stories of the Gospels. 239
The significance of the appearance stories 246
Conclusion 251

Chapter 10. The Resurrection as History: What Actually Happened 253
Events... 253
Understandings... 261
Implications.. 263
Conclusion 266

Chapter 11. The Resurrection as Interpretation and Revelation . 269
Reactions to critical-historical scholarship...................... 270
Theological language 275
Events and meaning... 280
Resurrection as revelation.................................... 284
Conclusion 287

Suggested Further Reading.................................. 290
Notes 299

CHAPTER 1

The Problem Exposed

> "I'm just one hundred and one, five months and a day," said the White Queen.
> "I can't believe *that*!" said Alice ... "One *can't* believe impossible things."
> "Can't you?" the Queen said in a pitying tone. "I daresay you haven't had much practice. When I was your age, I always did it for half-an-hour a day. Why, sometimes I've believed as many as six impossible things before breakfast!"
>
> *Lewis Carroll,* Alice Through the Looking Glass

One reason why many people have difficulty, although possibly sympathetic to what they understand to be the values and moral teaching of Jesus, in accepting Christian doctrine is that they, like Lewis Carroll's Alice, feel that they are being asked to believe impossible things.

The intention of this book is to address this problem head-on. At the heart of the Christian faith there is the assertion that God raised Jesus from the dead. This assertion is deeply embedded in the New Testament. It is summarized in the Church's creeds and is widely held to be normative and indispensable. Given the centrality of resurrection faith, most Christians want to be able to say a clear "Yes" to the sceptic who challenges them with the question, "Do you really believe that God raised Jesus from the dead?" But some of us find this difficult. Others even feel obliged to say, "No, I don't", because the post-Enlightenment scientific world view to which they are also committed has no place for the idea of divine intervention interrupting and reversing the natural order. And somewhere in between the extremes of confident affirmation and outright denial there are those, including the author, who believe that it is possible to affirm the resurrection with integrity, but only if we are allowed to explain what this affirmation means and how it can be compatible both with a modern view of reality and also with the very earliest Christian traditions. In addition, although fully committed to a modern scientific world view, we want to point out that modern science and philosophy have anyway moved on far beyond simple, reductionist scientism.

The problem is that the sceptic's question is deceptive in its apparent simplicity. It goes beyond history into the realm of theology or "God-talk". In speaking of God, believers and unbelievers alike are entering territory of whose complexity few of them are aware. What sounds like a simple historical question referring to a specific historical person turns out to be nothing of the sort. Christian theological claims impinge on history, but they use language in a variety of different ways. To affirm or deny the resurrection of Jesus it is necessary to be clear what is and is not meant. Over the years, the resurrection of Jesus has been understood in different ways, not all of which are legitimate. For example, it is quite commonly supposed that resurrection means the resuscitation of the dead Jesus; that is, that after his death Jesus was restored to life in a normally functioning human body, much as a crashed car might be repaired and put back on the road. As we shall see, this is not what the New Testament texts say about Jesus (in contrast to Lazarus). The belief that the resurrection of Jesus involved the restoration or resuscitation of his dead body to its former state of physicality was never part of the earliest tradition, nor has it ever been normative Christian doctrine. Likewise, there are various different understandings concerning the action of God in history. Christians who reject the idea of God delivering messages to humankind by miraculously intervening and overturning the natural order have an obligation to explain how they believe that knowledge of God *is* disclosed to humans. This means exploring the ways in which meaning may be located in historical events and the ways in which revelation might be delivered through the perception of meaning attaching to historical events. If asked why we have to extend and complicate the discussion in this way, we reply that the question we are addressing involves both history and theology, and we must be allowed to reply in the same vein.

Authors owe their readers some indication of their working assumptions. As a former physicist, this author subscribes to a world view that discounts the idea of divine interference in natural, historical processes. At the same time, as someone now engaged in the field of New Testament studies and theology, he celebrates the achievements of modern critical-historical biblical scholarship and admires the thoroughness and integrity of New Testament historians and theologians. In terms of philosophy, he would describe himself as a common-sense critical realist; that is, as someone who believes that there are realities independent of our perception of them, but that objectivity is something that has to be worked for. And yet, as a Christian he believes that there is more to the matter of Christian origins than either scientists can measure or historians can describe. Specifically, he believes there is something significant and rational to be said about the action of God in connection with Jesus and the emergence of resurrection faith—something over and above the conclusions arrived at by the application of critical-historical method, which can never speak explicitly and normatively about God. It follows that if Christians are to provide clear and convincing answers to the questions posed by secularists, they need urgently to find a way of understanding and affirming resurrection faith that is compatible with modern scientific and critical-historical methods and assumptions, that allows for the possibility of a revelation of God in and through history, and that is congruent with the beliefs of Jesus' followers as we discover them embedded in the very earliest texts and traditions, particularly those which antedate the formation of the Gospels.

Pre-Enlightenment world views

The critical scrutiny of traditional Christian beliefs is not a new phenomenon. It has its immediate origins in eighteenth-century Enlightenment values and thinking, and in the somewhat earlier emergence of science based on experimental observation, but as far back as the seventeenth century, radical new understandings concerning nature and humanity's relationship to the created order were already challenging established thinking. Increasingly, explanations of natural phenomena were being based on theory and reasoning allied to accurate experimental observation, and on the establishment of mathematical relationships between data, rather than on appeals to revelation and divine governance.

Implicit in this combination of observation, theory, and mathematics—as exemplified, for example, in Galileo's heliocentric astronomy and in Newtonian physics—was a changed understanding of the status and nature of humankind. In the mediaeval world view, men and women had been regarded as the pinnacle of all created being. For the new science of the seventeenth century this framework and its implications were no longer felt to be adequate. An intellectual transition was under way. Although humans had not yet been fully assimilated into the natural realm, they were already being gradually displaced from their former position of cosmic significance based on the twin assumptions of hierarchical supremacy and universal centrality.

Likewise, the role of God in relation to creation was being redefined. If, as it increasingly appeared, the world functioned as a law-abiding machine, one had to ask how God acts in relation to this law-abiding world. One might allow that God initially created the machine and set it in motion. One might also allow that God is always invisibly holding creation in being. One might go even further and allow that God occasionally intervenes to correct and adjust natural processes in line with his particular providential intentions. But otherwise, it seemed, God's role in relation to nature was simply to sit back and observe what he had set in motion. Latent in the emergent seventeenth-century scientific world view was a new metaphysic potentially capable of displacing God altogether and explaining the whole of reality by means of scientific concepts. The issue of whether there ever had been, or ever could be, such a thing as a miracle in the form of a specific, local, divine intervention, one of the issues then held to be pivotal to Christian belief and especially to belief in the resurrection of Jesus, was not yet centre stage. But it was waiting in the wings.

Throughout the eighteenth century, the new science continued to develop in such a way as eventually to affect and decisively influence virtually every sphere of Enlightenment thought and activity. There was never any set Enlightenment scientific manifesto or agenda, because the Enlightenment was above all a philosophical and political mood or mindset rather than a movement. Nevertheless, there emerged as hallmarks of Enlightenment thinking carried over into the realm of science:

- first, the appeal to reason as man's defining characteristic and the assumption of human autonomy and freedom to criticize existing understandings and traditions;
- second, the understanding of nature as a self-sufficient, impersonal mechanism;
- and third, epistemological and metaphysical reductionism, that is, the belief that natural phenomena are governed by scientific laws, and that reality is constituted by its smallest components.

An example of the new scientific paradigm was the work of Pierre-Simon, marquis de Laplace (1749–1827), who visualized reality in terms of matter in motion. For Laplace, reality was a mechanical, deterministic system of cause and effect. It was governed in its entirety by inflexible and invariant scientific laws. The whole of nature and the entire universe operated as a self-sufficient system requiring no external intervention. When Napoleon asked Laplace why he made no mention of God in his writings, Laplace memorably replied that, so far as he was concerned, God was an unnecessary hypothesis. Where there were gaps in scientific understanding, it was taken for granted that in due course scientific research would supply the missing answers. There was therefore no need for recourse to explanations predicated on belief in a divine being or miraculous divine intervention.

From the time of Locke onwards the Enlightenment had been characterized by the acceptance of reason as the primary source of legitimacy, but radical atheism such as that of Laplace was not widespread, nor were Enlightenment thinkers universally or generally hostile to religion. There was much criticism and questioning of religious institutions and authorities, but there was little outright opposition to religious belief as such. Insofar as there was a wider or more general agenda, it was principally a concern—arising out of the memory of the horrors of the Thirty Years' War (1618–1648)—to ensure that religious controversy never again spilled over into politics. There was therefore little general rejection of the concept of a revealed religion and the associated possibility of miraculous divine intervention, although the tendency in religious thought was increasingly away from theism and towards deism and atheism. Nevertheless, full-blown atheism was rare and was generally regarded as potentially politically subversive. Even so, implicit in the assertion of the primacy of human reason and in the scientific understanding of the universe as a self-sustaining mechanism are fundamental questions concerning the nature of human existence. Who are we, these rational observers of the external world? What are our origins, and how are we related to the natural order upon which we entirely depend, and yet nevertheless observe as something distinct from ourselves?

By the end of the eighteenth century, the scientific world view was poised to undergo further radical change. Although the science-based technologies and industries were expanding exponentially and appeared to be carrying all before them, in the fields of geology and biology new ideas were also emerging. Sir Charles Lyell's *Principles of Geology* (1830–1833) was predicated on the axiom that the laws of nature are constant across time and space. Lyell demonstrated clearly how slow, steady, and apparently minor natural processes had acted over extended periods of time in such a way as to bring about significant changes in the structure of the earth's crust and in the natural environment. The idea of gradual natural processes bringing about major change over extended periods of time had obvious implications for naturalists, who had for some time been trying to reconcile the apparent stability of biological forms with the observed diversification of the species, both in nature and in the fossil records. From the later eighteenth century and onwards into the nineteenth, various writers published theories concerning natural organic change and the adaptation of species to their environment. Eventually Charles Darwin (1809–1882) and Alfred Russel Wallace (1823–1913) effectively solved the problem by independently proposing that the mechanism underlying evolution was that of natural selection by survival of the fittest in response to environmental pressures.

Although Darwin did not directly address the question of human evolution in his 1859 book, *On the Origin of Species by Means of Natural*

Selection, the implications were evident from the outset. His theory of natural selection by the survival of the fittest directly contradicted the traditional argument from design for the existence of God, which William Paley had popularized using the well-known "watchmaker analogy". Moreover, for Darwin, nature was a dynamic process. This meant that human beings, as an integral part of the natural process, must be amenable to examination and analysis in terms of categories derived from the biological sciences. In his 1871 book, *The Descent of Man*, Darwin therefore went on to spell out the implications of evolutionary theory for human as well as for animal origins. Hitherto, it had been widely assumed that men and women had a unique status, either by virtue of their possession of an immortal soul, or for some other unspecified reason. It was taken for granted that some element or aspect of a human being existed outside and apart from nature. Darwin himself did not force the issue, but it was already apparent that he was effectively closing the gap between human and animal. To many Christians, Darwin therefore appeared simultaneously to be undermining the uniqueness of human beings, challenging the authority of scripture, and demolishing the basis of ethics.

Towards the end of the nineteenth century and in the early decades of the twentieth, the triumph of the physical and life sciences appeared to be complete. All the basic understandings were in place, or so it was widely assumed. The new scientific world view was firmly established. Step by step the laws of nature were being unravelled, and all that remained was a matter of filling in the gaps. Science had triumphed, and it had triumphed because it was objective. That is, it was based on sense-data acquired by painstaking observation, and it had no interest in abstract speculations incapable of verification by scientific methods. Accordingly, it followed—and this was tacitly agreed by many on both sides of the divide—that there could be no legitimate point of contact between science and theology. Science and theology belonged to quite different realms of human experience. An uneasy truce in the warfare between science and religion ensued.

The rejoicing over the triumph of science proved to be premature. During the twentieth century, there was another seismic shift in the scientific world view. Most especially, the concept of the detached, objective observer was challenged and eventually had to be abandoned. It is now accepted that, as observers and scientists, we can never have access to the essential nature of things. The structure of reality has proved to be altogether more complex than was formerly supposed, and the naïve realism implicit in the theory of the detached observer is no longer sustainable. Einstein's theories of relativity have brought into relationship with each other and with the observer the quantities of mass, space, and time, entities previously thought to be fundamental, stand-alone aspects of reality. Quantum theory and indeterminacy have also undermined the concept of the detached, autonomous observer, it now being apparent that the act of observation necessarily changes both the observer and that which is observed. In effect, we now see that scientific knowledge arises out of an interactive relationship between the observer and the observed, and that there is no such thing as objective knowledge of the essential nature of reality. Knowledge is reduced to statements concerning our relationship with that which is known.

More recently it has become apparent that yet another fundamental world view change may be in the offing. In 1957, the American physicist Hugh Everett III proposed a novel interpretation of quantum theory. Initially Everett's work attracted little attention, but as subsequently developed by Bryce DeWitt, John Archibald Wheeler, and others, it led to what is now called the "many-worlds" interpretation of quantum physics. The possibility that reality as a whole may be functioning as a single quantized entity, or as one gigantic, quantized "molecule", has implications for understanding the nature of time. It also fuels contemporary speculations about possible multiple realities or "multiverses". Although regarded by many as inherently unverifiable, the "many-worlds" interpretation of quantum theory has its supporters. There is also now experimental evidence, not available to Everett, indicating that systems many orders of magnitude greater than single particles or molecules (systems comprising 10^{16} atoms or more) can indeed function as single, quantum-entangled entities. To this extent, theory and experiment seem to be suggesting that reality should be conceptualized in terms of incremental transitions between quantum states rather than as matter in motion. If the modern scientific world view does shift significantly in this direction, there will be major implications for our understanding of the nature of the historical process.

Enlightenment and post-Enlightenment historiography

We now need to backtrack slightly. One of the principal features of Enlightenment thinking on the Continent was its commitment to rationalism, and in Britain to empirical investigation. This applied in the field of history as much as it did in the field of the natural sciences. In pre-Enlightenment Christian Europe, insofar as there was a philosophy of history over and above the chronicling of past events, thinking was dominated by the concept of teleology, the explicit or implicit assumption that events were being guided by purpose and directed towards a goal, usually (but not necessarily) conceived of as divinely ordained. Historiography had therefore been primarily descriptive, but within the framework of a Christian teleology. Or, to put it another way, history was regarded as the arena within which God was working his purposes out. It now appeared that the search for meaning or purpose in history ought to be based not on teleological assumptions about direction, purpose, and ends, but on rational and empirical enquiry akin to that which had proved so effective in the natural sciences. Accordingly, in the second half of the eighteenth century, and increasingly in the nineteenth century, there emerged in France, Germany, and England a new critical-historical science, whose hallmark was a commitment to the objective examination and questioning of sources (hence the term "critical-historical" science). Allied to this was the assumption that historical events are part of an ongoing process; that is to say, genuinely historical events always have antecedents (or causes) and sequents (or after-effects).

One immediate consequence of this assumption is that miracles, as supposed events without causes located within the historical process, cannot qualify to be regarded as historical events. David Hume (1711–1776) had already gone further in his own thinking by dismantling altogether the idea of necessary connection between events. Hume substituted instead the concept of inference based on experience and evidence. In the case of miracles this was even more disturbing for traditional religious thinkers, because Hume argued that the evidence for a miracle must always be insufficient. By definition, miracles are single events occurring at particular times and places. It follows that the evidence for a supposed miracle will always be outweighed by the evidence for the law of which the miracle is supposed to be a transgression:

> The plain consequence is (and 'tis a general maxim worthy of our attention), "That no testimony is sufficient to establish a miracle, unless the testimony be of such a kind, that its falsehood would be more miraculous, than the fact, which it endeavours to establish; and even in that case, there is a mutual destruction of arguments, and the superior only gives us an assurance suitable to that degree of force, which remains, after deducting the inferior."
>
> *An Enquiry Concerning Human Understanding*[1]

For many Christians the application of critical-historical science to the examination of Christian origins was deeply disturbing. In the 1770s, the Enlightenment philosopher Gotthold Ephraim Lessing (1729–1781) published a series of extracts by an author whose identity, according to Lessing, was unknown. (It was not until some years later that it became known that the author was Hermann Samuel Reimarus (1694–1768), a rationalist philosopher and Deist physico-theologian, who had been a professor of Oriental languages at the élite *Gymnasium* in Hamburg.) The essays published by Lessing, known as the *Wolfenbüttel Fragments*, were extracted from Reimarus's *Apologie*, an unpublished manuscript in which he had set out his private views on religion. The full text of the *Apologie* (using a late manuscript different from that used by Lessing) was not published until 1972. The seventh *Wolfenbüttel Fragment* caused a sensation: Reimarus argued that the key criteria by means of which the truth or falsity of historical testimony should be established were internal consistency, coherence, and freedom from contradiction. Applying these criteria to the New Testament, he drew attention to the way in which the Gospel accounts of the message and intention of Jesus are influenced and coloured by the beliefs and concerns of the early Church. Reimarus also examined the historical evidence for the resurrection of Jesus, subjecting the accounts of the resurrection in the four Gospels and the other New Testament resurrection traditions to concise, accurate, and deadly critical analysis. Exposing contradiction after contradiction in the biblical testimony, he then issued the following challenge:

> Reader, you who are conscientious and honest, tell me before God, could you accept as unanimous and sincere this testimony concerning so important a matter that contradicts itself so often and so obviously in respect to person, time, place, manner, intent, word [and] story?[2]

This challenge has to be set against the background of Reimarus's belief that the miracles reported in scripture, including the supposed miracle of the resurrection, are not susceptible of proof, and are incapable of establishing even one basic article of faith. As to how and why this confused and improbable biblical testimony had come about, Reimarus advanced the theory that the reports of the resurrection of Jesus were a deliberate and calculated fabrication on the part of the apostles, who had secretly spirited away and hidden the corpse of Jesus. The intention of the apostles was to secure for themselves, by means of this fraud, the wealth and power which they believed they had been promised by Jesus. This wealth and power, they assumed, would accrue to them by virtue of the leadership they would exercise in the coming Messianic kingdom.

The theory that the apostles must have stolen and disposed of the body of Jesus, and then conspired fraudulently to create the legend of his resurrection, depends on the incorrect assumption that the dubious story in the Gospel of Matthew concerning the guard at Jesus' tomb was written by an apostle. Nevertheless, Reimarus's analysis of the texts and, in particular, his highlighting of the inconsistencies and lack of coherence in the appearance stories and the resurrection narratives, was thorough, detailed, and perceptive. Many of his questions still have the capacity to trouble traditional Christian believers today.

Nor was it just a matter of discrepancies in the testimony adduced in support of the claimed miracle of the resurrection. At the heart of Reimarus's historical analysis of the traditions concerning the resurrection of Jesus there is the vexed question of the relationship between faith and history. By applying purely historical techniques to the traditions enshrined in the Gospels, and by everywhere exposing the tensions between the figure of the historical Jesus and that of the Jesus Christ of the Church, Reimarus was touching a raw nerve. The claim that God acts in history seems to imply that at least one particular historical event must be an example of such action. But how is that event ever to be known with certainty when the outcome of historical enquiry is always relative rather than absolute certainty? Lessing summarized this problem neatly when he spoke of there being an ugly, broad ditch between the contingent truths of history and the necessary truths of reason.

Albert Schweitzer memorably described Reimarus's work as a magnificent overture in which are announced all the motifs of the future historical treatment of the life of Jesus. Reimarus stimulated Lessing, but he scarcely influenced thinking concerning the relationship between the history of Christian origins and the truth of Christian theology. His significance lies in his non-supernaturalist, historical account of Christian origins. He anticipated many of the insights of later twentieth-century research and identified issues of which some are still problematic today.

In respect of critical-historical investigation of the Gospels, David Friedrich Strauss (1808–1874) may be regarded as Reimarus's greatest successor. In his massively influential book *Das Leben Jesu, kritisch bearbeitet* ("The Life of Jesus Critically Examined"), published in 1835, Strauss identified various different types of "mythical" material. He applied to the Gospels as a whole what he called the "mythical" mode of interpretation, an approach which had previously been applied only to Greek literature, to the Hebrew scriptures, and to the beginnings and ends of the Gospel narratives. Strauss expressed little interest in establishing or investigating the residue of historical data he accepted in the Gospels. Although he saw Jesus as a human figure about whom much could be known, his main interest was in translating or reinterpreting the "mythical" material in the Gospels into the Hegelian idea of the unity of the human and the divine, and finally in re-applying this concept to the human race rather than to the individual Jesus.

Strauss's treatment of the traditions concerning the resurrection of Jesus illustrates his technique. Like Reimarus, he homes in on the numerous inconsistencies and divergences in the evangelists' accounts of the discovery of the empty tomb and the subsequent appearances of the risen Christ. He discusses—and dismisses as unconvincing –various attempts to harmonize the conflicting data. Emphasizing the lack of any credible, independent witnesses, and stressing the need to escape from "the magic circle of the supernatural", he concludes that the resurrection traditions must be understood as "mythical". That is, they are unhistorical. Nevertheless, in this particular instance, Strauss offers his own alternative historical hypothesis. He suggests that the emergence of resurrection belief was driven by psychological necessity. After the crucifixion of Jesus, the disciples found themselves unable to reconcile the brutal reality of Jesus' unexpected death with the messianic ideals to which they were so fervently committed. In present-day terminology, they experienced extreme psychological dissonance.

Somehow this dissonance had to be resolved. Initially the disciples fled from Jerusalem to save their lives, but in due course they reassembled in Galilee. There they began to examine the Hebrew scriptures, seeking out passages which might support the idea of a suffering and dying Messiah, a concept hitherto entirely foreign to their thinking. After a period of reflection, they came to believe that Jesus' death served God's purpose and was therefore not the disaster it appeared to be. They became convinced that Christ was alive and invisibly present with them. A heightened sense of this presence of the living Christ led eventually, when their mental state had become sufficiently excited, to self-generated, subjective visions of the risen Christ. Finally, under the influence of certain key texts in the Hebrew scriptures, the disciples arrived at the conclusion that the body of Jesus could not have remained in the grave where it had first been placed, but must have been raised by God on the third day after his death. At the same time, said Strauss, the tradition (under the influence of pious enthusiasm) became embellished with additional details, until finally we arrive at the received Gospel texts.

Strauss's principal strength is the thoroughness with which he applies his chosen method of analysis to the Gospels taken as a whole. Reimarus's assumption that conflicting testimony had no historical value ruled out of court a whole swathe of potentially important evidence. Strauss also shook traditional beliefs about the Bible's reliability. By his questioning of the dependence of Christianity on historical testimony, he also reignited the questions about Christian origins and the nature and foundations of

Christian faith. It was through Strauss that historical criticism entered the mainstream of New Testament studies. His insistence that the emergence of resurrection faith is an after-effect or response to the totality of the life of Jesus is especially significant. Although supernaturalist Christians would continue to maintain that the resurrection involved some form of miraculous divine intervention, others would henceforth follow Strauss in arguing that the resurrection visions of the risen Christ were the product rather than the basis of faith. There would also be those who would argue that the relationship between the visions and historical memories of Jesus is more complex than Strauss supposed.

It was Ferdinand Christian Baur (1792–1860), Strauss's one-time teacher, rather than Strauss himself who most clearly articulated the idea of a historical theology and pioneered the critical-historical investigation of primitive Christianity. Following Hegel, Baur had no doubt that faith must have a proper object transcending the individual's religious consciousness. He was convinced that God's self-mediation is historical, not in the form of sudden miraculous intervention, but in the form of revelation mediated through historical process. Unlike Hegel, he believed that obtaining access to the historical Jesus and subsequent historical developments is essential, and that this implies a wholehearted commitment to the critical-historical analysis of all the available sources. Baur was critical of Strauss's failure to engage in critical analysis of the aims of the Gospel texts themselves before talking about the history they report. He was also critical of Strauss for discounting the testimony of the texts simply on account of their evident inconsistencies and contradictions. Baur reaffirmed the anti-supernaturalism of Reimarus and Strauss, asserting unequivocally that miracles, as events lacking historical causes, must necessarily be beyond the scope of historical investigation. Of the resurrection of Jesus, Baur said:

> The question as to the nature and reality of the resurrection lies outside the sphere of historical enquiry. History must be content with the simple fact, that in the faith of the disciples the resurrection of Jesus came to be regarded as a solid and unquestionable fact. It was in this faith that Christianity acquired a firm base for its historical development. What history requires

as the necessary antecedent for all that is to follow, is not so much the fact of the resurrection of Jesus, as the belief that it was a fact.[3]

For Baur, the primary historical datum was resurrection faith, because historical science can only be concerned with events that have both historical causes and historical outcomes. Nevertheless, whilst rejecting the idea of God miraculously intruding himself into history, Baur also opposed the kind of rationalism which dissolves history into a mere sequence of disconnected moments. He regarded history as a process of significant change within overall continuity. Therefore, although accepting Enlightenment anti-supernaturalism, Baur saw the historian's task as being to penetrate the inner significance and meaning of particular events. He set the Gospels, as the primary testimony to the historical Jesus, in the mainstream of the development of early Christian thought, focusing on the ways in which each of the different Gospel compilers had shaped and modified material to give expression to his own particular understanding or "tendency". Baur contributed significantly to the historical-critical study of Christianity, which liberal historical theologians have since carried forward in their ongoing quest for the Jesus of history and the origins of Christian belief.

The Jesus of History and the Jesus Christ of the Church

The liberal quest for the historical Jesus proved less successful than its protagonists expected. One might have supposed that as the critical-historical method was progressively developed and refined, and as successive generations of scholars built on the foundations laid by their predecessors, a more and more accurate picture of the historical Jesus would gradually have emerged. If anything, the outcome was almost the opposite. It was not that the Jesus of history was collapsing and vanishing under the pressure of hostile interrogation. For the most part, the critical questioning was neutral, expert, and intended only to elicit the truth. The problem was that the straightforward picture of the historical Jesus which scholars had sought to discover steadfastly refused to come into focus. Even when supported by a much-improved understanding of Jesus'

Jewish context, decades of intensive Jesus research seemed only to yield more and more possibilities, with fewer and fewer certainties.

Reviewing the disappointing outcome of the previous generation's critical-historical study of the life of Jesus, Albert Schweitzer (1875-1965) wrote:

> The Jesus of Nazareth who came forward publicly as the Messiah, who preached the ethic of the kingdom of God, who founded the kingdom of heaven upon earth and died to give his work its final consecration, never had any existence. He is a figure designed by rationalism, endowed with life by liberalism, and clothed by modern theology in an historical garb. This image has not been destroyed from without, it has fallen to pieces, cleft and disintegrated by the concrete historical problems which came to the surface one after another, and . . . refused to be planed down . . . and were no sooner covered over than they appeared again in a new form.[4]

Schweitzer was not saying that there is no historical way back through the Gospels to the historical Jesus. Indeed, he had his own historical interpretation of Jesus as a deluded apocalyptic fanatic. What he was saying is that the eighteenth- and nineteenth-century liberal critical historians' depictions of the human Jesus reflected their own predilections. Other scholars, from Bruno Bauer (1809-1882) to William Wrede (1859-1906), were even more radical than Schweitzer in their scepticism. They argued that much of the Gospel narrative, formerly accepted as basically historical, reflects not history but rather the theological interests and understandings of the early Christian community. This scepticism focused attention on a new problem. If the Jesus of history could not be recovered, the liberal theologians' agenda (which was to rebase Christian faith on the Jesus of history rather than the Christ of the Church) was fatally undermined.

Around 1920, the attack on liberal life-of-Jesus research was sharpened by the claim of some critics that the earliest pre-Gospel Christian traditions contain only vestigial traces of the historical Jesus. First and foremost, it was claimed, the Jesus of the New Testament is the post-Easter community's living Lord. As such he is an immortal, spiritual being. He is Christ, the Lord, Son of God, and Son of Man. He rose from the dead and is now supremely exalted in heaven, where he has been given a name that is above every name; he is seated at God's right hand, crowned with glory. As a heavenly being the risen Christ outranks all angels, princes, and heavenly powers. He was pre-existent—that is, he had his being prior to the creation of heaven and earth—and he will continue to exist, even when the earth and the heavens have passed away. Directly and indirectly, it was argued, these exalted christological convictions exercised a powerful retroactive influence on the formation of the tradition and on the writing of the Gospels. They directly influenced each individual author's depiction of Jesus, his purpose, and his intentions. They indirectly exercised a controlling influence on the communal remembrance of Jesus. In effect, they filtered the tradition, removing and suppressing what were assumed to be superfluous details, and retaining for onward transmission only material assumed to be relevant to the community's needs or in some way supportive of its understandings. They also provided a rationale for the modification of existing, probably authentic sayings of Jesus, and for the creation and retrojection into the tradition of additional sayings reflecting these later christological insights.

In the light of these developments, we have to ask how a human Jesus, about whom little can be known with certainty, is to be reconciled with the earliest Christians' convictions concerning the exalted person and functions of the heavenly Jesus Christ. Can faith in this exalted Christ ever be securely and safely grounded in historical uncertainty? These questions have been addressed in a variety of different ways, but essentially there are two basic approaches. The first is to cut the Gordian knot by permitting—implicitly or explicitly—some measure of disconnection of Christian faith from history. In the twentieth century, Karl Barth (1886–1968) and Rudolf Bultmann (1884–1976) have both, in different ways, adopted this approach. Detaching Christian theology from dependence on Jesus as reconstructed by historians makes it possible for the primary datum for faith to be located either in personal or collective religious experience, and/or in the Jesus Christ of faith as encountered in the present-day proclamation of the Church, or in scripture. The second approach is to reject the assumption that religious truth is truth of a different kind and order from historical truth, and to accept the provisionality of all the results of rational enquiry. Accepting that historical enquiry into Christian origins can yield only provisional outcomes need not, then, necessarily invalidate our seeking to bridge the gap between the historical Jesus and the Jesus Christ of the Church both at the historical and the theological levels.

The suggestion that the liberals' search for the Jesus of history has ended in failure must therefore be challenged. Admittedly, few historically reliable biographical details concerning Jesus are to be found in the Gospels, but that is by no means the end of the matter. We have in the Gospels some credible echoes of the teaching of Jesus, especially in his parables. We can see the main thrust of his message concerning the coming and already-inaugurated kingdom of God. We can observe Jesus' attitude of directness, the immediacy of the authority which he displayed in his various encounters and in his clear assertion of human responsibility in the face of God's coming judgement. And we can be confident about Jesus' absolute commitment to what he believed to be the purposes of God. No doubt some of the substance and many of the details of this material have been retrojected into the Jesus tradition by the primitive Christian community. Nevertheless, we can be reasonably confident that we are hearing a voice that is clearly individual and substantially authentic. We also have the advantage of now being able to access a great deal of new information about Second Temple Judaism. Too often in the past, Christians have sought to emphasize the discontinuity between Jesus and Judaism. Today we are more sensitive to the Jewishness of Jesus. We recognize that both the Jesus of history and the theological understandings clustered around the figure of the heavenly Jesus Christ of the Church must be interpreted within the context of first-century Judaism and Hellenism.

The way forward

The starting point must be the one certain historical fact, that is, the death of Jesus. When Jesus was suddenly and unexpectedly killed, his followers, who had forsaken everything to follow him during his ministry, had somehow to make sense of the radically changed situation in which they now found themselves. They had shared Jesus' belief in the imminently coming kingdom of God. They had also shared (perhaps without fully understanding) his belief that he himself was the anticipatory point of presence, here and now, of the imminently coming kingdom. Their experience of Jesus during his lifetime—his teaching, his personality, his ministry, and his mission—had now to be reconciled with the shocking reality of his unexpected death.

First and foremost, they must have wondered what had happened to Jesus himself. Jesus had died and his body had been buried, but where was Jesus himself, and what was now the future of his "project".

In formulating answers to these urgent questions, Jesus' followers were able to draw on a wide variety of existing Second Temple afterlife beliefs. These included belief in heaven, earth and *Sheol*, the underworld depository of the dead; the belief that the boundary between heaven and earth was sometimes porous; the belief that humans might be transformed into angels and vice versa; and the strange concept of action on earth proceeding in parallel with equivalent action in heaven. There is evidence that it was also believed that there might be special privileges, after death, for exceptionally important and heroic figures. For example, it was believed that faithful martyrs might bypass *Sheol* and go directly to heaven, and/or that God would vindicate by exaltation the unjustly persecuted righteous man, either in this life or in the next. There was also a tradition—possibly of ancient origin—of a mighty, manlike angelic being endowed with delegated divine powers. This figure, some supposed, would come suddenly from heaven in power, accompanied by angels, to execute judgement on the wicked and inaugurate a new era of blessedness and righteousness, either in heaven or here on a radically transformed earth. These ideas will be examined closely in the following three chapters, because some or all of them could have influenced the thinking of Jesus' disciples in the period immediately after his death.

We then move on to consider Jesus' own future expectations, focusing in particular on his teaching concerning the coming kingdom or rule of God, and on what he apparently believed was going to happen in the very near future. Discovering that the teaching of Jesus cannot be separated from the person of Jesus will open up a whole raft of further questions. Who was Jesus? How was he regarded by the ordinary people, by his opponents, and by the inner circle of his closest followers? Who or what did he suppose himself to be? And what specific role, if any, did he envisage that he himself would be playing in the implementation of the coming kingdom or rule of God?

References to the resurrection of Jesus from the dead first appear in letters written by Paul, mainly in the fifties. In addition to providing evidence of his own resurrection and afterlife beliefs at the time of writing, Paul's letters contain "embedded" historical testimony—direct and indirect—that in some instances takes us back through the fifties and forties to the period very shortly after the death of Jesus. This "embedded" testimony includes a short, powerful and multiply-attested formulaic assertion to the effect that God has raised Jesus from the dead. It also includes apparently pre-Pauline christological hymns, or fragments of hymns, that speak powerfully of the heavenly exaltation of Jesus without making any reference to his resurrection. There is an early Aramaic prayer for the coming or return of Jesus from heaven. And, most especially, there is a very early tradition concerning appearances of the risen Jesus to his disciples, a tradition differing significantly from the much later appearance stories in the Gospels.

The primary objective must therefore be to identify, analyse and evaluate these different strata or layers of historical testimony—which include Paul's rather reticent references to his own very early experience of encounter with the risen Jesus Christ—in such a way as to give maximum weight to the earliest and most reliable strands of evidence. Only when this task has been completed shall we be in a position to assess the testimony of the Gospels, where we first encounter narrative accounts of the discovery of Jesus' empty tomb.

Examination of the texts will lead to the conclusion that these narratives and the associated appearances stories were almost certainly in the first instance two independent streams of tradition. It will also confirm the conclusion of most modern scholars that the Gospel traditions cannot be harmonized either with one another or with the much earlier appearances tradition in Paul's first letter to the Corinthians. Nevertheless, although of very limited value for historical purposes, the appearance stories of the Gospels are theologically important. Using motifs drawn from the Hebrew scriptures and Jewish tradition they are designed to protect the identity of the risen Christ of the Church and the Jesus of history whilst communicating the theological conviction that in dealing with the risen Jesus there is an experience of encounter with divine being.

Finally, in the concluding chapter, we revert to the question with which we started; that is, how can modern Christians share and affirm the resurrection faith of Jesus' first followers without abandoning their commitment to a modern scientific world view? Whilst accepting that the possibility of some form of miraculous quasi-historical event can never be disproved, we argue that the historical evidence certainly does not point in this direction. On the contrary, historically speaking, resurrection faith appears to have emerged as a theological interpretation of historical events. We see no reason to attempt to "row back" against the force of this conclusion. Instead, we shall argue that a purely historical approach to the resurrection of Jesus, although legitimate and necessary, will always be less than adequate because it fails to connect with a whole dimension of significance and revelatory experience. In effect, a purely historical approach delivers a one-dimensional understanding of a two-dimensional reality.

We therefore decline to be drawn any further into debate on historical issues which are incapable of resolution and which were anyway no part of earliest resurrection belief. Instead, we focus on the theology of the resurrection, not seeking to persuade unbelievers into belief, but seeking rather to demonstrate the rationality of faith that extends beyond the boundary of reason alone. To this end, we consider the nature, function, and ownership of theological language and the ways in which divine revelation may be "delivered" and articulated. Resurrection faith then and now, we shall argue, originates in real experience of encounter with the divine, experience mediated through the human perception of intrinsic or transcendent significance in historical events.

CHAPTER 2

Resurrection and Immortality

Ideas of bodily resurrection and the immortality of the soul begin to emerge and assume prominence during the course of Second Temple Judaism; that is, the period commencing with the return of the exiles from Babylon in the late sixth century BCE and ending with the final destruction of the Jerusalem temple by the Romans in 70 CE. At the time of the Babylonian exile, most Jews would have subscribed to the ancient Israelite and Judahite idea of the dead existing as vestigial shades in *Sheol*, the shadowy underworld and place of no return, a concept closely paralleling the Greek concept of Hades. There are scattered examples, dating from before, during, and after the exile, of reputed miracles of resurrection and/or the bodily assumption of living human beings directly into heaven. These stories do not appear to have been part of any systematic pattern of belief. They are best regarded either as ancient fables or isolated expressions of the pious conviction that YHWH's power may, at times, be exerted even over death itself.

In addition to these fables and stories, there are a number of instances in the Hebrew scriptures in which affirmations of anticipated national and individual salvation or restoration are found couched in the language of deliverance from *Sheol* or resurrection from the dead. There are also expressions of piety indicative of belief in a profound relationship of continuing communion with YHWH, a relationship which even death and *Sheol* are powerless to disrupt. Although suggestive, these scattered hints and intimations also fall well short of any systematic or general belief in the resurrection of individuals to bodily life after physical death. The historical data suggest that in ancient Israel and in early post-exilic Judaism the general belief was that the dead resided permanently in *Sheol* as shadowy vestiges of their former selves. The best that any man could hope for after death was therefore to rest in peace and to be remembered with respect and affection by his living descendants.

The Hellenization of Palestine and the Maccabean Insurgency

In the later Second Temple period the historical data paint a very different picture. There is evidence that during this period, belief in some form of immortality or resurrection to life after death became commonplace, at least in some circles within Judaism. To understand how and why this came about, a brief historical digression is necessary.

The development of Second Temple Judaism has to be set in the context of the ongoing progressive Hellenization of the whole of the eastern Mediterranean seaboard and hinterland. The coastal cities of Palestine appear always to have been allowed a considerable measure of commercial if not political freedom. They were therefore wide open to external cultural influences throughout the period in question. Politically, the Jewish nation—newly restored after the exile in Babylon—was a fragile and vulnerable plant, a pale shadow of its former self. Numerically small, territorially restricted, and politically impotent, it was very much at the mercy of events. In the late fifth and fourth centuries, trade between Palestine and Greece was rapidly accelerating and geographically expanding, even before Alexander the Great's victory at Issus in 333 BCE and the consequent surrender of Jerusalem two years later. Greek merchants and settlers had long-established homes and warehouses in the Phoenician coastal cities. Pottery of all kinds, including cooking pots, lamps, bowls, and amphorae, were marketed not just along the coast, but also inland in Galilee and Judaea. Greek wine was imported into Palestine in large quantities. The archaeological evidence of Greek cultural influence includes buildings and even whole towns designed and laid out according to Greek plans, together with devotional and cultic objects, and an abundance of coins, seals, and miscellaneous artefacts.

This opening up of Palestine, including Judaea, to Hellenistic influence meant that Greek ideas and thinking became widely disseminated and easily accessible. Even in Jerusalem and its surrounding Jewish territories there was an ongoing process of cultural osmosis. Many people were more or less bilingual and were therefore exposed to both Jewish and Hellenistic cultures, not least in the theological and intellectual spheres where the mutual exchange of ideas seems to have been especially vigorous.

Different groups within Judaism reacted to Hellenization in different ways and at different levels, both directly and indirectly. Although some Jews embraced Hellenization with fervour, for the most part Aramaic-speaking Judaism was only selectively receptive to Hellenistic influences and Hellenizing tendencies. A determined minority of Jews, notably the traditionalist Hasidim, maintained a posture of opposition amounting to outright defiance. But even this opposition was to some extent conditioned and coloured by that which it sought to oppose. Taken as a whole, Second Temple Judaism was a complex and turbulent phenomenon, very far from uniform in belief and practice, and very different from later, so-called normative Judaism. For all practical purposes it must be assumed that from the mid-third century onwards (and certainly by the turn of the era), all Judaism, including Palestinian Judaism, was to some extent Hellenistic Judaism—or, at the very least, that Judaism as a whole was conditioned either positively or negatively by Hellenistic influences.

In the large and wealthy Jewish communities of the Diaspora, the process of Hellenization was even more rapid and far-reaching. In many communities, Greek was the language of choice for daily life. In Egypt, during the third and second centuries BCE, the expanding Jewish population was sufficiently Hellenized for the Hebrew scriptures to be translated into Greek (the translation now known as the Septuagint or LXX) and for this Greek translation to be read alongside the Hebrew scriptures in synagogues. One of the more remarkable manuscripts to have come to light in recent years is an Armenian version of what appears to be a first- or second-century "Jonah and the Whale" sermon, originally delivered in Greek, probably to the congregation of an Alexandrian synagogue on the Day of Atonement. The style is crisp, economical, and to the point. It could be reused today in any synagogue or church without the slightest difficulty.

The Hellenization of Judaism reached its apogee in Jerusalem and the surrounding Jewish territories early in the second century BCE. By then, Jerusalem had been captured by the Seleucid king, Antiochus the Great, who was an enthusiastic proponent of Hellenization. He granted permission for the building of a gymnasium in Jerusalem, with all that that implied in terms of the public display of nakedness. His decision polarized opinions and generated communal tension. A poisonous, long-running dispute between two of the chief families of Jerusalem, concerning the right of appointment to the office of high priest and the custody of the Temple's sacred treasures, culminated in serious public rioting and armed insurrection. Antiochus IV Epiphanes, successor to Antiochus the Great, reacted swiftly and decisively, if not wisely. Deciding that the only way to put a stop to the unrest was to enforce a programme of complete Hellenization, Antiochus embarked on a campaign of ruthless suppression of Judaism and other local religions and cults. It was during this clampdown (in 167 BCE) that the Jerusalem temple was deliberately desecrated and defiled. The possession of a Torah scroll was made punishable by death. This prompted an armed insurrection, which developed into the ultimately successful war of resistance waged under the leadership of the Maccabee family.

Resurrection for reward or punishment

The book of Daniel marks a further stage in the development of ideas. The book exists in more than one version, and the text is unusual, being written partly in Hebrew and partly in Aramaic. To make matters more complicated, there are versions written in Greek which contain additional material that English Bibles normally relegate to the Apocrypha. There may also have been one or more Hebrew-Aramaic manuscripts which are now lost. It is generally agreed that the Hebrew-Aramaic version dates, in its final form, from the early second century, possibly 167 BCE and almost certainly no later than 165 BCE. The importance of Daniel is that it reflects the circumstances of the Maccabean insurgency, which had either just begun, or was just about to begin. It can also be dated fairly precisely because it is apparently unaware of the rebels' success and the resulting rededication of the Jerusalem temple in 164 BCE. Daniel contains stories and accounts of apocalyptic visions with matching interpretations. The theme of the stories is that God is supreme over human history and that he will rescue his people from the tyranny of foreign rulers. The visions involve the revelation and interpretation of heavenly secrets concerning the rise and destruction of four great world kingdoms. Whilst the visions and their interpretations date from the second century, it seems likely that many of the stories are of more ancient origin.

Using language and ideas drawn from the book of Isaiah, including material from Isaiah 26, Daniel contains what may be the earliest explicit evidence in the Hebrew scriptures for belief in the resurrection of individuals. A coming time of unprecedented distress is predicted, followed eventually by national deliverance:

> "At that time [the prince-angel] Michael, the great prince, the protector of your people, shall arise. There shall be a time of anguish, such as has never occurred since nations first came into existence. But at that time your people shall be delivered, everyone who is found written in the book. Many of those who sleep in the dust of the earth shall awake, some to everlasting life, and some to shame and everlasting contempt. Those who are wise shall shine like the brightness of the sky, and those who lead many to righteousness, like the stars for ever and ever."
>
> *Daniel 12:1–3*

The first thing to be said is that this is not an affirmation of belief in the general resurrection of all mankind for final judgement at the end of time. In Daniel, resurrection involves the resurrection of some, but not all, dead people. This limited resurrection will apparently serve two very specific purposes. Firstly, it will enable the righteous Jews who have died defending their faith to be reunited with their living colleagues. Those whose names are found to be "written in the book"—that is, the righteous who are still living—and their resurrected, righteous dead colleagues will then together enjoy the blessings of life in the kingdom which God will bring about through the agency of the prince-angel Michael. Secondly, this resurrection serves justice. The exceptionally wicked are also to be raised. Their resurrection is stated to be "for shame", but condign punishment is implied. Exactly who comprises this second group is not made clear. The use of the term "shame" suggests that the reference may be to quisling, Hellenizing Jews who have given aid and comfort to the nation's persecutors. But it may also include the persecutors themselves.

The concept of resurrection for punishment constitutes a landmark development in Jewish religious thought. It is not found in Isaiah, nor is it found in any of the other afterlife material scattered in earlier texts. The author introduces this innovatory idea without any supplementary explanation or comment, which suggests that it was probably already in circulation at the time when he was writing—or, at the very least, that it was an idea already known to those for whom he was writing.

There are other points of interest. The statement about resurrection is followed by the comment that "those who are wise shall shine like the brightness of the sky, and those who lead many to righteousness, like the stars for ever and ever". The meaning is much debated. In Jewish apocalyptic tradition, "stars" often serves as code for "angels" or "the angelic host". The text may be suggesting that the resurrection of some or all of the righteous martyrs will be spiritual resurrection to an angelic or angel-like life in heaven, rather than physical resurrection to a restored human life on earth. On the other hand, the meaning may simply be that within the total group of resurrected righteous martyrs returned to human life on earth, these special ones will be "stars" or "celebrities" in the modern sense. One of the problems in interpreting Daniel is that the author draws together and amalgamates a variety of material from a number of different sources. The passage in question may originally have been an independent unit of tradition, envisaging direct resurrection from *Sheol* to heaven, in which case, the present ambiguity may simply be reflecting the way in which the tradition has been adapted for incorporation into the final text of Daniel.

The democratization of resurrection

Strong confirmation that the concept of resurrection in Daniel had gained widespread currency within Judaism during the second and first centuries is afforded by the Second Book of Maccabees, an abridged version of a five-volume work by Jason of Cyrene. The date of 2 Maccabees is debated:

Jason could have been an eyewitness to the events he describes, but he was probably writing about forty to one hundred years later. The book of 2 Maccabees is an intensely partisan account of the Maccabean revolt, overloaded with gratuitously gruesome detail. In one extended section, the author tells the ostensibly historical, but almost certainly fictional, story of Antiochus's attempt to compel a mother and her seven sons to eat swine's flesh. Under torture, the sons declare that they will die rather than transgress the Law of Moses. Antiochus is enraged. One by one, the seven sons are killed before their mother's eyes; then the mother also is slain.

Embedded in this story are numerous references to the sons' and the mother's expectation of vindication by resurrection. They closely parallel the ideas and motifs already encountered in the book of Daniel. For example, the second brother says to Antiochus:

> "You accursed wretch, you dismiss us from this present life, but the King of the universe will raise us up to an everlasting renewal of life, because we have died for his laws."
>
> *2 Maccabees 7:9*

When the third son is commanded to put out his tongue and hold out his hands for the executioner's sword, he says:

> "I got these from Heaven, and because of his laws I disdain them, and from him I hope to get them back again."
>
> *2 Maccabees 7:11*

Similarly, the fourth son says:

> "One cannot but choose to die at the hands of mortals and to cherish the hope God gives of being raised again by him. But for you there will be no resurrection to life!"
>
> *2 Maccabees 7:14*

The mother of the seven significantly links resurrection to creation, saying:

> "Therefore the Creator of the world, who shaped the beginning of humankind and devised the origin of all things, will in his mercy give life and breath back to you again, since you now forget yourselves for the sake of his laws."
>
> 2 Maccabees 7:23

Finally, the youngest son rebukes the king:

> "For our brothers after enduring a brief suffering have drunk of ever-flowing life, under God's covenant; but you, by the judgement of God, will receive just punishment for your arrogance."
>
> 2 Maccabees 7:36

Although nothing is said about when, where, and how the resurrection of the seven sons will take place, the restoration of amputated limbs suggests an expectation of eventual bodily resurrection, as does the restoration of "life and breath". On the other hand, the youngest son's reference to his brothers having already drunk of "ever-flowing life under God's covenant" suggests that his dead brothers, and perhaps all the Maccabean martyrs, were supposed to have already entered—presumably at the moment of death—into some form of blessed afterlife envisaged in terms of immortality of the soul rather than resurrection of the physical body. The underlying ideas are not entirely consistent. A similar but reverse situation arises in Wisdom of Solomon 3:1–9 and 5:15–16 where the concept of identifiable bodily resurrection, albeit to life in the heavenly court rather than renewed life on earth, obtrudes into a text otherwise dominated by the concept of immortality of the soul.

We have to be careful not to jump to conclusions about the origins of the apparently quite different concepts of bodily resurrection and spiritual resurrection or immortality. The assumption used to be that the concept of bodily resurrection to restored life on earth was the earliest and most authentically Jewish form of resurrection belief, and that the idea of the resurrection of the spirit to immortality immediately upon death was a later Hellenistic concept. The ambivalence of Daniel, 2 Maccabees, and The Wisdom of Solomon gives us pause for thought. It could be the other way around. The idea of immediate spiritual resurrection to immortality may have been an early stage in the movement of Hebrew thought that later generated the idea of bodily resurrection. Or perhaps the two ideas were running together in parallel over an extended period of time, each concept serving at times to support the other.

There are two other significant references to resurrection in 2 Maccabees. There is the story of Razis, one of the elders of Jerusalem: cornered by his enemies, Razis resolved to die honourably by falling on his sword. Tearing out his own entrails, he called upon "the Lord of life" to give them back to him again, implicitly by resurrection (2 Maccabees 14:37–46). There is also an account of the rebel leader, Judas Maccabaeus, providing a sin-offering for the dead Jewish warriors upon whose corpses forbidden idolatrous tokens and charms had been found (2 Maccabees 12:39–45). The author approves of Judas's action, saying:

> In doing this he [Judas] acted very well and honourably, taking account of the resurrection. For if he [Judas] were not expecting that those who had fallen would rise again, it would have been superfluous and foolish to pray for the dead. But if he was looking to the splendid reward that is laid up for those who fall asleep in godliness, it was a holy and pious thought. Therefore he [Judas] made atonement for the dead, so that they might be delivered from their sin.
>
> *2 Maccabees 12:43b–45*

In both cases it appears that bodily resurrection to renewed life on earth is anticipated, not resurrection in the sense of the survival of an immortal soul.

In 2 Maccabees resurrection serves to vindicate the conduct of the righteous. The law of God, the king of the universe, necessarily takes precedence over the dictates of any earthly ruler. The book of 2 Maccabees also introduces two important ideas which are not part of the understanding of resurrection in either Isaiah or Daniel. First, the seven brothers and Razis profess faith in their own resurrection. This is unprecedented. Second, there is an implied extension of resurrection hope to the generality of martyrs and also, perhaps, to others who have "fallen asleep in godliness". This too is unprecedented. It seems that resurrection belief is becoming democratized as it gains in general acceptance.

To some later Hellenistic Jews, the rather literal and physical understanding of resurrection in 2 Maccabees appeared simplistic and naïve. In the mid-first century CE, 2 Maccabees was rewritten in the form of a Greek philosophical treatise, now designated 4 Maccabees. The Jewish author emphasizes the rule of reason over the passions and seeks to persuade Hellenized Jews (not Greeks) that Jewish religion and practice not only can be, but should be, regarded as Greek wisdom. In 4 Maccabees, references to the resurrection of the body are systematically eliminated and replaced by statements about the immortality of the soul. Death by martyrdom becomes "rebirth for immortality". Under torture, the seven brothers are "running the course towards immortality". When they are dead, they and their mother receive "pure and immortal souls from God". The author is not repudiating his Judaism, but he is very definitely overlaying it with a veneer of Greek philosophy.

The necessary vindication of the persecuted righteous man

The Wisdom of Solomon also seeks to bridge the gap between Hellenistic and Jewish philosophy not by eliminating the latter, but by bringing about a marriage between the Hellenistic concept of the immortality of the soul and Jewish apocalyptic traditions about judgement and heavenly exaltation. The basic theme of the first six chapters is that righteousness leads to life and immortality, whereas unrighteousness leads to death and destruction. This theme is illustrated by an extended story about the suffering, vindication, and final exaltation of a righteous man, and the ultimate fate of his wicked persecutors (Wisdom of Solomon 2:6–20). The wicked and ungodly persecutors advance the very modern argument that since death means extinction, nothing matters. One might as well enjoy life here and now, even to the extent of persecuting and oppressing the righteous. The wicked men plan an experiment which, they believe, will verify their theory. They decide to put an anonymous, righteous man to the test. Together they conspire to bring about his disgrace and death, saying:

> Come, therefore...
> Let us oppress the righteous poor man;
> let us not spare the widow
> or regard the grey hairs of the aged.
> But let our might be our law of right,
> for what is weak proves itself to be useless.
> Let us lie in wait for the righteous man,
> because he is inconvenient to us and opposes our actions...
> Let us test him with insult and torture...
> Let us condemn him to a shameful death...
>
> *Wisdom of Solomon 2:6,10-12,19-20*

So they kill the righteous man. But, says the author, what they have failed to realize is that man is created for incorruption. Men bear the image of God's eternity in the form of a pre-existent and immortal soul. It follows that although a righteous man may die, death cannot be the end of him:

> But the souls of the righteous are in the hand of God,
> and no torment will ever touch them.
> In the eyes of the foolish they seemed to have died...
> but they are at peace.
> For though in the sight of others they were punished,
> their hope is full of immortality.
>
> *Wisdom of Solomon 3:1-4*

Here the concept of resurrection is becoming merged with that of immortality. The dead souls of the righteous retain recognizable identity and in due course they are to be rewarded, apparently on earth. Resurrection, or some form of angelomorphic transformation, seems to be envisaged. Nevertheless, the distinction between restored life on earth and life in heaven is apparently of little or no significance:

> Having been disciplined a little, they [the righteous
>   dead] will receive great good . . .
> In the time of their visitation they will shine forth,
> and will run like sparks through the stubble.
> They will govern nations and rule over peoples,
> and the Lord will reign over them for ever.
>
> Wisdom of Solomon 3:5–8

The author now applies this belief to the specific instance of the persecuted righteous man. In the second half of the story, it emerges that everyone is now dead. The scene is set for a post-mortem confrontation between a (or the) righteous man and his former persecutors. It is immediately apparent that the tables have been turned. The righteous dead are now discovered to be highly exalted, honoured, and numbered among the children of God; that is, the angels. Faced with the evidence of this new reality, and quaking in anticipation of dreadful retribution, the ungodly persecutors now confess the error of their ways. The implied scene is a heavenly courtroom, but significantly God is not the judge and this is not general judgement at the end of time. It is the resurrected righteous who are the judges and who condemn their former persecutors. The function of immortality in the Wisdom of Solomon, as with resurrection in Daniel, is to serve the purpose of justice. Not only must the suffering, righteous man be vindicated, he must be seen by everyone to have been vindicated. Likewise, it is essential that before they are struck down, and before the memory of them is erased for ever, the wicked men should be clearly seen to have been in the wrong. Therefore, when the wicked men see the vindication and exaltation of those whom they have persecuted and murdered, they are obliged to confess:

> "These are persons whom we once held in derision
> and made a byword of reproach—fools that we were!
> We thought that their lives were madness
> and that their end was without honour.
> Why have they been numbered among the children of God?
> And why is their lot among the saints?
> So it was we who strayed from the way of truth,

and the light of righteousness did not shine on us . . ."
Wisdom of Solomon 5:4–6

Setting aside the incomplete merging of the concepts of immortality and bodily resurrection, the Wisdom of Solomon exhibits clear parallels with the motifs of the suffering and subsequently vindicated servant of God in Isaiah, and the resurrection of the martyred Hasidim and their wicked persecutors in Daniel. In this respect the conceptual background is thoroughly Jewish, not Hellenistic.

In late Second Temple Judaism, the motif of the vindication of the righteous man can be observed in many different texts, flexibly combined and entwined with the idea of resurrection for universal judgement. Analysis reveals that there were originally two separate traditions. Firstly, there was a traditional story of ancient origin, which appears in the Hebrew scriptures in many variant forms, concerning a righteous, wise Jew who is maliciously accused and brought to the brink of death. In the nick of time, he is vindicated of the charges brought against him. Subsequently he is exalted to a position of high honour and his enemies are punished. This story evolves over time, with vindication on earth becoming, in later variants, vindication and reward by resurrection and heavenly exaltation after death. Secondly, there is a traditional heavenly judgement scene, initially for the purpose of securing justice in a specific situation rather than for general judgement at the end of time. As in the case of the vindication of the righteous man in the Wisdom of Solomon, combinations of these two basic motifs serve as vectors for the onward transmission and development of Jewish belief in resurrection and immortality.

Afterlife belief in 1 Enoch

The first book of Enoch is a composite work, part of the collection of writings known as the *Pseudepigrapha* and dating from the mid- or late-third century BCE down to 100 CE, or slightly later. The first book of Enoch, according to its final editor, is addressed to those who are faithfully observing the law "in the last days". In the concluding vision, an interpreting angel tells Enoch that the spirits of sinners and blasphemers will be destroyed, whereas the spirits of the righteous dead who have remained faithful will be vindicated and recompensed with honour:

> "I shall bring them out into the bright light, those who have loved my holy name, and seat them each one by one upon the throne of his honor; and they shall be resplendent for ages that cannot be numbered; for the judgement of God is righteousness, because he will give faith—as well as the paths of truth—to the faithful ones in the resting place. Then they shall see those who were born in darkness being taken into darkness, while the righteous ones shall be resplendent. (The sinners) shall cry aloud, and they shall see the righteous ones being resplendent; they shall go to the place which was prescribed for them concerning the days and the seasons."
>
> 1 Enoch 108:12–15[5]

Notable features of this concluding revelation include similarities with Daniel (the honouring of the righteous in heaven and their shining brightness) and parallels with the Wisdom of Solomon (resurrection of the spirit and the crying out of the doomed sinners at the sight of the vindicated righteous). That the spirits of the dead are to be raised is evident, but whether this resurrection includes their bodies is uncertain. The imagery associated with judgement and reward seems to imply some form of bodily resurrection, or at least that the righteous and the wicked will be in some way recognizable. The post-mortem honouring of the extremely righteous with heavenly thrones is a motif which also appears in the Christian scriptures. The Gospels of Luke and Matthew both contain a saying of Jesus in which "the twelve" are promised that they will sit on thrones judging the twelve tribes of Israel:

> "You are those who have stood by me in my trials; and I confer on you, just as my Father has conferred on me, a kingdom, so that you may eat and drink at my table in my kingdom, and you will sit on thrones judging the twelve tribes of Israel."
>
> Luke 22:28–30; cf. Matthew 19:28

Taken as a whole, 1 Enoch reflects a wide range of eschatological and afterlife expectations. The Book of Watchers, a section of 1 Enoch dating from circa 200 BCE or even earlier, contains an account of the judgement on earth of the righteous and the wicked. God will come down from heaven with mighty power, the wicked ones will be destroyed, and the righteous will be rewarded. There is no suggestion of resurrection, nor is there any implication of eternal life or immortality. But there will be no return to sin, and there is a clear promise of future blessedness in the form of happiness, peace, and disease-free, extended life:

> In those days [of judgement] . . . to the elect there shall be light, joy, and peace, and they shall inherit the earth . . . And they shall not be judged all the days of their lives; nor die through plague or wrath, but they shall complete the (designated) number of the days of their life. And peace shall increase their lives and the years of their happiness shall be multiplied forever in gladness and peace all the days of their life.
>
> *1 Enoch 5:6–7,9–10*[6]

The Similitudes, another section of 1 Enoch, are particularly important for our present purposes. Estimates vary widely, but the probability is that they date from the end of the Herodian period (37–4 BCE) or slightly later. The Similitudes represent afterlife either in terms of the resurrection of the spirit to immediate life in the presence of God, or in terms of the resurrection of the body to renewed life on earth. For example, the legendary human being Enoch is represented as having been carried up to heaven by a whirlwind (cf. Genesis 5:24). There he sees the dwellings of the holy ones (the angels) and the spirits of the righteous humans with them. Judgement on earth may be imminent, but it has not yet taken place, because the righteous and blessed humans in heaven:

> . . . interceded and petitioned and prayed on behalf of the children of the people [on earth] . . .
>
> *1 Enoch 39:5*[7]

A few lines later we read that:

> ... all the righteous and chosen were mighty before him [God] like fiery lights.
>
> *1 Enoch 39:7*[8]

This closely parallels Daniel's statement that the resurrected righteous will shine "like the stars for ever and ever", but there is no suggestion of bodily resurrection. It appears that the spirits of the righteous have been taken straight to heaven without any preliminary period of waiting in *Sheol*.

By way of contrast, a little later in the Similitudes there is a scene of eschatological judgement and renewal, reminiscent of Daniel and Isaiah, in which the bodily resurrection of the righteous dead to new life as humans on a gloriously transformed earth is more or less explicit:

> In those days, Sheol will return all the deposits which she had received and hell will give back all that which it owes. And he shall choose the righteous and the holy ones from among (the risen dead), for the day when they shall be selected and saved has arrived. In those days, (the Elect One) shall sit on my throne ... And the earth shall rejoice; and the righteous ones shall dwell upon her and the elect ones shall walk upon her.
>
> *1 Enoch 51:1–3,5*[9]

The figure called the "Elect One" is not God, but a mighty heavenly being. This figure and its significance will be discussed in Chapter 3. For the moment, the relevance of the passage is its reference to resurrection and afterlife. The text of 1 Enoch contains other important references to the afterlife, some of which are ambivalent on the question of the physicality or otherwise of resurrection. The Animal Apocalypse, the second section of the Dream Visions, is an extraordinary text dating from about the time of Daniel. In the Animal Apocalypse, angels are depicted as humans, and humans as animals. The climactic scene is the judgement of angels and men by the Lord of the Sheep (God). The wicked angels and men are then cast into the fiery abyss, and the Jerusalem temple is replaced by a greater and glorious edifice where men of all nations assemble to worship God:

> All those which have been destroyed [the righteous dead] and dispersed, and all the beasts of the field and the birds of the sky were gathered together in that house; and the Lord of the sheep rejoiced with great joy because they had all become gentle and returned to his house.
>
> *1 Enoch 90:33*[10]

In this case, the reference to the gathering in of those who have been destroyed is almost certainly a reference to the bodily resurrection of the righteous dead Israelites to new human life on a radically transformed earth.

Less certain in its implications is the exhortation to the souls of the righteous dead in the first-century BCE Epistle of Enoch, another constituent of 1 Enoch. In a passage bearing striking similarities to the Wisdom of Solomon, Enoch urges the souls of the righteous dead in *Sheol* to have courage because:

> ... good things and joy and honour have been prepared and written down for the souls of the pious who have died ... your lot will exceed the lot of the living. The souls of the pious who have died will come to life, and they will rejoice and be glad; and their spirits will not perish ...
>
> *1 Enoch 103:3–4*[11]

Whether these souls will be restored to their former bodies to live a new life on a transformed earth or whether they will rise as spirits directly to heaven is unclear. There is a similar lack of specificity in an immediately following exhortation addressed to the righteous who are still alive. Once again, the influence of Daniel is apparent. Enoch says:

> Take courage, then; for formerly you were worn out by evils and tribulations, but now you will shine like the luminaries of heaven; you will shine and appear, and the portals of heaven will be opened for you.
>
> *1 Enoch 104:2*[12]

Taking 1 Enoch as a whole, instances of the resurrection or exaltation of the spirit directly to heaven immediately after death, and instances of resurrection of the body to new human life on a transformed earth seem to be fairly evenly balanced. There is, however, one noteworthy new development in the Epistle of Enoch. Here, for the first time, we encounter a significant broadening in the function of resurrection. Whereas in Daniel God raises the righteous dead because they have suffered martyrdom for his sake, in the Epistle of Enoch the righteous dead are raised simply because they have suffered unjustly. In other words, martyrdom is no longer the precondition for resurrection. In the Epistle of Enoch, resurrection speaks to the problem of suffering and oppression more generally than it does in Daniel.

Sheol as a temporary waiting place

The notion of resurrection, especially general resurrection for judgement at the end of time, has consequences for the concept of *Sheol*. *Sheol* can no longer be regarded as the universal and permanent realm of the dead, becoming instead a temporary habitation for shades of the dead pending resurrection and judgement. Another idea that gains currency is the concept of different grades of accommodation in *Sheol*. That in *Sheol* the shades of the circumcised are separated from those of the uncircumcised is an idea of ancient origin, but as the idea of resurrection gained ground, it became more generally accepted. Concepts of preliminary blessing or torment for the souls or shades in *Sheol* also begin to emerge. For example, in the second- or third-century BCE Book of Watchers, Enoch has a vision of a mountain where the souls of the dead are segregated into four separate underground hollow places, or "corners", according to the degree of their wickedness. One of the hollow places is full of light and contains a fountain of water for the relief of the righteous souls:

> Then I went to another place [under the mountain], and he [the angel] showed me on the west side a great and high mountain of hard rock and inside it four beautiful corners; ... Rufael ... said to me, "These beautiful corners (are here) in order that the

> spirits of the souls of the dead should assemble into them . . . until the day of their judgment and the appointed time of the great judgment upon them." . . . I raised a question, . . . "For what reason is one separated from the other?" And he replied . . . "the souls of the righteous are separated (by) this spring of water with light upon it, in like manner, the sinners are set apart . . ."
>
> *1 Enoch 22:1–4,8–10*[13]

The passage goes on to discriminate between sinners who have already suffered for their offences and those who have escaped justice during their lifetimes. For the latter there will be no resurrection. They are doomed to destruction. The idea of the separation of righteous and wicked shades or souls actually taking place at the time of death reappears somewhat later in a more developed form in the Similitudes, where the elect and righteous dead are referred to as presently dwelling in the "Garden of Life".

The idea of *Sheol* as a place of preliminary separation and anticipatory blessing or punishment was apparently shared by Jesus, who is represented as having told a traditional story about a poor man called Lazarus (Luke 16:19–31). During his lifetime Lazarus was treated with contempt by a certain rich man. When they both died, the tables were turned. The rich man found himself in Hades (i.e. *Sheol*), tormented in flames, whereas the poor man found himself carried away by the angels to enjoy blessed felicity in the presence of Abraham:

> The poor man died and was carried away by the angels to be with Abraham. The rich man also died and was buried. In Hades, where he was being tormented, he looked up and saw Abraham . . . Abraham said, ". . . between you and us a great chasm has been fixed, so that those who might want to pass from here to you cannot do so, and no one can cross from there to us."
>
> *Luke 16:22–26*

Here the separation of souls is absolute, and it serves the purpose of justice. Nevertheless, there is no suggestion that this is final judgement.

The Gospels also contain clear evidence that, at the time of Jesus, the Jewish sect known as the Pharisees believed, too, in the preliminary separation of souls and in some form of resurrection of the dead. This is confirmed by the Jewish historian, Josephus. Josephus was a Hellenized Palestinian Jew who served as a senior Jewish military commander before defecting to the Romans. As a significant participant in many of the events he describes, his graphic, eyewitness narratives make impressive reading. In his account of the beliefs and practices of the Pharisees, he says:

> They believe that souls have power to survive death and that there are rewards and punishments under the earth for those who have led lives of virtue or vice: eternal imprisonment is the lot of evil souls, while the good souls receive an easy passage to a new life.
> *Antiquities of the Jews, XVIII:14*[14]

Probably with an eye to the inclinations and wishes of his wealthy Roman patrons, Josephus is here superimposing on Jewish beliefs terminology and concepts derived from Greek philosophy. Nevertheless, this passage shows that he clearly understands the Pharisees to believe in rewards and punishments "under the earth" (that is, in *Sheol*) and in some form of resurrection or ongoing new life for the souls of the righteous dead.

Bypassing *Sheol* and going straight to heaven

If *Sheol* is understood to be a waiting-place rather than a final state or destination, it becomes possible to envisage bypassing *Sheol* altogether. Instead of waiting underground in *Sheol* pending general resurrection and final judgement on the last day, why should not exceptionally righteous and heroic dead individuals go straight to heaven, with or without their earthly bodies? Towards the end of the Second Temple period there is evidence that this was believed to be possible. For example, in 2 Maccabees the puzzling reference to "our brothers" having already "drunk of overflowing life" makes good sense when it is interpreted as meaning that the righteous martyrs had already bypassed *Sheol* and gone straight to heaven. In the Fourth Book of Ezra, which dates from shortly after the fall of the Second Temple in 70 CE, Ezra is advised:

> "Lay up in your heart the signs that I have shown you, the dreams that you have seen, and the interpretations that you have heard; for you shall be taken up from among humankind, and henceforth you shall live with my Son and with those who are like you, until the times are ended."
>
> *4 Ezra/2 Esdras 14:8–9*

The passage is Jewish, not Christian, and the reference to "my Son" has nothing to do with Jesus of Nazareth. The reference is to a messianic heavenly redeemer, a figure closely similar to—or identical with—the mighty angelic figure referred to as the "Elect One" in 1 Enoch 51:1–5 (see above). Traditions concerning this heavenly being may have played a pivotal role in the emergence of Christian belief in the resurrection and exaltation of Jesus, but for the moment the point of interest is that this is another example of the belief that a human being could, in certain circumstances, bypass *Sheol* and be taken directly to heaven.

The same idea finds vivid expression in the first-century CE Apocalypse of Zephaniah. Zephaniah is depicted as having a visionary experience in which he escapes from *Sheol* and reaches the gates of heaven. An angel welcomes him, and he finds that other righteous heroes of faith have similarly bypassed *Sheol*:

> Then a great angel came forth having a golden trumpet in his hand, and he blew it three times over my head, saying, "Be courageous! . . . For you have . . . escaped from the abyss and Hades. You will now cross over the crossing place. For your name is written in the Book of the Living." . . . Then he [the angel] ran to all the righteous ones, namely, Abraham and Isaac and Jacob and Enoch and Elijah and David. He spoke with them as friend to friend speaking with one another.
>
> *Apocalypse of Zephaniah 9:1–5*[15]

Likewise, in the Animal Apocalypse it appears that Noah was believed to have bypassed *Sheol* and been transformed into an angel. When the floods receded and the doors of the ark were opened:

> Then the snow-white cow [that is, the man Noah] which became a man [that is, an angel] came out from that boat together with three cows [humans].
>
> *1 Enoch 89:9*[16]

A little later in the same text there is an account of the death of Moses. Here also the implication is that the human Moses had been transformed into an angel, this transformation possibly having taken place before he died. The text reads:

> (There) that sheep [that is, Moses] who was leading them—the one who had become a man [that is, an angel]—departed from them, and all of them went to sleep. (Then the rest of) the sheep sought him; and there took place a great cry over him.
>
> *1 Enoch 89:38*[17]

The statement that the rest of the sheep were seeking Moses and lamenting over him seems to reflect the scriptural tradition that the site of Moses' burial has always remained unknown. The implication is that Moses, when he died, was assumed directly into heaven. There are also traces of an assumption of Moses tradition in the writings of Philo and other ancient authors. Taking the evidence as a whole, it seems that by the turn of the era it was possible to believe that exceptionally righteous or significant individuals might have bypassed *Sheol* and gone straight to heaven, either after or even before death.

The realized eschatology of the Qumran community

In sharp contrast to the documents already cited, the Dead Sea scrolls contain few references or allusions to afterlife belief. Given the abundance of the material recovered from the caves and other sites adjacent to the community buildings at Qumran—in whole or part there are some 850 documents dating from 180 BCE to 68 CE—this almost total lack of reference to resurrection belief is puzzling, to say the least. The reason appears to be that the members of the Qumran community were strongly committed to an alternative belief system, which rendered resurrection faith largely irrelevant. According to the sectaries, that which resurrection faith signified had already happened, or was already happening. So far as they were concerned, the blessings of the end of the age and the afterlife were already accessible here and now in the present.

Belief of this kind, often called realized eschatology, is of ancient origin. It is implicit in some of the poetic writings concerning deliverance from *Sheol*. The underlying premise is the believer's personal experience of an intense, self-authenticating encounter or relationship with God. This experience is so powerful and immediate that it is inconceivable to the believer that anything could ever negate it. This intense personal piety is evident in a number of the Qumran scrolls. For example, the author of the Community Rule speaks of the spiritual blessings bestowed on the Qumran sectaries and of their corporate worship being joined with that of the angels and inhabitants of heaven:

> God has given them to His chosen ones as an everlasting possession, and has caused them to inherit the lot of the Holy Ones. He has joined their assembly to the Sons of Heaven . . .
>
> *1QS XI, 7–8*[18]

Similar sentiments appear in the Qumran Thanksgiving Hymns. The author of Hymn 10 gives thanks to God for rescuing him from "the Pit" and the "hell of Abaddon", metaphors signifying either death or a state of sinfulness equivalent to death:

> Thou hast cleansed a perverse spirit of great sin
> that it may stand with the host of the Holy Ones,
> and that it may enter into community
> with the congregation of the Sons of Heaven.
>
> *1QH XI, 21[19]*

The depictions of angelic worship in the fragments collectively known as "The Songs for the Sabbath Holocaust" also imply the simultaneity of worship on earth and in heaven. One fragment seems actually to merge the existential status of the human sectaries ("the sons of the world") with that of the community of divine beings:

> In accordance with the mercies of God, according to His goodness and wonderful glory, He caused some of the sons of the world to draw near (Him) . . . to be counted with Him in the com[munity of the "g]ods" . . .
>
> *4Q181[20]*

A similar idea appears in the Qumran fragment sometimes called "The Song of Michael and the Just". The identity of the speaker is not given, but he lays claim to extraordinary exaltation, including—apparently—heavenly enthronement:

> . . . a throne of strength in the congregation of "gods" so that not a single king of old shall sit on it, neither shall their noble men . . . my glory is incomparable, and apart from me none is exalted. None shall come to me for I dwell . . . in heaven, and there is no . . . I am reckoned with the "gods" and my dwelling-place is in the congregation of holiness.
>
> *4Q491, fragment 11[21]*

The text is difficult to interpret, but it seems that the speaker is either a heavenly being or that the boundary between earth and heaven has been dissolved and a human speaker is regarding himself as already having been in some way divinized by transformation into a heavenly being. The Qumran sectaries appear to have understood their community to be an outpost of God's coming kingdom embedded in present time. Interestingly, Jesus of Nazareth appears to have had a somewhat similar perception of himself as the anticipatory point-of-presence of the coming kingdom of God.

The evidence of Josephus

Josephus's account of the afterlife views of the Essenes closely parallels what he says about the Pharisees. Superficially, what Josephus says bears little relation to the evidence of the Qumran documents. According to Josephus, the Essenes believed souls to be immortal; they inhabit the human body much as a person might inhabit a prison. Once released from their bodily imprisonment, souls wing their way to a blessed habitation beyond the ocean. This is almost certainly another example of Josephus's Hellenizing tendency. It sheds little light on the actual beliefs of the Essenes other than to confirm that they believed in some form of afterlife. Whether their belief involved spiritual or physical resurrection we cannot say.

Much more interesting are Josephus's personal views on the afterlife. These are set out in *The Wars of the Jews* in a section in which he strongly condemns suicide:

> The bodies of all men are indeed mortal, and are created out of corruptible matter; but the soul is ever immortal, and is a portion of the divinity that inhabits our bodies ... Those who depart out of this life according to the law of nature, and pay that debt which was received from God, when he that lent it us is pleased to require it back again, enjoy eternal fame ... their souls are pure and obedient, and obtain a most holy place in heaven, from whence, in the revolutions of ages they are again sent into pure bodies; while the souls of those whose hands have acted madly against themselves are received by the darkest place in Hades ...
> *The Wars of the Jews*, III:8.5[22]

In his *Life Against Apion*, embedded in a somewhat self-serving account of his surrender to the Romans, Josephus speaks of reward for faithful martyrs taking the form of renewed life after death:

> Each individual, relying on the witness of his own conscience and the lawgiver's prophecy, confirmed by the sure testimony of God, is firmly persuaded that to those who observe the laws and, if they must needs die for them, willingly meet death, God has granted a renewed existence and in the revolution of the ages the gift of a better life.
>
> *Contra Apion, II:218*[23]

The scheme is typically Pythagorean. Souls are divine and incarnation is temporary. After death, souls live on, bad souls being punished and good souls being rewarded. In due course, good souls may be granted new life by reincarnation. Josephus's descriptions of the afterlife beliefs of the Sadducees, Essenes, and Pharisees are cleverly contrived to make them appear to conform to the teachings of the Epicurean, the Pythagorean, and the Stoic schools of Greco-Roman philosophy. Nevertheless, it would be unwise to assume that his accounts of his own personal beliefs are similarly contrived. Josephus's stated beliefs accord quite well with what one would expect of any sophisticated, Hellenized, first-century Jew.

For present purposes, the importance of Josephus lies elsewhere. He describes the Sadducees as disputatious and practically atheists. The Sadducees did not believe in the immortality of souls; they rejected the idea of resurrection, and they denied any possibility of reward or punishment in Hades or *Sheol*. Interestingly, the Gospels of Matthew, Mark, and Luke all contain the same account of a group of Sadducees denying the possibility of resurrection and challenging Jesus' teaching on the subject. If there had been no widespread popular belief in resurrection, the fact that one particular sub-group denied the possibility would scarcely have warranted comment. The naming and shaming of the Sadducees by Josephus and, independently, by Jesus in the Christian Gospels indirectly confirms the prevalence of resurrection belief in first-century Judaism.

Conclusion

The evidence suggests that there were a wide variety of afterlife beliefs in Second Temple Judaism. We observe different ideas and tendencies gradually coming into focus. Belief in *Sheol* as the permanent resting place of the dead can be observed morphing into belief in *Sheol* as the temporary abode of dead souls pending bodily resurrection, either at the commencement of a new age or at the end of time. A concept of preliminary punishments or rewards emerges and takes its place alongside traditional belief in *Sheol*. There are also scattered examples of the belief that exceptionally righteous or significant individuals might sometimes bypass *Sheol* altogether and go straight to heaven, either before or after death.

The idea of resurrection first appears clearly in the book of Daniel. It is not general resurrection, but resurrection of the exceptionally wicked and the exceptionally righteous for preliminary punishment and reward. Resurrection for reward or punishment addresses the problem of theodicy. Justice must be done, and justice must be seen to be done. In particular, the wicked must be punished and the righteous martyrs of faith must be vindicated and seen to be vindicated. The recurring motif of the necessary vindication of the righteous man, before or after death, is especially important, because it functions as a vector for the onward transmission of resurrection belief.

The texts suggest that resurrection was a rather fluid concept. Sometimes it seems to be envisaged in terms of future bodily resurrection, either to life in heaven or to ongoing life on a transformed earth. At other times, it appears to be envisaged as the raising of the spirit or soul to heavenly life immediately after death on earth. Under the impact of Hellenization, the concept of resurrection begins to merge with the idea of belief in the immortality of the soul, and we observe a number of instances in which both ideas are flexibly combined in an indeterminate way. Meanwhile, the Qumran sectaries were apparently believing that, within the worship of their own exclusive community, the boundary between heaven and earth was already dissolved and that they were presently united with the hosts of heaven in a fellowship which death was powerless to disrupt or dissolve. Overall, the impression is one of diversity, complexity, and fluidity. The data resist harmonization, and there appears to have been no particular orthodoxy. In many cases, ancient beliefs are brought forward and continue to coexist in parallel with much later ideas. Apparently incompatible images and concepts—such as bodily resurrection, spiritual resurrection, and immortality of the soul—are found to be juxtaposed without any apparent sense of strain. There is no real sense of any particular developmental trajectory, nor is there any impression that radical change is imminent.

CHAPTER 3

Angels and Angelomorphic Transformation

The previous chapter focused on the emergence of resurrection and afterlife beliefs in Second Temple Judaism. We noted examples of belief in bodily resurrection to new life on a transformed earth, and of belief in bodily or spiritual resurrection to life in heaven. Towards the end of the period, we encountered the idea of the pre-existence and immortality of the soul, according to which, when its owner dies, a soul sheds the prison of a mortal body and flies upwards or downwards for divine reward or punishment. We also observed a number of instances in which the ideas of resurrection and immortality were combined or conflated, with no apparent sense of strain. Now we need to widen the scope of the enquiry by examining the ways in which transitions to the afterlife were believed to take place. In the first instance, we focus on the concept of heaven and its inhabitants, on the relationship of events on earth to events in heaven, and on traffic between earth and heaven, or vice versa, whether by resurrection or by any other means.

The location of heaven

In heaven angels dwell in the presence of God, but where is heaven, and who or what are the angels? For many modern men and women such questions are meaningless. We take it as axiomatic that God, if there is a God, is external to the reality we experience, and exists in some other realm or state of being where concepts of space and time do not apply. It was not so for the ancients. For the writers who compiled the Hebrew scriptures, heaven was an integral part of reality. Moreover, it was inside space and time, and its whereabouts were well known. By day, one could look up at the over-arching blue dome of the sky, which was the floor or pavement of heaven. And gazing up into the night sky, one could look in through the windows of heaven, and see the distant, glimmering lights of its myriad angel-inhabitants, whom we call stars. It follows that in principle, a man or woman could go up from earth to heaven as easily and naturally as he or she might go up today from Tel Aviv to Jerusalem. All that was needed was transport, someone to act as a guide, and perhaps a change of clothing. Heaven, like *Sheol*, was a real location. The difficulties in going from earth to heaven and heaven to earth were practical rather than conceptual.

The angelic hierarchy

Angels are more complicated. In Canaanite and early Israelite documents, we encounter a multiplicity of references to angels and other supernatural beings, benevolent and malicious. Angels may come from heaven to earth. On earth, they may appear in human form as messengers charged with the task of delivering specific messages to particular individuals, as in the case of the angels who came to Abraham and Sarah (Genesis 18–19). One of the Hebrew words for an angel, *mal'akh*, signifies messenger, as does its later Greek equivalent, *angelos*. Other terms signifying angels include "sons of god" (*benei elohim* or *benei elim*), "holy ones" (*qedoshim*), and "watchers" (*'irin*).

As it appears in ancient Israelite thinking, the concept of angelic beings seems to have originated, at least in part, in Canaanite polytheism and in the Canaanite concept of the divine council of the gods. The divine council comprised the gods of the nations and of individuals gathered together in solemn conclave. The historical data, such as they are, support the rather general thesis that there was a progressive development in thinking. Initially the God of Israel enjoyed parity with the other gods in the divine council. Then he became first among equals. Finally, he emerged as the absolute heavenly monarch possessing unchallengeable authority and power. Traces of all three stages survive in the literature.

Once the God of Israel was believed to be the one and only absolute heavenly monarch, there was no longer any role for the lesser gods of the Canaanite pantheon. Accordingly, in popular thinking, these lesser gods became downgraded or marginalized. Losing their autonomy, they began to take on the characteristics of officers and executives of a heavenly royal household. This change appears to have accelerated with the enforced exposure of Jews to the highly efficient, centralized bureaucracy of imperial Babylon. During the Second Temple period, therefore, alongside persisting older traditions we find increasingly elaborate and sophisticated depictions of the heavenly household. Angels become divided into categories, such as the *seraphim*, the *cherubim*, and the *ophanim*. These categories are further subdivided into functional hierarchies. Alongside messenger and interpreter angels, there are angels whose duty is to wait on the divine presence, others whose role is to guard the doors of heaven, others who are responsible for controlling the weather, and yet others who have oversight of kingdoms and individuals on earth. The countless myriads of these angelic beings serve a very definite theological purpose. In bureaucracies, then as now, numbers signify status. The multitudinous heavenly host enhances the majesty of the absolute divine monarch, and usefully distances him from personal involvement in the minutiae of human affairs.

The angel of Yhwh

In the Hebrew Bible, there are between seventy and eighty references to an angel called "the angel of Yhwh" or "the angel of *Elohim*". These appear in the books of Genesis, Exodus, Numbers, Judges, First and Second Chronicles, and Zechariah. One of the features of these so-called "angel of the Lord" traditions is that in a number of instances the figure is theophanic or angelomorphic. That is, the figure sometimes appears and acts or speaks as if it were a human being, sometimes as an angel, and sometimes as if it were God himself. For example, Genesis 18:1–15 tells how the aged Abraham and Sarah receive three visitors. These visitors are initially described as men. One of them tells Sarah that she will have a son—Sarah is disbelieving. It then transpires that one of the figures is God himself and the other two are angels. In the ensuing dialogue the angels and God speak with Abraham and Sarah. God, it seems, can appear and speak as if he were an angel, and an angel can appear and speak as if it were a human.

There are other instances of similarly fluctuating identity. In the Genesis 16:7–14 story of the runaway slave-girl Hagar, the angel of Yhwh orders Hagar to return. Hagar's reply makes it clear that in encountering the figure of the angel of Yhwh, she understands that she has encountered God (*El-roi*) himself. Likewise, in the Exodus story of Moses and the burning bush, an angel appears to Moses in a flame of fire, but a moment later it seems that the angel is God himself:

> There the angel of the Lord appeared to him in a flame of fire out of a bush; . . . Moses said, "I must turn aside and look at this great sight, and see why the bush is not burned up." When the Lord saw that he had turned aside to see, God called to him out of the bush, "Moses, Moses!"
>
> *Exodus 3:2–4*

Another striking example is the Exodus story of the escape of the people of Israel from Egypt. A pillar of cloud by day and fire by night leads and protects the people. yhwh himself is present in the pillar of cloud and fire (Exodus 13:21). A few verses later we are told that it was the "angel of *Elohim*", not Yhwh, who was in the cloud (Exodus 14:19). There is similar fluctuation in the story of Gideon. The angel of Yhwh appears in human form, sits in the shade of an oak tree, and talks with Gideon (Judges 6:11–22). Gideon is commissioned to deliver Israel from the Midianite oppressors. The commission is introduced with the words, "Then Yhwh turned to him and said . . ." (Judges 6:14). From then on there are alternating references to Yhwh and the angel of Yhwh, without any apparent distinction between the two. It appears that the angel and yhwh himself are one and the same being.

It appears that it was believed that God could at times appear as an angel designated the "angel of Yhwh". Furthermore, the "angel of Yhwh" could appear either as an angelic being or in human form. In due course, we shall explore other traditions in which humans similarly morph into angels, or even more exalted heavenly beings.

The Divine Name angel

The key to understanding this puzzling, intermittent loss of distinction between Yhwh himself and the "angel of Yhwh" may lie in a reference to another angel; that is, the angel of whom it is said that "he has God's Name in him". It was this angel who led the Israelites into the Promised Land. While they were still in the wilderness, God said to Moses:

> I am going to send an angel in front of you, to guard you on the way and to bring you to the place that I have prepared. Be attentive to him and listen to his voice; do not rebel against him, for he will not pardon your transgression; for my name is in him.
> *Exodus 23:20-21*

The text makes it clear that the angel "who has my name in him" is the angelomorphic "angel of yhwh" or "angel of *Elohim*". Custody of the Divine Name is very important. It signifies possession of at least some measure of divine authority, power, and being. The underlying concept is personification or hypostasis. Hypostasis in this context means that an aspect or property of some greater whole is being represented as an independent, autonomous entity or actor. For example, the Wisdom and Word of God are at times depicted as divine hypostases. As such, they can be thought of and experienced and talked about as if they were independent entities. In the case of the angel who "has God's Name in him", the underlying idea seems to be that this angel is freighted with divine power, authority, and being to such a degree that in encountering him one is, in effect, encountering God himself.

There is also some evidence (stronger in some cases than in others) to suggest that other divine attributes such as the Glory, the Spirit, and the Power of God were also sometimes understood to be divine hypostases. For example, in the book of Ezekiel, the Glory of God assumes the form of a manlike angel, albeit an angel of extraordinarily exalted status. Ezekiel's description of this figure is freighted with details intended to emphasize its supreme, quasi-divine status. Overhead is the crystal dome of heaven. Subordinate ministering angelic beings having both animal and human features surround a chariot-throne of unimaginable splendour. It has wheels, and wheels within wheels. There is fire, thunder, and lightning:

> And above the dome over their heads there was something like a throne, in appearance like sapphire; and seated above the likeness of a throne was something that seemed like a human form. Upwards from what appeared like the loins I saw something like gleaming amber, something that looked like fire enclosed all round; and downwards from what looked like the loins I saw something that looked like fire, and there was a splendour all round ... This was the appearance of the likeness of the glory of the LORD.
>
> *Ezekiel 1:26-28*

A little later in Ezekiel, the same figure appears as a majestic but unenthroned messenger angel. Later still, the same angelic being (or a closely similar figure) appears for a third time, depicted in terms which correspond almost exactly with the description of the figure on the chariot-throne. Whatever its origins, Ezekiel's description of the enthroned Glory of God exerted a significant influence on a number of later apocalyptic texts, including a theophany in 1 Enoch 14:18ff. in which Enoch enters the innermost circle of heaven and sees the awful majesty of the enthroned Great Glory, the Excellent and Glorious One, surrounded by blazing fire and myriads of angels. This Enochian theophany probably influenced the description of the judgement scene in Daniel 7:9–10, an important text which will be considered in a later chapter.

The book of Exodus also contains a number of accounts of theophanies in which the Glory of God, presented as an apparently autonomous entity, is substituted for what otherwise might have been references to God himself. The principal purpose served by maintaining a distinction between God and the Glory of God is that God himself must necessarily always be invisible, whereas the Glory of God may—in principle—be seen by humans. When the Law is given to Moses on Mount Sinai, Moses begs to be allowed to see the Glory of God. The subtext is that Moses could not ask to see God himself because the experience would have been fatal, but he could aspire to see the Glory of God. God's reply to Moses effectively confirms this understanding, although in this instance Moses had to realize that he could not be exposed to even the Glory of God without protection:

> "... you cannot see my face; for no one shall see me and live." And the LORD continued, "See, there is a place by me where you shall stand on the rock; and while my glory passes by I will put you in a cleft of the rock, and I will cover you with my hand until I have passed by..."
>
> *Exodus 33:20-22*

Angels with names

As the concept of the polytheistic divine council gave way to that of the monotheistic heavenly court or household, the most senior angels began to take on individual identities and assume personal names. Responsibility for different functions was assigned to specific, named angels. The texts testify to there being four—or sometimes seven—principal angels. The names of the four are Michael, Raphael, Gabriel, and either Sariel or Phanuel. Additionally, there are Uriel, Reuel, and Remiel, bringing the total up to seven. References to named angels appear regularly from the second century BCE onwards. By the turn of the era, angels are remarkable mainly for their extraordinary variety and for the ever-increasing complexity of their roles and functions. The Qumran War Scroll, for example, requires the military angel-commanders to list by name the individual angel-warriors in their cohorts. They are ordered to emblazon slogans such as "Mighty Hand of God", "Splendour of God", and "Vengeance of God" on the apparatus of war, slogans which are probably the names of the respective angelic commanders. In its present form the third Book of Enoch dates from the sixth century CE or even later, but it contains traditions which are almost certainly considerably earlier. These traditions include lists of angels and their functions. In many instances the individual names, powers, and duties of the angels are specified in minute detail. Interestingly, the higher angels are depicted as having human characteristics and appearance.

The great angelic prince

The model of heaven as a royal household lent itself to the further idea that one of the principal angels must be supreme over all the others. The evidence indicates that at different times and among different groups, various angelic figures or heavenly powers were regarded as supreme, but it is Michael who gradually emerges as the principal figure. In Daniel, Michael is a great angelic prince (Daniel 12:1), protector of the faithful Israelites, and the commander of the heavenly armies.

The book of Daniel contains an account of a vision in which a mighty and glorious heavenly figure, described as "one like a human being" or "one like a son of man", is seen coming to God and being appointed to rule over an everlasting kingdom:

> I saw one like a human being
> coming with the clouds of heaven.
> And he came to the Ancient One
> and was presented before him.
> To him was given dominion
> and glory and kingship,
> that all peoples, nations, and languages
> should serve him.
> His dominion is an everlasting dominion
> that shall not pass away,
> and his kingship is one
> that shall never be destroyed.
>
> *Daniel 7:13–14*

The identity and significance of this figure is much debated. It may be that the figure is an individual being, a supreme angelic power, God's heavenly lieutenant and enforcer of the divine will on earth. Alternatively, the figure may be a symbol either for the previously suffering but now vindicated people of Israel, or for the angelic host. If the figure represents a specific individual, that figure is probably Michael, the prince-angel of Israel, or Melchizedek. One of the Qumran scrolls (11Q13) describes Melchizedek as a supreme heavenly prince, a god or divine being (*Elohim* or *El*) second only to God himself.[24] Melchizedek's functions are to deliver the righteous from captivity and then to pass definitive final judgement on all beings in heaven and on earth. Melchizedek appears also to have an earthly counterpart who acts as his herald. The implications of this partnership or duality for early Christian understandings of Jesus will be discussed in a later chapter, but for the moment we note that two other Qumran texts (the Community Rule and the War Scroll) make it clear that Michael, Melchizedek, and another figure called the "Prince of Light" are all one and the same heavenly being.

The most extraordinary of these angelic beings is Metatron. References to Metatron appear in a number of documents, the most important being 3 Enoch. Although falling well outside the period with which we are concerned, the figure of Metatron—who may originally have been Michael—is a fascinating example of a heavenly grand vizier. According to the tradition in 3 Enoch, Metatron was once a young man called Enoch. As Enoch, he was taken from earth to heaven and transformed into Metatron, a heavenly power of unimaginable splendour, enthroned and surrounded by his own hosts of ministering angels. So great is Metatron's splendour that he is described as "the lesser Yhwh". That is, he has God's Name in him. Events spiral out of control when a foolish angel called 'Aher oversteps the mark:

> ... he saw me [says Metatron] seated upon a throne like a king, with ministering angels standing beside me as servants and all the princes of kingdoms crowned with crowns surrounding me. Then he opened his mouth and said, "There are indeed two powers in heaven!" Immediately a divine voice came out of the presence of the Shekinah and said, "Come back to me, apostate sons—apart from 'Aher!" Then ... the dreadful Prince [another great angel]

came at the command of the Holy One, blessed be he, and struck me [Metatron] with sixty lashes of fire ...

3 Enoch 16:2–5[25]

The offence for which Metatron was punished was allowing his subordinate angel to suggest that there were two supreme powers in heaven. This was serious heresy because no one, not even the most exalted angelic power, may be compared with God.

Parallel action in heaven and on earth

The concept of human action on earth taking place in parallel with angelic action in heaven is probably of Canaanite origin. Nations on earth were believed to have their own individual heavenly mentors, or guardian angels, whose sphere of influence reflected the boundaries of the nation. For example, the Song of Moses in Deuteronomy says:

> When the Most High apportioned the nations,
> when he divided humankind,
> he fixed the boundaries of the peoples
> according to the number of the gods;
> the LORD's own portion was his people,
> Jacob his allotted share.
>
> *Deuteronomy 32:8–9*

This raises an obvious question. If national boundaries are fixed by divine decree, what happens when nations make war on nations, and national boundaries change in consequence? The answer, strange as it may seem, is that when armies make war on earth, their heavenly mentors are fighting one another in heaven. Victory on earth therefore reflects a successful outcome in heaven—and vice versa. In the book of Daniel there is an account of a vision in which the eponymous Daniel is told that two great angels have been battling together in heaven against the angel-prince of Persia. One of them (possibly Gabriel) breaks off fighting to speak briefly with Daniel. When the conversation is concluded, he says:

> Now I must return to fight against the prince of Persia, and when I am through with him, the prince of Greece will come... There is no one with me who contends against these princes except Michael, your [i.e. Israel's] prince.
>
> *Daniel 10:20–21*

The text makes it clear that these battles in heaven are proceeding in parallel with corresponding battles between the human nations on earth.

In another dream-vision, Daniel sees four terrifying, supernatural beasts, probably representing the warrior-angels of the nations opposed to Israel. The beasts crawl up out of the "great sea", which probably signifies *Sheol*, the realm of the dead. The beasts make war against the holy ones of the Most High (the good angels) and initially the beasts are successful. Meanwhile, in parallel on earth the faithful Israelites are being hard-pressed by their human adversaries. Then God intervenes. He delivers decisive judgement in favour of the good angels and against the terrifying beasts. As a result, the tide of war is turned:

> As I looked, this horn [great beast / warrior angel] made war with the holy ones [the good angels] and was prevailing over them, until the Ancient One came; then judgement was given for the holy ones of the Most High [good angels], and the time arrived when the holy ones gained possession of the kingdom.
>
> *Daniel 7:21–22*

When the holy ones of the Most High (the good angels) are victorious in heaven, the people of the holy ones (the faithful Israelites) are likewise victorious on earth. As a reward, both they and the good angels receive the gift of an everlasting kingdom:

> "The kingship and dominion and the greatness of the kingdoms under the whole heaven shall be given to the people of the holy ones of the Most High; their kingdom shall be an everlasting kingdom, and all dominions shall serve and obey them."
>
> *Daniel 7:27*

The relationship between the "holy ones of the Most High" in heaven and the "people of the holy ones" on earth is pivotal: the good angels and the faithful Israelites are yoked together in a parallel, symbiotic relationship.

Similar examples of parallel action in heaven and on earth appear scattered throughout the literature of the period. In Isaiah there is a depiction of a climactic battle in which God lays waste the whole earth, scattering its inhabitants far and wide. It is a time for retribution and settling scores. The wicked angels of the nations are therefore punished by God in heaven, whilst their parallel beings, the wicked kings of the human nations, are punished here on earth:

> On that day the LORD will punish
> the host of heaven in heaven,
> and on earth the kings of the earth.
> They will be gathered together
> like prisoners in a pit;
> they will be shut up in a prison,
> and after many days they will be punished.
>
> *Isaiah 24:21–22*

Sometimes the parallel action is so much taken for granted that distinctions begin to collapse. In the Song of Deborah—part of the book of Judges—the victory of the kings of Israel over their enemies, Sisera and the kings of Canaan, is celebrated. In parallel, the stars of heaven (the good angels) are described as having fought, not—as one might expect—against Sisera's angels, but against Sisera himself:

> "The kings came, they fought;
> then fought the kings of Canaan,
> at Taanach, by the waters of Megiddo;
> they got no spoils of silver.
> The stars [angels] fought from heaven,
> from their courses they fought against Sisera."
>
> *Judges 5:19–20*

The logical culmination of this process would be for the distinction between action in heaven and parallel action on earth to collapse altogether. Towards the end of the book of Deuteronomy, the dying Moses blesses the Israelites. Reflecting on Israel's past victories and giving glory and credit to God, Moses tells the Israelites that God came down from Sinai with myriads of holy angels, who fought not just for the Israelites, but in and amongst them and even under their command:

> The LORD came from Sinai . . .
> With him were myriads of holy ones;
> at his right, a host of his own.
> Indeed, O favourite among peoples,
> all his holy ones were in your charge;
> they marched at your heels,
> accepted direction from you.
>
> *Deuteronomy 33:2–3*

A closely similar idea appears in the Qumran War Scroll:

> . . . the King of Glory is with us together with the Holy Ones. Valiant [warriors] of the angelic host are among our numbered men, and the Hero of war is with our congregation; the host of His spirits is with our foot-soldiers and horsemen.
>
> *1 QM XII. 7–8*[26]

Personal angels

People as well as nations could have individual angelic guardians or intercessors. This idea is of ancient origin, and it derives from the concept of the council of the gods, where human beings were supposed to have their own representatives or protagonists. Scattered references to angelic intercessors, guardians, and guides are found in Job, Zechariah, Tobit (part of the Apocrypha), and elsewhere. In one of the dream visions in the Similitudes of Enoch, the inhabitants of heaven—angels and transformed humans—pray to God on behalf of humans on earth. That

Jesus of Nazareth shared this common belief in personal angels is evident from his severe denunciation of those who abuse or despise the innocence of little children. Children may appear to be vulnerable and defenceless, says Jesus, but beware—they have powerful protectors in heaven:

> "Take care that you do not despise one of these little ones; for, I tell you, in heaven their angels continually see the face of my Father in heaven."
>
> *Matthew 18:10*

The angelomorphic transformation of humans

Given the belief that God could assume angelic form and that angels could assume human form, we have to ask whether it was also believed that humans could, either temporarily or permanently, be transformed into angels or some other form of heavenly being. The answer is that, in some circles at least, it was. The classic instance of temporary angelomorphic transformation of a living human being is Moses on Mount Sinai:

> As he came down from the mountain . . . Moses did not know that the skin of his face shone because he had been talking with God. When Aaron and all the Israelites saw Moses, the skin of his face was shining, and they were afraid to come near him . . . When Moses had finished speaking with them, he put a veil on his face; but whenever Moses went in before the LORD to speak with him, he would take the veil off, until he came out . . .
>
> *Exodus 34:29–34*

Moses was temporarily transformed by his encounter with God. His face shone with the reflected light of the divine Glory. This early biblical tradition is probably one of the factors underlying later speculations concerning the transformation and heavenly exaltation of Moses after his death.

There are a number of other instances in which angelomorphic transformation is either explicit or implicit. The mid-first-century

Jewish author Pseudo-Philo has two stories involving the temporary angelomorphic transformation of humans. The first occurs in his account of the victory of the Israelites over the Amorites. The leader of the victorious Israelites is called Kenaz:

> And Kenaz arose, and the spirit of the Lord clothed him . . . he was clothed with the spirit of power and was changed into another man . . .
>
> *Pseudo-Philo 27:9–10*[27]

This transformation is more than metaphorical. Kenaz is armed with a sword which is described as shining "like a lightning bolt". Assisted only by two other angels, he personally slaughters the entire Amorite army.

The second instance occurs in Pseudo-Philo's retelling of the story of David's victory over the Philistine giant, Goliath. As Goliath lies dying, David commands him to open his eyes and look at him. Goliath looks and sees an angel standing beside David:

> And the Philistine [Goliath] looked and saw an angel and said [to David], "Not you alone have killed me, but also the one who is present with you, he whose appearance is not like the appearance of a man." *And* then David *cut off his* [Goliath's] *head*. Now the angel of the Lord had changed David's appearance, and no one recognized him.
>
> *Pseudo-Philo 61:8–9*[28]

The change in David's appearance seems to imply some form of angelomorphic transformation, while the angel standing alongside David is probably to be understood as David's personal guardian angel or his heavenly alter ego. The manner in which this angel has assisted David is not stated, but the implication may be that his victory over Goliath had been accompanied by a parallel victory between their respective guardian angels fighting in heaven.

In all these stories there is a tension between metaphorical and literal significance. Sometimes the balance tilts one way and sometimes the other. There are also instances in which, although the primary sense is clearly metaphorical, nevertheless there are indications that something more literal is also being hinted at. In the book of Zechariah, the eponymous prophet has a vision in which he sees Joshua, the high priest, standing in the presence of the angel of Yhwh. Joshua is dressed in filthy clothes:

> The angel said to those who were standing before him [other angels], "Take off his filthy clothes." And to him [Joshua] he said, "See, I have taken your guilt away from you, and I will clothe you in festal apparel." ... So they put a clean turban on his head and clothed him in the apparel; and the angel of the Lord was standing by.
>
> *Zechariah 3:4-7*

Superficially the account is metaphorical. Joshua is in the presence of the angel of the Lord and other angels. The angels help him to discard his dirty clothes and vest him in the raiment appropriate to a high priest. The changing of Joshua's raiment undoubtedly serves as a metaphor for forgiveness and the removal of guilt. But there are also hints that he may be undergoing some form of transformation because, in the immediately following verses, Joshua is granted rights of access to God equivalent to those accorded to the angels. In exercising the functions of high priest, Joshua—it seems—has quasi-angelic status (Isaiah 63:9; cf. Jubilees 31:14).

There are other instances where the high priest is extravagantly praised in language reminiscent of that used of angels. For example, in Ecclesiasticus there is a description of the high priest emerging from the innermost sanctuary of the Jerusalem temple, the Holy of Holies, on the Day of Atonement:

> How glorious he was, surrounded by the people, as he came out of the house of the curtain. Like the morning star among the clouds, like the full moon at the festal season; like the sun shining on the temple of the Most High, like the rainbow gleaming in splendid clouds ...
>
> *Ecclesiasticus/Ben Sirach 50:5-7*

Behind this lavish hyperbole, there may again be echoes of an ancient angelomorphic tradition. On the Day of Atonement, the high priest would have been magnificently vested in regalia which included a turban bearing the Divine Name. When he emerged from the Holy of Holies, it was customary for him to utter the Divine Name, otherwise never spoken by anyone at any time. Hecataeus of Abdera, a non-Jewish fourth-century BCE writer on the history of Jews and Judaism, describes how the onlookers prostrated themselves and reverenced the high priest. This ritual prostration, implying reverence akin to worship, calls to mind the traditions about the Divine Name angel, the angel who has God's Name in him. Ecclesiasticus may be unwittingly reflecting an ancient understanding that the high priest, vested in his regalia and undertaking his high-priestly duties on the Day of Atonement, was temporarily transformed into a quasi-angelic being.

There is a further example of a human being acquiring angelic characteristics in Joseph and Aseneth, a Hellenistic-Jewish romance probably dating from between 100 BCE and 130 CE. The author describes the young couple's meeting with the elderly Jacob:

> ... Jacob was exceedingly beautiful to look at, and his old age (was) like the youth of a handsome (young) man, and his head was all white as snow ... and his eyes (were) flashing and darting (flashes of) lightning, and his sinews and his shoulders and his arms were like (those) of an angel ...
>
> *Joseph and Aseneth 22:7*[29]

The terminology suggests that Jacob, having undergone some form of transformation, is now simultaneously both a human and a quasi-angelic being. This may seem far-fetched, but a similar idea is found in the fragmentary Prayer of Jacob, a work probably dating from the first century CE. It appears that the human Jacob has in some way been transformed into an immortal, earthly angel:

> Fill my heart with good things, Lord; as an ear[th]ly angel, as [hav]ing become immortal, as having recei[ved] the gift which (is) from [yo]u, [a]men, amen.
>
> *Prayer of Jacob 18–19*[30]

The so-called "transfiguration" of Jesus may be regarded as another instance of temporary angelomorphic transformation. The author of Mark, in whose Gospel the earliest version of the story appears, undoubtedly believed that he was reporting an actual event (Mark 9:2–8). Nevertheless, there are parallels with the account of the transfiguration of Moses in the book of Exodus which are clearly intentional. Mark tells how Jesus took three of his disciples up a mountain to a place where they could be alone together:

> And he [Jesus] was transfigured before them, and his clothes became dazzling white, such as no one on earth could bleach them. And there appeared to them Elijah with Moses, who were talking with Jesus... Then a cloud overshadowed them, and from the cloud there came a voice, "This is my Son, the Beloved; listen to him!"
>
> *Mark 9:2–4,7*

Apparently, Jesus was temporarily transformed into a heavenly being, or—momentarily—he was being seen for the heavenly being that he was and always had been. The authors of Matthew and Luke expand Mark's story, adding the detail that Jesus' face also was transformed and shining. Their obvious intention is to emphasize still further the parallels with the transfiguration of Moses. The story concludes with the voice from heaven declaring Jesus to be the Son of God. Then the heavenly visitors depart, the glory fades, and Jesus is an ordinary human again. A number of highly significant motifs are entwined in this important story. For the moment, we note that this is another instance of a first-century CE Jewish story in which a living human undergoes temporary angelomorphic transformation.

When these findings are set alongside the evidence of 1 Enoch (see previous chapter), it seems clear that in the first and second centuries of the Common Era, at least in some circles within Judaism, it was believed that exceptional persons, such as prophets, priests, and kings, might undergo temporary as well as permanent angelomorphic transformation.

Transformation and heavenly ascent

There is a significant body of evidence testifying to the belief that humans could undergo angelomorphic transformation, not just on earth, but also by virtue of temporary or permanent entry into heaven. Accounts of these angelomorphic transformations are usually set within the conceptual framework of progressive ascent through the seven heavens, heaven being envisaged either as a temple, or as a royal court. So-called "ascent apocalypses" are common from the third century BCE to the second century CE. Typically, on arrival in heaven the seer is granted access to understandings and truths beyond the range of normal human knowledge, these insights being delivered either by an interpreting angel, or by God himself. The seer then comes back to earth, bringing with him the understandings that he has received. A motif frequently encountered in ascent apocalypses is that of discarding old clothing and putting on glorious new raiment, the change of raiment signifying that the seer is temporarily assuming angelic or quasi-angelic status. The seer's face may be described as radiant and shining. He may be initiated into the language of the angels, and he may be enabled to participate in the worship of God in heaven. In effect, the seer becomes an angelic being for the duration of his visit.

A turn-of-the-era text known as the Apocalypse of Zephaniah is typical. It describes the seer arriving in heaven and putting on an angelic garment. He is enabled to understand the language of the angels, speaking with them and joining in their prayers. Zephaniah describes his arrival at the crossing place into heaven:

> Thousands of thousands and myriads of myriads of angels gave praise before me. I, myself, put on an angelic garment. I saw all

of those angels praying. I, myself, prayed together with them, I
knew their language, which they spoke with me.

Apocalypse of Zephaniah 8:2–4[31]

The Martyrdom and Ascension of Isaiah, a composite, partly Jewish and partly Christian text, tells the story of Isaiah's temporary ascent into heaven. Isaiah, accompanied by an interpreter angel, ascends from the first to the seventh heaven. As he ascends, his appearance is transformed. He is shown (but does not put on) the glorious garment which is ready and waiting against the moment when he will have shed his earthly body. Once he has put on these garments, he is told, he will become equal to the highest of the angels:

> And he [the interpreting angel] took me up into the third heaven, and . . . the glory of my face was being transformed as I went up from heaven to heaven . . . And he [the angel] said to me "Hear then this also from your companion: [when from the body by the will of God you have come up here], then you will receive the robe which you will see, and also other numbered robes placed (there) you will see, and then you will be equal to the angels who (are) in the seventh heaven." . . . And he led me into the air of the seventh heaven, and moreover I heard a voice saying . . . "The holy Isaiah is permitted to come up here, for his robe is here." . . . And he took me up into the seventh heaven, and there I saw a wonderful light, and also angels without number. And there I saw all the righteous from the time of Adam onwards . . . stripped of (their) robes of the flesh; and I saw them in their robes of above, and they were like the angels who stand there in great glory.
>
> *Martyrdom and Ascension of Isaiah 7:24—9:9*[32]

In another composite document, the Testament of Levi, Levi twice dreams that he has entered heaven. First he dreams that God is conferring on him the blessing of priesthood. Then he dreams that seven men in white clothing are placing upon him the vestments of priesthood in preparation for his return to earth. Levi describes his experience thus:

> The first [angel] anointed me with holy oil and gave me a staff.
> The second [angel] washed me with pure water, fed me by hand with bread and holy wine, and put on me a holy and glorious vestment.
>
> *Testament of Levi 8:4–5*[33]

The angels continue the process of vesting Levi in his priestly garments, then they give him gifts signifying his new appointment and exalted status. The combination of motifs appears to imply angelomorphic transformation.

Angelomorphic transformation after death

There are numerous accounts of the angelomorphic transformation of human beings after death. A selection will suffice to illustrate the general principles. In Daniel there is the promise of future resurrection for the righteous dead Hasidim:

> "Many of those who sleep in the dust of the earth shall awake ... Those who are wise shall shine like the brightness of the sky, and those who lead many to righteousness, like the stars for ever and ever."
>
> *Daniel 12:2–3*

Given that the term "stars" frequently signifies "angels", the probable meaning is that the resurrected righteous martyrs will be transformed into angelic beings. The transformation in question is either for life in heaven, or for renewed life on a restored and radically transformed earth.

In the second of the three parables in the Similitudes of Enoch there is an account of *Sheol* giving up the dead for the last judgement. The righteous and holy ones are separated from those who are doomed to destruction. The righteous and holy ones, we are told, are destined to become angels in heaven, and their faces will shine with joy. In the third parable, this judgement scene is depicted in greater detail. Confronted with the enthroned Son of Man, the wicked kings, governors, and officials who have tyrannized the righteous of Israel will be condemned and then consigned to the angels for destruction. The righteous and the elect from among the presently living and the newly risen dead will put on garments of glory which will never wear out. Angelomorphic transformation is explicit:

> The righteous and elect ones shall rise from the earth and shall cease being of downcast face. They shall wear the garments of glory. These garments of yours shall become the garments of life from the Lord of the Spirits. Neither shall your garments wear out, nor your glory come to an end before the Lord of the Spirits.
>
> *1 Enoch 62:15-16*[34]

In the fourth book of Ezra, also called 2 Esdras, an interpreting angel teaches Ezra about death and the afterlife. He explains that the blessed dead have seven orders of foreknowledge concerning their impending resurrection and blessedness. The sixth order of blessedness is foreknowledge of impending angelomorphic transformation:

> The sixth order, when it is shown them how their face is to shine like the sun, and how they are to be made like the light of the stars, being incorruptible from then on.
>
> *4 Ezra/2 Esdras 7:97*

The second book of Baruch has an extended section concerning the nature of the resurrection life on and after the day of God's judgement. The unknown author addresses with extraordinary precision issues associated with heavenly transformation. He discusses how the resurrected righteous dead will be able to recognize one another, how they will be able to perceive presently invisible worlds, and the way in which they will be able to access times past and times future in addition to time present. The righteous dead will be astonishingly transformed and glorified, their dazzling splendour exceeding that of the angels:

> Also, as for the glory of those who proved to be righteous on account of my law [says God] ... their splendour will then be

> glorified by transformations, and the shape of their face will be changed into the light of their beauty so that they may acquire and receive the undying world which is promised to them.... they will be like the angels and be equal to the stars ... and the excellence of the righteous will then be greater than that of the angels.
>
> *2 Baruch 51:3,10–13*[35]

There are also examples of belief in the angelomorphic transformation of specific individuals. As noted in the previous chapter, the Qumran scrolls have little to say about resurrection because they reflect the community's strongly realized eschatology. Consequently, there are few opportunities for the motif of transformation to manifest itself. Nevertheless, there is a potentially important fragment from Qumran Cave 4. An unknown figure describes himself as being already enthroned in the heavens and already reckoned as being among the gods:

> ... a throne of strength in the congregation of "gods" so that not a single king of old shall sit on it, neither shall their noble men ... my glory is incomparable, and apart from me none is exalted. None shall come to me for I dwell in ... heaven, and there is no ... I am reckoned with the "gods" and my dwelling-place is in the congregation of holiness.
>
> *4Q491, fragment 11*[36]

The text is complex and difficult to interpret and translate. The figure who is speaking is either a heavenly being (perhaps Michael) or a human being who has undergone angelomorphic transformation and exaltation. Other motifs entwined in this text may be implying priestly or messianic status.

The Testament of Abraham, a late first- or early second-century text, depicts the archangel Michael taking Abraham up to heaven in a chariot borne by angels. Adam and Abel are already there, transformed into glorious and exalted heavenly beings. Outside the gates of heaven, Michael and Abraham see Adam seated on a golden throne, separating the souls of men as they come before him. Abraham rejoices at the sight of the righteous who are selected for salvation, but he laments over the fate of the sinners who are being condemned to eternal punishment and destruction:

> And outside the two gates of that place, they saw a man seated on a golden throne. And the appearance of that man was terrifying, like the Master's [God's] . . . Then Abraham asked the Commander-in-chief [Michael], "My lord Commander-in-chief, who is this most wondrous man, who is adorned in such glory?". . . The incorporeal one [Michael] said, "This is the first-formed Adam . . ."
>
> *Testament of Abraham 11:4,8-9*[37]

An almost identical story follows immediately. The only significant differences are that in the second story the enthroned figure is Abel rather than Adam, and that the throne is between the gates of heaven rather than outside them. Again, the angels are separating souls, either for blessing or destruction. The figure on the throne is majestic, and the throne appears to be made of crystal:

> And upon it sat a wondrous man, bright as the sun, like unto a son of God . . . And Abraham said, "My lord Commander-in-chief [Michael], who is this all-wondrous judge?". . . The Commander in-chief said, "Do you see, all-pious Abraham, the frightful man who is seated on the throne? This is the son of Adam, the first-formed, who is called Abel . . . he sits here to judge the entire creation. . ."
>
> *Testament of Abraham 12:5;13:1-3*[38]

The text makes it clear that the angelomorphic transformations of Adam and Abel have taken place after their human death. However, there are other instances in which angelomorphic transformation appears to have taken place either before death or at the moment of death. In the Animal Apocalypse, Enoch describes the ending of the flood:

> Then the water began to descend . . . until that boat [the ark] settled upon the earth, the darkness vanished, and it became light.

> Then the snow-white cow [Noah] which became a man [an angel] came out from that boat together with three cows [Noah's sons].
>
> *1 Enoch 89:8–9*[39]

It is not clear whether Noah's angelomorphic transformation has taken place while he was in the ark, or whether it happened at the time of his death. There is some evidence that Noah may sometimes have been regarded as an angelic being during his lifetime. In what is thought to be a fragment of an independent work called the Book of Noah, now embedded in the 1 Enoch corpus, there is an extraordinary story concerning Noah's birth. Even as a newborn baby, Noah was (it seems) a quasi-angelic being:

> And after some days my son, Methuselah, took a wife for his son Lamech, and she became pregnant by him and bore him a son. And his body was white as snow . . . and as for his eyes, when he opened them the whole house glowed like the sun . . . And his father, Lamech, was afraid of him and fled and went to Methuselah his father; and he said to him, "I have begotten a strange son: He is not like an (ordinary) human being, but he looks like the children of the angels of heaven to me; his form is different, and he is not like us."
>
> *1 Enoch 106:1–5*[40]

A variety of traditions concerning ascent into heaven and heavenly transformation are also clustered around the figure of Moses. Given Moses' exalted status and the very clear statement in the Hebrew scriptures that his burial place remained unknown (Deuteronomy 34:6), this is perhaps not surprising. In the Animal Apocalypse, Moses—like Noah—is depicted as an animal (that is, a human) who becomes a man (that is, an angel). After he has ascended to the summit of a "great rock" and received the tablets of the covenant, Moses is transformed into an angel. As such, he builds a "house for the Lord of the sheep" (that is, he builds the Tabernacle). Moses then continues to lead the people forward on their journey to the promised land, which he sees away beyond the river Jordan, but does not enter:

> Then coming into a pasture, they approached a stream of water. (There) that sheep who was leading them—the one who had become a man—departed from them ... (Then the rest of) the sheep sought him; and there took place a great cry over him.
>
> *1 Enoch 89:37–38*[41]

The author of the Animal Apocalypse supposes the initial angelomorphic transformation of Moses (cf. Exodus 34:29–35) to have been permanent, and that it lasted until Moses "departed from them". There are other traditions which envisage the angelomorphic transformation of Moses taking place at the time of his death. Josephus says that a cloud suddenly appeared and stood over Moses, who disappeared and "went to God" (*Antiquities of the Jews*, IV 8.48). In Ezekiel the Tragedian, a second-century CE work, the human Moses dreams not just of transformation, but of heavenly enthronement:

> On Sinai's peak I [Moses] saw what seemed a throne
> so great in size it touched the clouds of heaven.
> Upon it sat a man of noble mien,
> becrowned, and with a scepter in one hand
> while with the other he did beckon me.
> I made approach and stood before the throne.
> He handed o'er the scepter and he bade
> me mount the throne, and gave to me the crown;
> then he himself withdrew from off the throne.
> I gazed upon the whole earth round about;
> things under it, and high above the skies.
> Then at my feet a multitude of stars
> fell down, and I their number reckoned up.
> They passed me by like armèd ranks of men.
> Then I in terror wakened from the dream.
>
> *Ezekiel the Tragedian, 68–82*[42]

The scene is the heavenly enthronement of Moses after his death. Having undergone angelomorphic transformation, Moses now becomes a heavenly being surrounded by other heavenly beings (the angel-stars).

This is confirmed in the immediately following lines, where Moses' father-in-law says to him, "You shall cause a mighty throne to rise, and you yourself shall rule and govern men . . . all things present, past and future you shall see." That a tradition of Moses being highly exalted in heaven was already current in first-century Hellenistic Judaism is confirmed by Philo, who describes Moses as worthy to be called the "Father and Maker of the universe". Philo's understanding is that by coming close to God Moses has become a quasi-divine being. In a later Samaritan text, called the Samaritan Liturgy, Moses is assigned the Divine Name and has the status of angel of the Lord.

Given his dramatic assumption into heaven, one might expect to find angelomorphic traditions also clustered around the figure of Elijah in much the same way that they are around the figure of Enoch (see below). Surprisingly, this is not the case. Elijah's ascent into heaven certainly points to his highly exalted status, but there is little or no evidence of any belief in angelomorphic transformation. Elijah was a fiery prophet. He exited this world wreathed in flames, and was expected to return before the coming Day of Judgement to promote reconciliation between the generations and the restoration of the tribes of Israel. Perhaps because of this expectation of return, Elijah is never represented as having undergone any angelomorphic transformation on entry into heaven.

There are, however, important angelomorphic speculations associated with the shadowy figure of Melchizedek. Little is known about Melchizedek—he makes a brief appearance in Genesis 14:18–20, where he is apparently the human king of Jerusalem and a priest of "God Most High". He apparently received tithes from (or granted tithes to) Abraham. There is also a passing reference to Melchizedek in Psalm 110:

> The LORD [God] says to my lord,
> "Sit at my right hand
> until I make your enemies your footstool" . . .
> "You are a priest for ever according to
>   the order of Melchizedek."
>
> *Psalm 110:1,4*

There is a more extended reference to Melchizedek in the Christian epistle to the Hebrews. There the priesthood of Jesus is contrasted with that of Melchizedek. Jesus, we are told, became a priest like Melchizedek, "not through physical descent ... but through the power of an indestructible life" (Hebrews 7:15–16). As already noted above, one of the Qumran texts depicts Melchizedek as a powerful heavenly prince. He is a divine redeemer, an eschatological judge, and the instrument of God's vengeance. Other Qumran texts identify Melchizedek with the angel-prince, Michael, who is also described as the Prince of Light. We infer that at Qumran Melchizedek was understood to have undergone angelomorphic transformation when he made his transition from life on earth to life in heaven.

Dual identity: Michael–Melchizedek and Jacob–Israel

The Qumran identification of Melchizedek with Michael raises questions about their supposed relationship at the time when Melchizedek was a human being on earth and Michael an angel in heaven. How could one and the same figure, Michael–Melchizedek, be in two different places at the same time? Common sense suggests that the identification of Michael with Melchizedek must be mistaken. In fact, the identification is robust. It seems that the authors of the relevant texts were able to accept and live comfortably with the extraordinary notion that a being might have simultaneous existence in heaven and on earth.

If this were the only instance of the concept of dual identity, it could be dismissed as an isolated oddity. However, there are other examples of similar duality. In the Prayer of Joseph we encounter the hybrid figure of Jacob–Israel. Compare the figure of Jacob who, in the Prayer of Jacob (see above), is said to be an "earthly angel", who has already received the gift of immortality. In the Prayer of Joseph, Jacob appears to be a human being having a parallel identity and existence in heaven, where he is an archangel called Israel. Jacob in his human mode is unaware of this parallel angelic identity until it is disclosed to him by the angel Uriel. Uriel explains that although Jacob had always been the angel Israel, when he, Jacob, descended from heaven to earth he was known to others and to himself only as Jacob. Having now been made aware of his highly exalted status, Jacob becomes angry. He wrestles with the angel Uriel in order to establish his now apparent supremacy, saying:

> "I, Jacob, who is speaking to you, am also Israel, an angel of God and a ruling spirit . . . because I am the *firstborn of every living thing to whom God* gives life . . . [Am I not] Israel, *the archangel of the power of the Lord* and the *chief captain* among the sons of God?"
>
> *Prayer of Joseph, A:1–3,7*[43]

Dual identity: Enoch and the Son of Man

According to the book of Genesis, Enoch—the son of Cain—by-passed death and *Sheol* and went straight to heaven:

> Enoch walked with God; then he was no more, because God took him.
>
> *Genesis 5:24*

This ancient tradition made Enoch a natural focus for speculations about heaven and its inhabitants. Traditions concerning the angelomorphic transformation of Enoch are found embedded in texts spanning many centuries. A tradition in the Similitudes of Enoch (1 Enoch 37—71) apparently identifies the human Enoch, after his translation into heaven, with a figure called the "Son of Man". This "Son of Man" is an exalted heavenly power superior even to the angels. When he arrives in heaven, Enoch is granted a vision of the blessedness of the righteous and chosen ones. In his vision, he joins in the heavenly worship of the angels and apparently undergoes angelomorphic transformation:

> In those days, whirlwinds carried me off from the earth, and set me down in the ultimate ends of the heavens . . . I saw a dwelling place underneath the wings of the Lord of the Spirits . . . And at that place (under his wings) my eyes saw others who stood before

> him sleepless (and) blessed (him) . . . And my face was changed on account of the fact that I could not withstand the sight.
>
> 1 Enoch 39:3,7,13–14[44]

In this case, it is not clear whether the transformation of Enoch is temporary and protective or permanent. However, towards the end of the Similitudes there is an account of another of Enoch's visions. It describes his final ascent from earth to heaven in a chariot borne on the wind. On arrival in heaven, he sees rivers of fire, myriads of angels, the storehouses of the sun, the moon, and the stars, and the heavenly palace wherein is the throne of God's glory. Finally, he sees (because he is no longer human) the Antecedent of Time—that is, God himself. There is now no doubt. Enoch's transformation is permanent:

> And he [Michael] took my spirit—even me, Enoch—to the heaven of heavens, and I saw there as it [a house] built of hailstones, and between those stones were tongues of living fire . . . And I saw angels that could not be counted, thousands and thousands and ten thousand times ten thousand; they were surrounding that house . . . And out of that house came Michael and Raphael and Gabriel and Phanuel and many holy angels without number. And with them was the Head of Days [God], and his head was white and pure as wool, and his apparel was indescribable. And I fell on my face, and my flesh melted, and my spirit was transformed.
>
> 1 Enoch 71:5–11[45]

In the Second Book of Enoch, a somewhat later work, there is another description of Enoch's ascent into heaven. When Enoch arrives in heaven, God instructs Michael to divest Enoch of his earthly clothing (that is, his human body), to anoint him with oil, and to clothe him in garments of glory. Enoch is transformed and becomes like one of the angels:

> And the Lord said to Michael, "Take Enoch and extract (him) from his earthly clothing. And anoint him with the delightful oil, and put (him) into the clothes of glory." And Michael extracted me from my clothes. He anointed me with the delightful oil . . .

> And I gazed at all of myself, and I had become like one of the glorious ones, and there was no observable difference.
>
> *2 Enoch [A] 22:8-10*[46]

The much later Third Book of Enoch is only indirectly relevant to the present study. Nevertheless, it contains yet another dramatic transformation scene. Enoch is brought up from earth to the heavenly heights and is transformed into Metatron, prince of the Divine Presence, the lesser YHWH (see above). Enoch describes what this transformation involved:

> The angel Metatron, Prince of the Divine Presence, the glory of highest heaven, said to me [i.e. Enoch]: When the Holy One, blessed be he, took me to serve the throne of glory, . . . at once my flesh turned to flame, my sinews to blazing fire, my bones to juniper coals, my eyelashes to lightning flashes, my eyeballs to fiery torches, the hairs of my head to hot flames, all my limbs to wings of burning fire, and the substance of my body to blazing fire.
>
> *3 Enoch 15:1*[47]

This text (3 Enoch) is late, and well outside the period with which we are concerned. But even in the much earlier Similitudes, it appears that Enoch may always have had a dual identity, like that of Jacob-Israel. Immediately after Enoch has been "translated" from earth to heaven and has prostrated himself before God and been transformed into a heavenly being, he is identified as the "son of man" and "that son of man":

> And that Head of Days came with Michael and Raphael and Gabriel and Phanuel and thousands and ten thousands of angels without number. And that angel [Michael] came to me and said to me, "You are that son of man who was born for righteousness, and righteousness dwells on you, and the righteousness of the Head of Days will not forsake you . . . And there will be length of days

with that son of man, and there will be peace for the righteous . . . in the name of the Lord of Spirits for ever and forever."

1 Enoch 71:13-14,17[48]

The text is corrupt, and the interpretation and translation may be flawed, but it appears that it is being revealed to Enoch that he is one and the same being as the Son of Man who, throughout the Similitudes, has been represented as a majestic, enthroned, pre-existent heavenly being variously designated as the Chosen One, the Anointed One (Messiah), and the Righteous One. The function of this Son of Man is to exercise delegated divine powers. On behalf of God, he is to judge all beings, whether in heaven or on earth, protecting the righteous and executing vengeance on sinners. He is to be a light to the Gentiles, and the hope of those who are sick in heart.

The obvious question that has to be asked is, how could Enoch have been a human being on earth whilst at the same time being (unknown to himself) a mighty, pre-existent, enthroned power in heaven? How could he have two different identities and been in two different places at one and the same time? And how could each identity apparently be unaware of the other?

The concept of dual identities is exceedingly strange, but it becomes slightly less so when set in the context of the belief that significant action proceeds in parallel in heaven and on earth, and that nations and individual humans have individual heavenly partners or guardian angels. When the latter are in heaven and the former are on earth, the distinction between them is easily maintained, and there is no problem. But when the human being (Enoch in this case) is transported to heaven and undergoes angelomorphic transformation, the distinction between the one who was formerly human (Enoch here) and the parallel heavenly alter ego necessarily collapses. The two former identities (earthly and heavenly) have to become fused into one ongoing heavenly identity. On arrival in heaven and undergoing angelomorphic transformation, the human Enoch discovers that he has always been the heavenly Son of Man, just as Jacob discovers that he has always been the heavenly Jacob–Israel.

Conclusion

Important findings have emerged. Heaven, it seems, was not envisaged as a separate realm of being: it was a location with borders that could, at times, be porous. Heaven was inhabited by angels. There could be angelomorphic transformation: God might appear in angelic form, and angels in human form. There could be traffic in both directions between heaven and earth. Alongside continuing traditional beliefs, such as *Sheol* being the permanent abode of the dead, we have seen evidence indicating that in some circles it was believed that righteous martyrs and other significant figures had bypassed *Sheol*, entered directly into heaven, and been transformed into glorious angelic beings. Living humans also, it appeared, might sometimes undergo similar transformation. Heavenly transformation seems sometimes to have been visualized in terms of the discarding of old clothing and the putting on of glorious new garments. We have also observed the belief, extraordinary to us, that significant action may take place simultaneously in parallel in heaven and on earth. Even more extraordinary is the concept of "dual identity"; that is, the belief that an exceptional being may exist as a human on earth whilst enjoying parallel being as an angelic power in heaven. Finally, we noted in passing examples of the belief that one particular angelic power was uniquely exalted over all the others, possibly even to the extent of exercising delegated divine powers. In view of the ideas that become attached to Jesus after his death, this figure merits closer examination.

CHAPTER 4

The Heavenly Redeemer

In the previous chapter we suggested that one of the starting points for belief in angels was the ancient polytheistic concept of a divine council or assembly of the gods in heaven. Within the divine council, the god of Israel was probably initially no more than one among equals, but over time he came to be regarded as the supreme ruler over all the lesser deities. These lesser deities then become either subordinate angelic powers or nonentities.

The notion of heaven as the court and household of a supreme monarch lent itself naturally to the further idea that there was one especially powerful and exalted angel appointed to act as God's chief executive officer, vicegerent, or grand vizier. In passing, we alluded to traditions concerning just such an exalted heavenly being, second in power only to God. This figure is variously described in the ancient texts, but the two most salient common features are that the figure exercises delegated divine powers and has a redemptive function. It is supposed that this being will come from heaven to earth to exercise judgement on sinners, to redeem and restore God's righteous people, and to inaugurate an ongoing age of peace and plenty. In some instances, this exalted heavenly being is called "a son of man" or designated "the Son of Man".

In this chapter, we consider a number of specific traditions concerning this heavenly figure. In the first instance, we want to know what the texts say and whether the figures depicted in the texts are the independent literary inventions of individual authors, or whether they may be specific instances of an underlying seam of ongoing tradition. If there was a seam of ongoing tradition, this could have had a significant bearing on Jesus' own self-understanding, or it might have influenced the earliest beliefs of Jesus' followers concerning his true identity and significance, or both.

One like a son of man

The anthropomorphic figure of the chariot-enthroned Glory of God in Ezekiel 1 was mentioned briefly in the previous chapter. This figure apparently features four times in the book of Ezekiel. In the first chapter, there is the dramatic figure of the Glory of God enthroned on a multi-wheeled chariot. In the third chapter, there is the standing figure of the Glory of God (verse 23). In chapter 8, an angel brings Ezekiel into the presence of the Glory of God in Jerusalem. Finally, in chapter 10 the Glory of God, surrounded by angels, rises up and departs from Jerusalem. Directly or indirectly, the imagery associated with this figure has exerted a considerable influence on depictions of theophanies in later apocalyptic texts, including the theophany in Daniel 7. In his bizarre dream, Daniel sees a glorious heavenly figure described as "one like a son of man":

> I [Daniel] saw one like a human being [literally "son of man"]
> coming with the clouds of heaven.
> And he came to the Ancient One [God]
> and was presented before him.
> To him was given dominion
> and glory and kingship,
> that all peoples, nations, and languages
> should serve him.
> His dominion is an everlasting dominion
> that shall not pass away,
> and his kingship is one
> that shall never be destroyed.
>
> *Daniel 7:13-14*

The identity of this manlike angelic power is problematic. One of the difficulties is disentangling what are almost certainly multiple traditions underlying the present text of Daniel 7, which—unusually—is written in Aramaic rather than Hebrew. The analysis of the different sources involves complex issues and is a matter for experts. It seems possible that two different traditional motifs, both of extremely ancient Canaanite origin, have at some early, pre-literary stage become entwined. Then, at some later stage, they have been overwritten by the final author or redactor.

One of these traditional motifs concerns a war between the angels in heaven. Daniel's vision opens with four terrifying beasts crawling up out of the troubled sea, which in Canaanite mythology represents death. These demonic apparitions make war on "the holy ones", who must either be persecuted human Jews or their corresponding guardian angels. If the "holy ones" are guardian angels, the battle between the angels and the demonic powers must be taking place in heaven in parallel with battles on earth between wicked Gentiles and righteous Jews. Something similar appears in the book of Revelation where Michael and his angels make war in heaven against the terrifying seven-headed, star-destroying, red dragon and his wicked angels. This war in heaven proceeds in parallel with conflict on earth between the human saints of God and their wicked human oppressors (Revelation 12 and 13). In Daniel's vision, the good angels are initially losing the battle. Then God intervenes decisively in judgement, and the tables are turned. God rewards the good guardian angels of the Israelites by awarding them a kingdom in heaven. At the same time, he gives a parallel kingdom to the faithful Israelites on earth.

This narrative appears to be entangled with a second traditional story or motif concerning eschatological judgement. The controlling image in this second story is that of the Divine Council of the gods in heaven. Wheeled thrones are brought forward, and God—who is called "an Ancient of Days"—takes his place on his fiery throne, flanked by lesser deities and surrounded by multitudes of angels. He prepares to give judgement. At the last moment, another heavenly figure suddenly appears (Daniel 7:13–14). Whether this figure comes from elsewhere in heaven, or from somewhere on earth, is not stated. This heavenly figure is described as being "like a son of man", that is, he has a human appearance. He is presented before God, and God delegates to him everlasting dominion, glory, and kingship over all people and nations on earth. How this delegated role is connected with the impending eschatological heavenly judgement is not specified, but the implication seems to be that this manlike heavenly being will exercise his functions on earth in parallel with the Divine Council's judgement in heaven. He is a "heavenly redeemer", tasked first with rescuing and making safe the faithful human Israelites and then with reigning over all peoples and nations as God's vice-regent on earth. The figure is not named, but his role and functions suggest that he must be a major angelic power having a special relationship with the people of Israel. This conclusion, taken together with the evidence of other texts examined below, suggests that he could be either Gabriel or Michael, the latter being the guardian prince-angel of Israel and commander-in-chief of the heavenly armies.

This figure played a significant part in the thinking of Jesus' earliest followers, and perhaps of Jesus himself. As we shall see, it played a major part in the emergence of resurrection and exaltation faith, and parallel formation of belief in the *parousia* or second coming of Jesus. It also exerted a major influence on early christological thinking. One of the key issues is whether the earliest followers of Jesus believed the figure of the "one like a son of man" depicted in Daniel 7 to be an individual heavenly being, or whether they understood the figure to be a metaphor or symbol for the persecuted and suffering—but subsequently vindicated and rewarded—righteous people of Israel.

The symbolic interpretation is doubtful. The "holy ones" referred to in Daniel 7:18 are almost certainly angels, not formerly suffering humans. The central motif in the story of the war in heaven is God's decisive, saving intervention, not recompense for human suffering. More significantly, in the story of judgement before the Divine Council (Daniel 7:9–14) there is no suggestion that the "one like a son of man" has endured suffering or adversity before coming to God. On the contrary, he is presented as an established, heavenly being to whom God is now assigning additional plenipotentiary powers over all peoples and all nations on earth. The overarching conceptual framework is that of action proceeding in parallel on earth and in heaven. Within this framework, the terrifying beasts in Daniel's vision are more than merely symbolic figures. They are presented as realities, wicked angelic powers in partnership with the alien world-empires intent on the destruction of God's people on earth. War in heaven is proceeding in parallel with war on earth.

The principal difficulty which the "symbolic" interpretation cannot overcome is that the figure of a coming heavenly redeemer appears in variant forms in a number of later, derivative apocalyptic texts. Nowhere in any of these derivative texts is the heavenly redeemer figure ever regarded as symbolic, or as suffering, or as ever having suffered or been in any way disadvantaged. In every instance he is a mighty, individual, heavenly being who comes to earth to save and make secure the people of God.

Heavenly redeemer figures in the Qumran Scrolls

In the previous chapter, attention was drawn to the mysterious figure of Melchizedek, who appears only twice in the Hebrew scriptures: once as the human priest and king of Jerusalem who blesses Abraham, and once in Psalm 110 where the anticipated Davidic king is declared to be "a priest for ever according to the order of Melchizedek" (verse 4). Despite this paucity of reference, Melchizedek traditions become important in the Second Temple period, in early Christian thinking, and (later) in rabbinic Judaism. In the Qumran War Scroll, the archangel Michael is explicitly identified with another heavenly being called the "Prince of Light". On the basis of this identification, and of other references to the Prince of Light in the text known as the Community Rule, Michael and the Prince of Light are identified with the figure of the exalted, heavenly Melchizedek. Melchizedek himself appears in the Qumran scroll designated 11Q13, which dates from the first century BCE and is strongly influenced by Isaiah 61:1–2. This scroll depicts Melchizedek as an extraordinarily exalted heavenly being. He is called "head of the sons of heaven" (a role belonging to the archangel Michael), and he is represented as having a special relationship with the people of God (another of Michael's roles). According to the scroll, there is to be a great day of deliverance when Melchizedek will protect and liberate Israel, forgive sins, execute judgement on angels and men, and annihilate the forces of Belial:

> For this is the moment of the Year of Grace for Melchizedek. [And h]e will, by his strength, judge the holy ones of God, executing judgement as it is written concerning him in the Songs of David, who said, ELOHIM *has taken his place in the divine council; in the midst of the gods he holds judgement* (Psalms lxxxii,1).
>
> *11Q13:9–10*[49]

The scroll is complex, fragmentary, and difficult to interpret with certainty. In addition to describing Melchizedek and his functions, it appears to imply that Melchizedek has an associated earthly counterpart, a Spirit-anointed messenger or herald. The author goes on to quote and then interpret Isaiah 52:7:

> This is the day of [Peace/Salvation] concerning which [God] spoke [through Isa]iah the prophet, who said, [*How*] *beautiful upon the mountains are the feet of the messenger who proclaims peace, who brings good news, who proclaims salvation, who says to Zion: your* ELOHIM [*reigns*](Isa.lii, 7). Its interpretation; *the mountains* are the prophets . . . and *the messenger* is the Anointed one of the spirit, concerning whom Dan[iel] said . . .
>
> 11Q13:15–18[50]

The references here to Daniel and to the "Anointed one of the spirit" have nothing to do with the figure of the "one like a son of man" in Daniel 7:13–14. They point forward to Daniel 9:25, a passage which concerns "the time of an anointed prince". The statement that Melchizedek's messenger is "anointed with the spirit" implies messianic status. It appears that Melchizedek's messenger may be a human messiah distinct from the heavenly Melchizedek. Another possibility is that the whole text may be reflecting an understanding of Melchizedek as an angelomorphic being, someone who may simultaneously act and be spoken of as being both human and divine. The most significant connection between the Qumran scroll 11Q13 and Daniel 7:13–14 is that both texts appear to be describing an individual, exalted, heavenly being equipped with delegated divine status and functions. The similarities between the two exalted figures suggest that we may be seeing an early stage of what was to become an ongoing process. Daniel's figure of the "one like a son of man" is beginning to be drawn into a complex web of messianic interpretation.

The same phenomenon may perhaps be observed in another Qumran scroll designated 4Q246, which is thought to date from the last third of the first century BCE. This text, normally referred to as the "Son of God" fragment, is particularly difficult to reconstruct and interpret. Nevertheless, it is important because it apparently points forward, in terms reminiscent of Daniel 7, to an apocalyptic figure designated "Son of God" and "Son of the Most High":

> "Son of God" he shall be called, and they will name him "son of the Most High"... His [or its] kingdom is an everlasting kingdom and all his [or its] ways truth. He [or it] will judge the earth with truth and all will make peace. The sword will cease from the earth, and all cities will pay him [or it] homage. The great God will be his [or its] strength... His [or its] sovereignty is everlasting sovereignty...
>
> *4Q246, column 2*[51]

The figure referred to could be either human or angelic; if human, it could be a historical person. Opinions are divided. Nowhere is it stated explicitly that the figure is anointed, but the term "Son of God" is one of the designations used of the Davidic messiah. The functions ascribed to this figure—subduing the nations, ruling over an eternal kingdom, judging the earth, and exercising an everlasting dominion—are messianic. These and other considerations suggest that the figure may be a transcendent or superhuman being rather than a human king. Although there is no explicit reference to the figure of the "one like a son of man" in Daniel 7, there are similarities. If, as seems likely, the author of the Son of God fragment had the Danielic figure in mind, this would be important evidence that the merging of the concept of the Danielic "one like a son of man" with that of the Davidic messiah was well advanced, even before the time of Jesus.

The enthroned Son of Man in the Similitudes

The Similitudes of Enoch are something of a puzzle, because no trace of them is found among the Qumran documents. This may indicate that they were not composed until sometime after the destruction of the Qumran settlement in 68 CE. On the other hand, the internal evidence suggests that the Similitudes were probably composed during the Herodian period (37–4 BCE) or slightly later, perhaps around the turn of the era. Their omission from the Qumran corpus may be a matter of chance, or it could reflect the fact that the theology of the Similitudes was distasteful to the sectaries, whose own future expectations were articulated within the rather different framework of a partly realized eschatology.

The Similitudes purport to be Enoch's account of truths imparted to him in the course of visionary ascents into heaven. They are divided into three sections, each several chapters in length. Each section describes itself as a "parable"—hence the title, the "Similitudes". In addition to the three parables, there is a brief, formal preface and a two-chapter appendix (1 Enoch 70—71) describing the angelomorphic transformation of the human Enoch into the heavenly Son of Man. For present purposes, we focus on the three parables, that is on 1 Enoch 38—69.

The first parable is concerned with forthcoming judgement, the annihilation of the wicked, and the future heavenly home of the righteous. Enoch claims to be disclosing secret wisdom or knowledge imparted to him by the Lord of the Spirits [God]. This knowledge and wisdom, which has hitherto been withheld from mortal men, concerns the forthcoming appearance of a mighty heavenly being who will come to protect the righteous and elect people of Israel, and to execute judgement on sinners:

> ... and when the Righteous One shall appear ... he shall reveal light to the righteous and the elect who dwell upon the earth, where will the dwelling of the sinners be, and where the resting place of those who denied the name of the Lord of the Spirits? It would have been better for them not to have been born. When the secrets of the Righteous One are revealed, he shall judge the sinners, and the wicked ones will be driven from the presence of the righteous and the elect ... they shall not be able to behold the faces of the holy ones, for the light of the Lord of the Spirits has shined upon the face of the holy, the righteous, and the elect.
>
> *1 Enoch 38:2–4*[52]

Enoch is then carried up to heaven by a whirlwind. There he sees the dwelling place of the angels and beholds the righteous dead humans and angels interceding on behalf of the living humans. He also sees a mighty angelic being who is called "the Chosen One". This heavenly being dwells in the closest possible proximity with the Lord of the Spirits (God), apparently taking precedence over all other inhabitants of heaven:

> And in that place my eyes saw the Chosen One of righteousness and faith . . . And I saw his dwelling beneath the wings of the Lord of Spirits, and all the righteous and chosen were mighty before him like fiery lights [that is, angelic beings].
>
> *1 Enoch 39:6-7*[53]

The second and third parables contain graphic accounts of Enoch's further visionary experiences, together with references to heavenly beings, including good and bad angels, some named and others anonymous. Interest again centres on the figure of an extraordinarily exalted heavenly being who is variously called the "Righteous One", the "Chosen One", the "Son of Man", and the "Anointed One" (i.e. the Messiah). These expressions are not titles in the formal sense, but they are used in a way that makes it clear that they are denoting a specific, supremely exalted heavenly being. In the second parable, we are told that the figure called the Son of Man stands before God, and that he will be seated on a throne of glory judging the wicked. God will then transform the heavens and the earth, and the Son of Man will dwell among the blessed on earth. Enoch describes the person and the mission of the Son of Man in terms strongly reminiscent of Daniel 7:

> At that place [in heaven], I saw the One [that is, God] to whom belongs the time before time. And his head was white like wool, and there was with him another individual, whose face was like that of a human being. His countenance was full of grace like that of one among the holy angels. And I asked . . . "Who is this?" . . . And he [Enoch's interpreter angel] answered me and said to me, "This is the Son of Man, to whom belongs righteousness, and with whom righteousness dwells . . . [T]he Lord of the Spirits [God] has chosen him, and he is destined to be victorious before the Lord of the Spirits in eternal uprightness. This Son of Man . . . shall depose the kings from their thrones and kingdoms."
>
> *1 Enoch 46:1-5*[54]

In another passage, even more strongly reminiscent of Daniel 7, Enoch describes how the prayers of the righteous humans ascend into heaven where they become mingled with the praise and worship of the holy ones (that is, the angels). Judgement is then passed on those who have persecuted and shed the blood of righteous humans:

> In those days I saw the Head of Days as he took his seat on the throne of his glory, and the books of the living were opened in his presence, and all his host, which was in the heights of heaven, and his court, were standing in his presence.
>
> 1 Enoch 47:3[55]

The timeframe then shifts, and we find that Enoch, who is now revealed to be the Son of Man, was given a secret "Name" by God at the dawn of time:

> At that hour, that Son of Man was given a name, in the presence of the Lord of the Spirits . . . even before the creation of the sun and the moon, before the creation of the stars, he was given a name . . . All those who dwell upon the earth shall fall and worship before him . . . For this purpose he became the Chosen One; he was concealed in the presence of (the Lord of the Spirits) prior to the creation of the world, and for eternity.
>
> 1 Enoch 48:2–6[56]

Three related motifs, each highly significant in itself, are here entwined. The Son of Man receives a Name from God, the Son of Man is revealed to be a pre-existent being, and the Son of Man's true nature and Name are concealed from mankind until the time comes for their final revelation.

In the third parable, Enoch describes the enthronement of the Son of Man, who is the Chosen One, and the final great judgement presided over by the Son of Man seated on a throne of glory (or, possibly, seated on God's own throne). Again, there is the motif of the initial concealment and subsequent revelation of the Son of Man. This concealment was from the beginning of time until God chose to reveal the Son of Man, first to the holy and chosen ones (righteous angels and humans) and then, on the day of judgement, to all creation. As the high and mighty kings, governors, landlords, and other wicked humans are brought forward to be judged, they are challenged to recognize the Son of Man. It appears that the Son of Man was someone known to them, but hitherto his significance had gone unrecognized. But now that the Son of Man is revealed, the great and the good have to grovel and plead in vain for mercy:

> [T]hey will be terrified and will cast down their faces, and pain will seize them when they see that Son of Man sitting on the throne of his glory. And the kings and the mighty, and all who possess the land will bless and glorify and exalt him who rules over all, who was hidden . . . But the Lord of Spirits himself will press them, so that they will hasten to depart from his presence; and their faces will be filled with shame, and the darkness will grow deeper on their faces, <and he will deliver them> to the angels for punishment . . .
>
> *1 Enoch 62:5–6,10–11*[57]

It is difficult to know where this action is supposed to be taking place, the boundary between action in heaven and action on earth being indistinct. This lack of definition probably reflects the underlying conviction that heaven and earth taken together constitute the arena within which God's saving action takes place. In this case, the Son of Man is an exalted, enthroned heavenly being whose primary role is to execute judgement, whether in heaven or on earth.

One issue brought into focus by the messianic designation of the transcendent Son of Man in the Similitudes is the figure's apparent lack of any redemptive or saving role. The Son of Man is presented as a heavenly judge, but does he at any time play any part in rescuing and ensuring the ongoing safety of God's righteous and holy people here on earth? The answer is that the absence of a redemptive or saving role is only apparent. Judgement itself is redemptive because the outcome of judgement is salvation for those who are vindicated and freed from the curse of their oppressors. Without judgement, there can be no salvation or redemption. In any case, it seems to be envisaged that the Son of Man will act on earth as well as in heaven. For example, in the second parable Enoch is told that:

> This son of man whom you have seen—he will raise the kings and the mighty from their couches, and the strong from their thrones. He will loosen the reins of the strong, and he will crush the teeth of the sinners. He will overturn the kings from their thrones and their kingdoms ...
>
> 1 Enoch 46:4–5[58]

Also, a little later, Enoch has an extraordinary vision of the future in the form of six great mountains of metal, which represent the wealth and power of mankind. An interpreting angel explains that all the things Enoch has seen in his visions happen by the authority of God's Messiah, "so that he [the Messiah] may give orders and be praised upon the earth" (1 Enoch 52:4). Before the blazing wrath of the Messiah these mountains of metal will melt away, there being no way that accumulated wealth can serve as a protection for the wicked. The implication is evident: the Son of Man, the heavenly Messiah, will act on earth as well as in heaven. His action will be redemptive and saving. He is the heavenly redeemer of God's righteous people on earth.

To summarize, the Similitudes of Enoch provide early and unambiguous evidence that their author understood the figure of the "one like a son of man" in Daniel 7:13–14 to be an individual, heavenly being invested with supreme authority and delegated divine powers. The Similitudes go further than Daniel in their depiction of the Son of Man, identifying the Son of Man as the Messiah. They declare him to be pre-existent, chosen, and named by God before creation. He is the righteous one, pre-eminent before God and enthroned in glory. He may even be seated on God's own throne. None of these details appear in Daniel 7.

There is one other significant tradition in the Similitudes that is similarly without parallel in Daniel. This is the naming of the Son of Man and the climactic revelation of his Name. The description in the Similitudes of the revelation of the Name of the Son of Man comes immediately after a difficult passage depicting a scene set long ago in heaven. What was happening is unclear, but it seems that rebel angels had extracted from the archangel Michael secret knowledge concerning the never-to-be-spoken Name of God. This knowledge had in some way become incorporated into an oath, responsible for initiating and sustaining the whole created order:

> [By this oath] [t]he heaven was suspended before the creation of the world; and forever! By it the earth is founded upon the water . . . By that oath, the sea was created . . . By the same oath the sun and the moon complete their courses of travel, and do not deviate from the laws (made) for them, from the beginning (of creation); and forever!
>
> *1 Enoch 69:16–20*[59]

There are striking parallels here with the Genesis creation story, with the description of divine Wisdom in the book of Proverbs, and with the Word of God as the agent of God's creation in the prologue to the Gospel of John.

At this point the author of the Similitudes suddenly changes tack and introduces his description of the scene in heaven when the hitherto secret Name of the Son of Man is revealed:

> (Then) there came to them [the angels] a great joy. And they blessed, glorified, and extolled (the Lord) on account of the fact that the name of that (Son of) Man was revealed to them. He shall never pass away or perish from before the face of the earth. But those who have led the world astray shall be bound with chains . . . all their deeds shall vanish from before the face of the earth. Thenceforth nothing that is corruptible shall be found; for that Son of Man has appeared and has seated himself upon the throne of his glory, and all evil shall disappear from before his face . . .
>
> *1 Enoch 69:27–29*[60]

There are similarities with the (probably very early) christological hymn embedded in Paul's letter to the Philippians. This hymn also depicts the rejoicing in heaven when Jesus is exalted and rewarded by the donation of a "Name that is above every name":

> Therefore God also highly exalted him
> and gave him the name that is above every name,
> so that at the name of Jesus every knee should bend,
> in heaven and on earth and under the earth,
> and every tongue should confess that Jesus Christ is Lord,
> to the glory of God the Father.
>
> Philippians 2:9–11

"That man" in the Ezra Apocalypse

The Ezra Apocalypse, also known as 4 Ezra, is a Jewish document embedded in a later Christian framework. The work as a whole—that is, the Jewish core and its Christian framework—is included in the Apocrypha under the title 2 Esdras. The date of the Ezra Apocalypse is usually given as late first century CE, which means that it is not much later—and possibly earlier—than some of the Christian Gospels. It contains accounts of seven visions, each of which is interpreted to Ezra by his angelic guardian and guide. In the sixth vision (2 Esdras/Ezra chapter 13), Ezra sees a figure described as "that man" or "a man" emerging out of a storm-tossed sea. Flying with the clouds of heaven, the figure carves out for himself a commanding position on top of Mount Zion. A great army of heathen nations now gathers itself together and rushes forward to make war against the "man", who is also called the "Son of God" (or "my Son"). He has no weapons with which to defend himself, but he opens his mouth and belches out a torrent of flaming fire. The armies of the heathen are instantly annihilated; nothing remains except dust, ashes, and the smell of smoke (cf. Isaiah 11:4). The "man" now comes down from the top of Mount Zion and gathers together the faithful of Israel, including the descendants of the long-lost ten tribes. This peaceable multitude, we are told, will henceforth dwell together in the city which cannot yet be seen, but which will be revealed. That city is Zion, the new Jerusalem.

Ezra's *heavenly redeemer* figure is a secret being, apparently pre-existent and involved in creation, whom the Most High has been keeping hidden until the end of days. When Ezra prays for enlightenment, God tells him:

> "As for your seeing a man come up from the heart of the sea, this is he whom the Most High has been keeping for many ages, who will himself deliver his creation . . . Then he, my Son, will reprove the assembled nations for their ungodliness (this was symbolized by the storm) . . . and will destroy them without effort by means of the law (which was symbolized by the fire)."
>
> 4 Ezra/2 Esdras 13:25,37

What we seem to have in 4 Ezra 13 is an early instance of the assimilation of the son-of-man concept in Daniel 7:13 to the traditional figure of the Davidic messiah (as also, perhaps, in the Qumran "Son of God" fragment 4Q246—see pp. 88–89). The description of "the man" flying "with the clouds of heaven" is reminiscent of Daniel 7, where the one like a son of man comes to God with the clouds of heaven. In 4 Ezra the figure is clearly an individual being, not a symbol for the people of Israel. Unlike in Daniel, he is explicitly identified as the Messiah. In 4 Ezra 13 this identification is implicit in the attribution of messianic functions and in the use of the messianic title "Son of God", but elsewhere in 4 Ezra the figure's messianic status is explicit. That this messiahship is Davidic messiahship is confirmed by the use of the term "Son of God". Nevertheless, it is a novel form of Davidic messiahship in that there is no expectation of an ongoing dynasty. Deliverance, restoration, and salvation are anticipated, but nothing lasts for ever. Despite being pre-existent and despite having delegated divine powers and functions, including redeeming and making safe God's people, Ezra's figure is to some extent mortal. Even the messianic kingdom will be of limited duration. After four hundred years everyone and everything will die, including the Messiah. The world will then revert to primeval silence and nothingness, prior to reawakening for the last judgement (4 Ezra 7:28–44).

Ezra's messianic Son of God is therefore very different from the heavenly Messiah/Son of Man figure in the Similitudes. In the Similitudes, the heavenly redeemer is pre-existent, immortal, and a mighty, quasi-divine angelic power. Although he is called the Anointed One (that is, the Messiah), there is no suggestion that he is Davidic. Enoch and Ezra appear to be independently accessing and recycling Danielic material in their own different ways for their own purposes. Nevertheless, there are indications that there could be a shared interpretive tradition underlying both the Similitudes and the Ezra Apocalypse. Both authors interpret Daniel's figure in messianic terms and both understand the Danielic figure to be an extraordinarily exalted individual being, not a symbol. In both cases the figure has delegated divine powers and functions.

The man with a sceptre

The Fifth Sibylline Oracle is a Jewish text, probably originating in Egypt sometime around the end of the first century, or early in the second century CE. It is riddled with later Christian interpolations, but these are clumsy; they can easily be identified and set aside. Two sections of the Jewish text make specific reference to an eschatological, messianic saviour. In the second section, a "blessed man" comes from heaven with a sceptre given to him by God. He engages in warfare, burning the nations of the evildoers and razing their cities to the ground. He restores Jerusalem and the temple, and he builds a tower so high that it reaches up to the clouds:

> For a blessed man came from the expanses of heaven with a scepter in his hands which God gave him, and he gained sway over all things well ... And the city which God desired [that is, Jerusalem], this he made more brilliant than stars and sun and moon, and he provided ornament and made a holy temple, exceedingly beautiful in its fair shrine, and he fashioned a great and immense tower over many stadia [in height] touching even the clouds and visible to all, so that all faithful and all righteous people could see the glory of eternal God, a form desired.
> *Sibylline Oracle 5:414–427*[61]

As with the other texts we have been examining, there is evident dependence on earlier traditions, especially the figure in Daniel 7:13–14, the "one like a son of man" who comes to God with the clouds of heaven and is given dominion and lordship over all peoples. Like the Messiah in the Apocalypse of Ezra, the "blessed man" from heaven burns up his enemies with fire. He redeems and restores his people, executes judgement on their enemies, and then (by implication) rules over them for ever, thus ensuring their ongoing paradisal bliss and security. These functions imply messianic status; elsewhere in the Oracle messianic status is explicit. Although nothing is said about divine sonship, and although there is no reference to the establishment of an ongoing dynasty, the fifth Sibylline Oracle shows that by the end of the first century CE the tradition of the heavenly redeemer has become firmly and explicitly fused with traditions concerning the earthly messiah.

The statements that "the glory of eternal God" rested on the top of a great tower and that it had "form" (that is, shape or definition) suggest that "the glory" could be an angelomorphic hypostasis like the "Glory of the Lord" in Ezekiel. One possibility is that the "blessed man" (the heavenly redeemer figure) and "the glory" (eventually coming to rest on the top of the tower) are one and the same being. Whether this is so or not, the figure of the "blessed man from heaven" in the Fifth Sibylline Oracle is another example of an individual, messianic, heavenly redeemer whose attributes reflect the continuing influence of the figure of the "one like a son of man" in Daniel 7.

The victorious warrior-messiah

The Apocalypse of Baruch is a composite Jewish work comprising the first seventy-seven chapters of a Syriac text known as 2 Baruch. It exhibits a number of significant similarities with 4 Ezra, although the theology of the two texts is very different. Most scholars assume that 4 Ezra and the Apocalypse of Baruch reflect a common earlier source or tradition rather than either being dependent on the other. The date of 2 Baruch is uncertain, but it was probably written after the destruction of the temple in 70 CE, perhaps between 100 and 110 CE.

A large part of the Apocalypse of Baruch is given over to three extended visions and their interpretations. These visions could be earlier than their present setting and may even antedate the destruction of the Jerusalem temple. The visions announce the progressive revelation of the "Anointed

One" (Messiah), who is portrayed as an invincible, eschatological warrior. There will be wars and universal tribulations, but the "Anointed One" will come to deliver the righteous Israelites from their enemies, executing judgement on the persecuting nations. Then he will inaugurate and preside over the messianic kingdom, a new era of eternal peace and joy in a world liberated from the fear of illness and any kind of adversity:

> [W]hen . . . the time of my Anointed One comes, he will call all nations, and some of them he will spare, and others he will kill . . . And it will happen that after he has brought down everything which is in the world, and has sat down in eternal peace on the throne of the kingdom, then joy will be revealed and rest will appear. And then health will descend in dew, and illness will vanish, and fear and tribulation and lamentation will pass away from among men, and joy will encompass the earth.
>
> *2 Baruch 72:2, 73;1-2*[62]

Some form of prior existence may be implied, because Baruch's Messiah is a hidden figure who will be revealed only when the time is right. Associated with his appearance will be the resurrection of the righteous dead who have hoped for his coming, but are presently in *Sheol*:

> And it will happen that when all that which should come to pass in these parts has been accomplished, the Anointed One will begin to be revealed . . . And it will happen after these things when the time of the appearance of the Anointed One has been fulfilled and he returns with glory, that then all who sleep in hope of him will rise. And it will happen at that time that those treasuries will be opened in which the number of the souls of the righteous were kept, and they will go out and the multitudes of the souls [of the living and the resurrected dead] will appear together . . .
>
> *2 Baruch 29:3;30:1-2*[63]

There is no suggestion that Baruch's Messiah is mortal. His implied pre-existence, his coming from heaven with glory, his universal dominion and the associated resurrection of the dead, and the establishment of a future age of peace and prosperity from which pain and suffering are banished all point to a transcendent, heavenly being. Like the figure in Daniel 7:13–14, he exercises universal dominion and kingship. All peoples, languages, and nations will serve him. Baruch's Messiah is a heavenly being, an eschatological warrior whose function is to intervene decisively to protect God's people and establish an ongoing golden age.

The coming lord

Another heavenly redeemer figure features in a group of Jewish texts dating from the second half of the first century CE: this figure is the heavenly Jesus, as depicted in early Christian writings. The heavenly Jesus has many similarities with the exalted heavenly beings described in Daniel 7:13, the Qumran scrolls, the Similitudes, 4 Ezra, 2 Baruch, the Fifth Sibylline Oracle, and elsewhere. He is pre-existent before creation. He is a glorious and radiant heavenly being having human form and appearance. He is greater than the angels and supremely exalted by enthronement at God's right hand. He possesses delegated divine powers and he is called the "Son of Man", the "Son of God", and "Messiah". It is expected that he will come from heaven to earth accompanied by angels in majesty and with awesome power. He will make his people safe and initiate a blessed new era of peace and prosperity. Those who believe in him will be raised from the dead (cf. 2 Baruch 29:3; 30:1–2). In some of the texts he is described in terms evidently derived from Daniel 7:13–14, but he is an individual being, not a symbol for anyone or anything else. Like Enoch, prior to the revelation of his majestic heavenly status, Jesus lived on earth as a human, apparently unaware of his pre-existence as a heavenly being. The beliefs of Jesus' earliest followers concerning his heavenly origins and his post-resurrection heavenly exaltation are an integral part of the variegated Judaism of the Second Temple period, and for historical purposes they must be open to examination as such. They have no privileged status.

A heavenly redeemer tradition?

The question is, are the various heavenly-redeemer narratives examined in this chapter independent creations, or are they reflections of one ongoing, underlying tradition about a mighty being expected to come from heaven to rescue the people of God? This question is deliberately framed in general terms in order to avoid prematurely "closing off" discussion. For example, some scholars argue that the evidence of first-century texts slightly later than the time of Jesus ought to be discounted. This writer disagrees. Traditions—including much of the material in the Christian Gospels—have usually circulated in oral form for some time before becoming fixed in writing. Nor must otherwise relevant texts be arbitrarily excluded from consideration simply because they lack one particular key feature. For example, some scholars would reject the evidence of texts not containing the terms "Son of Man" or "Messiah", but it seems preferable to assess the evidence as a whole and on its merits. Finally, we must be aware of the latent ambiguity in the term "tradition". For present purposes, a tradition is defined as an ancient story or narrative having common essential characteristics, and appearing and reappearing over time in the same or different historical settings.

Given the variety in the descriptions of the heavenly redeemer figures cited above, it can scarcely be claimed that they constitute a single stream of stable ongoing tradition. On the other hand, it cannot be denied that they represent multiple instances of a broadly similar heavenly being, and that there is considerable consistency in many of the key motifs. In particular, in almost every case there is direct or indirect reference back to the figure of the "one like a son of man" in Daniel 7. The heavenly redeemer is, in almost every instance, depicted as an exalted being possessing and exercising extraordinary powers. He is irresistibly powerful, and frequently described as having a manlike appearance. He is either explicitly designated Messiah or he exercises what are clearly messianic functions: he exercises judgement, makes safe the people of God, and inaugurates a new era of peace and blessedness on earth. The regular appearance and reappearance of all these key motifs suggests that although we may not be observing repeated outcroppings of one single stream of tradition, there is an ongoing practice of repeatedly adapting the figure in Daniel 7:13-14 to reflect each particular interpreter's circumstances and concerns. Perhaps we should speak of an ongoing and developing exegetical tradition rather than an ongoing heavenly redeemer tradition.

Conclusion

In late Second Temple Judaism and the immediately following decades, there are at least seven different depictions of an individual, highly exalted heavenly being possessing extraordinary delegated divine powers. The figure may be described as "manlike", "the man" or "the Son of Man". He may also be called "Messiah" and "Son of God". The expectation is that he will come from heaven to earth in power to protect the righteous, to exercise judgement and punish the wicked, and thereafter to rule over a kingdom of peace and blessedness. The depictions of this figure reflect the influence of a number of scriptural texts, especially Daniel 7:13-14.

After his death, the risen and exalted Jesus of Nazareth was understood by his followers to be such a figure and to have similar functions. Given the possibility or probability that the concept of a coming heavenly redeemer was known to Jesus and his followers during his lifetime, and the certainty that after his death Jesus was believed to be such a figure, we need urgently to establish and examine Jesus' own beliefs, especially his teaching concerning the future. What was Jesus saying and how was he expecting the future to unfold? Did Jesus see himself as a spectator, as a herald, or as a participant somehow involved in bringing the future down into the present? And how did Jesus' own beliefs connect with what was believed about him by others, both during his lifetime and afterwards?

CHAPTER 5

Jesus' Vision of the Future

The content of Jesus' teaching concerning the future, and especially his teaching concerning the kingdom of God, has been continuously debated since the nineteenth century. Liberal theologians, conditioned by Enlightenment values and attitudes, rejected the idea that Jesus believed that the kingdom or rule of God would be brought about by supernatural revelation and miraculous intervention. Many also reacted against the notion that there could have been any apocalyptic or futurist aspect to the teaching of Jesus. They understood Jesus to have been saying that the kingdom of God was a state of being, existing—or capable of existing—within the natural order, and that this state of being was potentially attainable by human moral effort, albeit human moral effort acting in response to the promptings of divine grace.

The publication of Johannes Weiss's *Jesus' Proclamation of the Kingdom of God* in 1892 and Albert Schweitzer's *Quest of the Historical Jesus* in 1906 turned the tide against the liberals' understanding of Jesus and his kingdom of God sayings. Both Weiss and Schweitzer insisted that the teaching of Jesus must be interpreted against the background of Jewish apocalyptic traditions. The kingdom of God in Jesus' estimation, they said, was inherently eschatological. Jesus expected that the kingdom of God would be brought about by an imminent act of divine intervention, not by human moral striving.

During the twentieth century, "Jesus research" has passed through several phases. In the period of disillusionment after the First World War, some scholars were deeply sceptical about the historicity of the Gospels and others were pessimistic as to the value of any historical research. The quest for the historical Jesus was regarded by some as not just impossible, but wrong-headed. Some theologians, including the influential Rudolf Bultmann, effectively abandoned the older attempt to recover the historical Jesus, and adopted instead various forms of neo-orthodoxy and existentialism. In the second half of the twentieth century, there was a significant reaction against this negativity and a revival of interest in the question of the historical Jesus. The principal features of this revival were a greater awareness of the relationship between faith, history, and interpretation; an acceptance of sociology and sociological perspectives; and the development of more sensitive criteria for determining the authenticity of particular sayings of Jesus. The closing decades of the twentieth century were marked by yet more fragmentation and diversification. Liberalism re-emerged, with some scholars denying any element of apocalyptic eschatology in the teaching of Jesus. Other scholars have remained hopeful that valid historical conclusions are attainable, provided it is accepted that the primary datum is not the historical Jesus himself, but rather the primitive Christian community's response to the historical Jesus. One positive development in recent years has been the integration of Jesus-research with Jewish studies. It is now axiomatic that Jesus must be studied and evaluated in the context of late Second Temple Judaism.

Today there are a variety of alternative and to some extent irreconcilable perspectives. Nevertheless, subject to the necessary caveats, the quest of the historical Jesus continues. Moreover, there is now greater underlying agreement on matters of substance than the debate might suggest. In particular, although the metaphor or symbol of the "kingdom of God" as used by Jesus continues to be variously interpreted, there is now fairly widespread agreement that on any reasonable interpretation of the data it can be assumed:

- that the kingdom of God was the dominant theme of Jesus' preaching,
- that Jesus made both future and present statements about the kingdom of God,
- and that the concept of the kingdom of God must have been meaningful and familiar to Jesus' hearers, even though the exact phrase "the kingdom of God" is not found in the Hebrew scriptures and is relatively uncommon in other Jewish literature of the period.

The fact that Jesus at no time felt it necessary to explain the precise significance of the term is an indication that he felt able to take it for granted that his hearers understood perfectly well what he was talking about.

The kingdom of God: traditional views

Before we can assess the teaching of Jesus himself, we need to be aware that the concept of God's timeless kingship and supreme sovereignty over all the earth is deeply embedded in the Hebrew scriptures, and would have been familiar to Jesus and his contemporaries. First, there is the universal, timeless rule of God over all creation. For instance:

> The LORD has established his throne in the heavens,
> and his kingdom rules over all.
> *Psalm 103:19*

> I will extol you, my God and King...
> Your kingdom is an everlasting kingdom,
> and your dominion endures throughout all generations.
> *Psalm 145:1,13*

There are also well-known sayings that express the idea that God's universal kingship applies in a special and more interventionist way to Israel as God's chosen people. For example:

> The LORD will reign for ever,
> your God, O Zion, for all generations.
> *Psalm 146:10*

> Your solemn processions are seen, O God,
> the processions of my God, my King, into the sanctuary...
> Awesome is God in his sanctuary, the God of Israel;
> he gives power and strength to his people.
> *Psalm 68:24,35*

In troubled times, a natural extension of this concept was the linking of the expectation of hoped-for national salvation with expressions of God's anticipated kingship or rule. For example:

> How beautiful upon the mountains
> are the feet of the messenger who announces peace,
> who brings good news,
> who announces salvation,
> who says to Zion, "Your God reigns."
> . . . he has redeemed Jerusalem.
> The LORD has bared his holy arm
> before the eyes of all the nations;
> and all the ends of the earth shall see
> the salvation of our God.
>
> Isaiah 52:7,9–10

In some circles, under the constant pressure of external threats and internal political turmoil, the hope that national salvation would one day be delivered by a human king, even with divine assistance, mutated into the expectation that national salvation would be brought about by God's own direct, immediate intervention. Although this present age might be characterized by irredeemable unrighteousness and misfortune, God's people could take heart. Change was coming. God would intervene and establish his own direct rule and kingship over everything and everyone, in heaven and on earth:

> On that day the LORD will punish
> the host of heaven in heaven,
> and on earth the kings of the earth . . .
> Then the moon will be abashed,
> and the sun ashamed;
> for the LORD of hosts will reign
> on Mount Zion and in Jerusalem . . .
>
> Isaiah 24:21,23

> See, a day is coming for the LORD ... the LORD will go forth and fight against those nations as when he fights on a day of battle. On that day his feet shall stand upon the Mount of Olives ... Then the LORD my God will come, and all the holy ones with him ... And the LORD will become king over all the earth; on that day the LORD will be one and his name one.
>
> *Zechariah 14:1,3–5,9*

> And in the days of those [heathen] kings the God of heaven will set up a kingdom that shall never be destroyed, nor shall this kingdom be left to another people. It shall crush all these kingdoms and bring them to an end, and it shall stand for ever ...
>
> *Daniel 2:44*

In the Isaiah and Zechariah oracles cited above there is no mention of human involvement; the act of establishing divine kingship rests entirely with God. In the case of Daniel 2:44, the position is less clear-cut. It appears that it is God who will establish his kingdom on earth, and this kingdom will have the military capability to crush all other nations. In other words, the saving action is attributed to God, but this may not exclude the possibility of human striving playing a part.

This interpretation receives support from the depiction of the saving act of God in Daniel 7:

> As I looked, this horn [Israel's great enemy] made war with the holy ones and was prevailing over them, until the Ancient One [God] came; then judgement was given for the holy ones of the Most High, and the time arrived when the holy ones gained possession of the kingdom.
> ... [One of the attendants said,]
> "The kingship and dominion
> and the greatness of the kingdoms under the whole heaven
> shall be given to the people of the holy ones of the Most High;
> their kingdom shall be an everlasting kingdom,
> and all dominions shall serve and obey them."
>
> *Daniel 7:21–22,27*

However one interprets the references to the "holy ones" (who may be angels) and "the people of the holy ones" (who may be humans mentored by angels), and regardless of whether the passage is thought to be depicting parallel wars in heaven and on earth, the outcome is the same. The faithful human Israelites receive an everlasting kingdom and dominion over all peoples, but only after they have actively fought for it. Nevertheless, human action, like the action of the heavenly redeemer figures described in the previous chapter, takes place within the framework of the understanding that ultimately it is God who is establishing his kingdom or rule.

In non-biblical Jewish sources such as the Apocrypha, the Pseudepigrapha, and the Dead Sea Scrolls, there are other instances of the idea that God will act in concert with humans in the establishment of his kingdom or rule. One passage in the Qumran War Scroll, in which angels fight alongside men, has already been cited. Other examples include:

> For Thine is the power, and the battle is in Thy hands! . . . For our Sovereign is holy and the King of Glory is with us; the [host of his spirits is with our foot soldiers and horsemen.]
>
> *1 QM XVIII:10, XIX:1*[64]

Compare the following:

> And there shall arise for you . . . the Lord's salvation.
> He will make war against Beliar . . .
> And Jerusalem shall no longer undergo desolation,
> nor shall Israel be led into captivity,
> because the Lord will be in her midst
>   [living among human beings].
> The Holy One of Israel will rule over them . . .
>
> *The Testament of Dan 5:10,13*[65]

John the Baptist and the kingdom of God

Possibly more immediately relevant to Jesus' teaching about the kingdom of God is the influence of John the Baptist, out of whose circle of followers Jesus apparently emerged. The Christian scriptures and Josephus both represent John the Baptist as having political influence and religious significance. In terms of politics, John's involvement in a dispute between Herod Antipas and the king of Petra, and Herod's fear that John's popular influence might lead to an insurrection, eventually led to his imprisonment and death. So far as John's religious significance is concerned, his earlier activity is of particular interest. John appeared in the desert, proclaiming a message of impending judgement linked to the possibility of salvation through repentance and ritual cleansing. He baptized large crowds of followers in the river Jordan. According to the tradition in the synoptic Gospels, John's baptism was "for repentance and the forgiveness of sins" (Mark 1:4; Matthew 3:2; Luke 3:3). According to Josephus, it was for "the consecration of the body", the soul being already cleansed by right behaviour (*Antiquities of the Jews* XVIII:117).

All four Gospels have narratives concerning John and his ministry of baptism. In every case they are introduced by the citation of the oracle from Isaiah, which reads:

> A voice cries out:
> "In the wilderness prepare the way of the LORD,
> make straight in the desert a highway for our God.
> Every valley shall be lifted up,
> and every mountain and hill be made low..."
>
> *Isaiah 40:3-4*

In this Isaiah oracle God himself is the one for whose coming preparations are to be made. In the Christian application of the oracle this clarity of reference is missing. The one who is to come could be God, or could be a human agent. In the Q version of the Gospel tradition, John the Baptist says:

> "I baptize you with water; but one who is more powerful than I is coming; I am not worthy to untie the thong of his sandals. He will baptize you with the Holy Spirit and fire. His winnowing-fork is in his hand, to clear his threshing-floor and to gather the wheat into his granary; but the chaff he will burn with unquenchable fire."
>
> *Luke 3:16-17; cf. Matthew 3:11-12*

The reference to "sandals" is probably metaphorical, but taken literally it points to an anticipated human figure, or a figure having human aspect or appearance. The reference to baptism "with the Holy Spirit and with fire" has connotations of cleansing and purgation, probably in association with anticipated eschatological judgement. This suggests that the one who is expected may be a heavenly redeemer like one of the figures depicted in the previous chapter.

What is beyond doubt is that all the Christian sources represent John the Baptist as having delivered an uncompromising prophetic message of impending crisis and judgement. This message was evidently sufficiently compelling for John to attract large crowds of followers. That people should have been willing to undertake the long and arduous journey from Jerusalem down into the Jordan valley to be baptized by John is testimony to the urgency of his message. The present age, said John, was coming to an end. The Powerful One (God's agent or God himself) was about to come. Judgement was imminent. Only by repentance and ritual cleansing could a person be saved. Some, indeed, were already beyond redemption, the Pharisees and Sadducees in particular:

> [John said,] "You brood of vipers! Who warned you to flee from the wrath to come? . . . Even now the axe is lying at the root of the trees; every tree therefore that does not bear good fruit is cut down and thrown into the fire."
> *Luke 3:7–9; cf. Matthew 3:7–9*

As to what, in John's view, lay beyond this coming judgement, we have little information. The threshing and winnowing of wheat, the burning up of the chaff with unquenchable fire, and the gathering of the good wheat into the granary are vivid metaphors. What being gathered into the granary signifies is not stated, but it is evidently good news. That it implies entry into the coming kingdom—that is, a state of being under the direct or mediated rule of God—is a reasonable inference.

John the Baptist and Jesus

The testimony of the Gospels concerning the relationship between John the Baptist and Jesus is difficult to unravel, not least because the traditions underlying the Gospels have been shaped to a considerable degree by a contradictory desire. On the one hand, the writers wish to relate Jesus to John the Baptist, and yet, on the other hand, they clearly wish to distinguish and distance the two figures. That Jesus was baptized by John the Baptist seems certain, firstly because of the strength of the testimony, and secondly because the idea that Jesus might have needed repentance and cleansing evidently became a later source of embarrassment to Christians: Matthew is trying to protect later sensitivities when he represents John the Baptist as saying that he, John, ought to be baptized by Jesus, not Jesus by him (Matthew 3:13–15). That Jesus initially kept company with John the Baptist, and that Jesus and some of his first disciples were former followers of John, is also probable. According to the Gospel of John, Jesus subsequently engaged in his own ministry of proclamation and water-baptism in parallel with that of John the Baptist:

> After this Jesus and his disciples went into the Judean countryside, and he spent some time there with them and baptized. John also was baptizing at Aenon near Salim . . .
>
> *John 3:22–23*

There is no other evidence that Jesus himself ever baptized anyone with water. In passing, note the rather clumsy editorial attempt to amend the Johannine tradition:

> Now when Jesus learned that the Pharisees had heard, "Jesus is making and baptizing more disciples than John"—although it was not Jesus himself but his disciples who baptized—he left Judea and started back to Galilee.
>
> *John 4:1–3*

There is insufficient evidence uncontaminated by what has been called "the Christian takeover of John the Baptist" to establish John's estimation of Jesus with certainty. There must have been some continuing connection between them because, when he was in prison, John is reputed to have sent messengers to Jesus to ask, "Are you the one who is to come, or do we wait for another?" The reply attributed to Jesus—"Go and tell John what you have seen and heard; the blind receive their sight, the lame walk, the lepers are cleansed, the deaf hear, the dead are raised up. . ."—may reflect a later theological understanding, but that John asked such a question, and that Jesus replied, is probable (Matthew 11:2–6; Luke 7:18–23). John the Baptist had expected the arrival of God's mighty agent of eschatological judgement. Nothing had happened to justify this belief, and John now found himself in prison. His unhappiness and uncertainty are reflected in the question carried by messengers to Jesus. It matches the historical circumstances. The Gospel of John tells a quite different story: John the Baptist is depicted as testifying to Jesus as the "Lamb of God" and the "Son of God" (John 1:26–36; 3:27–36).

This means that establishing the popular understanding of John the Baptist and determining his significance in the estimation of Jesus is not easy. One has to go behind the understandings in the Jesus tradition and the possibly different understandings of the authors of the Gospels. There is also the problem of the testimony of Josephus, who makes no mention of John's message having any apocalyptic dimension. This, in itself, is probably not significant. Josephus tends to present Jewish beliefs using the terms and categories of Greek philosophy. He also seems deliberately to suppress information about aspects of Judaism that might alarm his Roman patrons.

There are no serious reasons for doubting that John the Baptist was widely held to be an eschatological prophet (Mark 11:29–32). The synoptic Gospels suggest that some people thought him to be the Messiah (Luke 3:15). Others, possibly including Jesus, believed that John might be Elijah (Mark 9:11–13; Luke 1:17), or, at least, that he was exercising the functions of Elijah, which were to turn the hearts of the children to their fathers and the hearts of the fathers to their children before the great and terrible day of the Lord's coming (Malachi 4:5–6). If Jesus believed John the Baptist to be Elijah, he must have been regarding John as the final representative of the old order rather than the first representative of the new. In the teaching of Jesus, the coming kingdom of God was to be an entirely new and radically different order of being (Matthew 11:7-14; Luke 7:28).

The Gospel of John, or the tradition underlying the Gospel, takes a rather different view of John the Baptist. The author is emphatic that John is not the Messiah. Neither is he Elijah, nor is he "the prophet". (The term "the prophet" may be a reference to the figure of the "prophet like Moses" in Deuteronomy 18:15,18. Alternatively, it may be an allusion to an expected prophet "like one of the prophets of old"—see Mark 6:15, 8:28, and Luke 9:8,19.) Although the Gospel of John has an account of Jesus' initial involvement with John the Baptist, the importance of John is not his identity, but his function of testifying to the inner significance of Jesus.

To get behind these various conflicting traditions is difficult. So far as the Baptist is concerned, the evidence of Josephus and the Gospels supports the understanding that John was a popular eschatological prophet, an advocate of social justice (Luke 3:10-14), and a powerful preacher of repentance. The Baptist was convinced that catastrophic, divinely-ordained judgement was imminent. A Powerful One was coming. This coming One was God's agent, who would execute decisive judgement on the unrighteous. This terrifying event would usher in a radically new dispensation. Despite the separation of their ministries and their very different lifestyles, there are indications that Jesus regarded himself as being in some sense linked with John the Baptist in a divinely ordained enterprise (Luke 7:20-23). Jesus seems also to have regarded his baptism by John (and some form of visionary experience associated with that baptism) as his own personal divine commissioning (Mark 1:9-11; 11:27-32), and apparently continued to align himself with John prior to establishing a mission or ministry of his own. The reasons for Jesus separating himself from John are not known, nor do we have any information concerning the differences between Jesus' ministry of baptism and proclamation and that of John. John's extreme asceticism may have been unpalatable to Jesus and to some others among John's disciples, but this is speculation. What matters is that Jesus first comes into view as a fully-fledged eschatological prophet and apocalyptic preacher, sharing John the Baptist's conviction that the present age was drawing decisively to a close, and that in the new era there would be great blessing for the righteous and for the penitent, but fitting punishment and destruction for the wicked.

Jesus' afterlife beliefs

From what little information we have, Jesus' general afterlife beliefs appear to have been conventional and broadly in line with those outlined in the previous chapters. For example, he believed that the dead would be raised. According to the authors of the three synoptic Gospels, he debated the question of resurrection with a group of Sadducees. He cut through their argument by declaring that when the dead were raised, marriages previously contracted on earth would be irrelevant. The risen dead, he declared, would be asexual like the angels (Mark 12:25; Matthew 22:30; Luke 20:36). The story of the Transfiguration of Jesus (Mark 9:2–8; Matthew 17:1–8; Luke 9:28–36) is an indication that Jesus' followers—and perhaps Jesus also—may have shared the belief that certain exceptional persons had bypassed *Sheol* and were already with God in heaven. In Luke's version of Jesus' exchange with the Sadducees, Jesus says that those who are worthy to be raised from the dead will live in a new age and that they will never die again, because they will be "like angels and are the children of God, being children of the resurrection". This resurrection appears to be resurrection not to life in heaven, but for renewed life on a transformed earth.

Jesus also told his own version of a well-known traditional story about the respective fates of a rich man and poor man (Luke 16:19–31). The rich man dies and goes to *Sheol*, where he is tormented in flames of fire. The poor man, who during his lifetime was treated despicably by the rich man, also dies. In *Sheol* the tables are turned: while the rich man is tormented the poor man is taken by the angels to be with Abraham. The implication is that Jesus believed in *Sheol* and in continuing identity after death. It additionally appears that he understood *Sheol* to have different compartments, with preliminary rewards for the virtuous and preliminary punishments for the wicked. Jesus also seems to have believed that individuals had personal angels. Using a child as a visual aid, he vehemently denounced those who hindered or abused "little ones who believe in me", saying that the angels of little children "continually see the face of my Father in heaven" (Matthew 18:10).

With all these occasional sayings of Jesus, there are issues of authenticity and interpretation. For example, in Matthew 18:10 the phrase "little ones" may be a metaphor signifying vulnerable new adult believers, rather than actual children. It would be unwise to draw from a few examples any hard and fast conclusions other than that the views attributed to Jesus by the authors of the synoptic Gospels and their traditions appear to fall well within the broad spectrum of Second Temple Jewish afterlife beliefs.

When we come to Jesus' own teaching concerning the future, the situation is very different. The central and distinctive theme is his proclamation of the imminent coming of what he called the kingdom (or rule) of God. There is also an important group of sayings in which he is represented as predicting the future coming of a mighty, heavenly redeemer called the "Son of Man". The Gospel writers clearly understand Jesus to be referring to himself. They assume that Jesus was predicting that he, the Son of Man, would die, and that after his death he would suddenly and unexpectedly return from heaven, accompanied by angels. He would make safe those who were his own; he would deliver judgement on the wicked; and, by implication, he would establish the kingdom or rule of God by irresistible force. These sayings have major implications for any assessment of Jesus' future expectations, not least because the figure of the coming, or returning, Son of Man is in many respects similar to that of the messianic heavenly redeemer figures examined in the previous chapter. There is a similar evident dependence on Daniel 7:13–14.

The authors of the Gospels have no doubt that Jesus' teaching concerning the kingdom of God and his sayings concerning the coming of the Son of Man lie at the heart of the gospel proclaimed by the community of his followers after his death. We therefore need to examine these two elements in his proclamation, starting with his teaching concerning the kingdom of God and then going on to consider the puzzling sayings concerning the coming of the Son of Man. In conclusion, we consider whether the two concepts are compatible or whether they may be reflecting two different streams of tradition having separate and independent origins.

Jesus and the kingdom of God

Jesus communicated his convictions concerning the coming kingdom of God directly by means of sayings and aphorisms, obliquely in stories and parables (notably the "seed parables" and the "parables of crisis"), and also by means of intentionally significant actions such as exorcisms and healings. For present purposes, it is sufficient to focus on his explicit sayings.

The basic data are well known. The phrase "the kingdom of God" or its variant "the kingdom of heaven" appears more than sixty times in the Gospels, although some of these instances are duplicates. It also appears in all the principal streams of tradition underlying the Gospels. No doubt some of the sayings are redactional, but the data leave us in no doubt that the concept of the kingdom or rule of God was a central—or *the* central— theme of Jesus' preaching. The great majority of the sixty-plus instances refer to the kingdom of God as a state of affairs or a state of being which, although imminent, has yet to come. Some of the sayings appear to refer additionally to the kingdom of God having a "presently impacting" as well as a future, "yet-to-be-fulfilled" aspect. The presently impacting aspect of the kingdom of God is Jesus' own conviction that here and now, in his own person and in the circumstances surrounding his present activity, there is a prolepsis, or anticipation, of the otherwise yet-to-be-fulfilled kingdom of God. Finally, there are one or two sayings which may refer to the eternal or timeless kingly rule of God over creation, or which may be implying that the kingdom of God has already been fully realized.

An example of a saying which appears to envisage the kingdom of God as an entirely future state is the initial petition in the Lord's Prayer, the only formal prayer specifically attributed to Jesus in the New Testament. The Lord's Prayer appears in slightly different versions in Matthew and Luke. The opening petition in the slightly shorter Lucan version is:

> "Father, hallowed be your name.
> Your kingdom come . . ."
>
> *Luke 11:2; cf. Matthew 6:9–10*

Scholars draw attention to the marked similarities between the Lord's Prayer and the ancient Aramaic Jewish prayer, the Kaddish. Like the Lord's Prayer, the Kaddish urgently petitions for the effective establishment of God's as yet entirely future reign, or eschatological kingdom, "speedily and soon" in present time.

In the gospel of Mark, the basic concept of the futurity of the kingdom of God is frequently conjoined with the additional theme of imminence. Jesus is represented as saying at the outset of his ministry, later at a major turning point, and finally just before his death:

> "The time is fulfilled, and the kingdom of God has come near; repent, and believe in the good news."
>
> *Mark 1:15*

> "Truly I tell you, there are some standing here who will not taste death until they see that the kingdom of God has come with power."
>
> *Mark 9:1*

> "Truly I tell you, I will never again drink of the fruit of the vine until that day when I drink it new in the kingdom of God."
>
> *Mark 14:25*

There is also a strong element of promise for the future in the ethical teaching of Jesus. In particular, the Beatitudes (often read as exhortations to patience or even as declarations of blessedness associated with low estate) are probably better construed as assurances of an imminent turning of the tables, and better times to come for those who are presently oppressed. There is no particular blessedness in hunger, meekness, or misery. Jesus seems to be promising imminent relief and the lifting of burdens from those who were presently suffering illness, oppression, and deprivation. In the coming kingdom of God, Jesus said, things will be different:

> "Blessed are you who are poor,
> for yours is the kingdom of God.
> Blessed are you who are hungry now,
> for you will be filled.
> Blessed are you who weep now,
> for you will laugh."
>
> *Luke 6:20–21*

There are a number of other sayings in which it appears that the future is impacting on the present, or that the future and the present are conjoined, so that the kingdom of God has in some sense already arrived. Examples include Jesus' reply to John the Baptist's messengers, his refutation of those who criticized him for casting out demons, and his reference to a vision in which he saw Satan falling from heaven:

> Jesus answered them, "Go and tell John what you hear and see: the blind receive their sight, the lame walk, the lepers are cleansed, the deaf hear, the dead are raised, and the poor have good news brought to them. And blessed is anyone who takes no offence at me."
>
> *Matthew 11:4–6*

> "... if it is by the finger of God that I cast out the demons, then the kingdom of God has come to you."
>
> *Luke 11:19–20*

> The seventy [followers of Jesus] returned with joy, saying, "Lord, in your name even the demons submit to us!" He said to them, "I watched Satan fall from heaven like a flash of lightning."
>
> *Luke 10:17–18*

There are no sayings that explicitly and unambiguously equate Jesus' concept of the kingdom of God with the generalized Jewish concept of the timeless kingly rule of God over all creation. The nearest contender is the Lucan saying about the futility of looking for signs of the coming of the kingdom of God. Looking for such signs is a waste of time, says Jesus, because the kingdom of God is among you:

> "The kingdom of God is not coming with things that can be observed; nor will they say, 'Look, here it is!' or 'There it is!' For, in fact, the kingdom of God is among you."
>
> *Luke 17:20–21*

The interpretation of this saying is contested. The issue being debated is not whether the kingdom of God will come, but the timing and the signs associated with its coming. There are two variants of the same saying in the probably early second-century non-canonical Gospel of Thomas. They tend to confirm the authenticity of the Lucan saying, but they throw no additional light on its original form or significance. The Greek text of Luke is ambiguous. It could be signifying that the kingdom of God is among Jesus' followers in the sense that it is present in their fellowship. Or it could mean that the kingdom of God is within them in the sense that it is in their individual minds and souls. Or, just possibly, it could mean that the kingdom of God has come "within range".

In proclaiming the imminent coming of the kingdom of God, Jesus was not proclaiming the imminent end of time, or even the end of the world. He was announcing the end of the present era and the imminent coming of a radically new dispensation. Nor was he denying the possibility of repentance. On the contrary, although the coming kingdom would involve a reckoning, it was also an opportunity to be grasped and a challenge to be met, even now in the present. Nevertheless, the coming of the kingdom of God was certain. God was acting even now. The present age was already drawing to a close. This was certain; it was non-negotiable.

Finally, one of the most marked and possibly significant features of Jesus' kingdom teaching is his apparent reticence concerning the specific events and processes involved in the coming of the kingdom. The primary focus is the certainty of the event itself. The additional clause, "Your will be done on earth, as it is in heaven", inserted into Matthew's version of the Lord's Prayer, may be a pointer to what was understood by Matthew and perhaps more generally. Nevertheless, Jesus gives no detailed description of events associated with the coming of the kingdom, and there is a surprising vagueness overall. Many questions are left unanswered. What was actually supposed to be going to happen? Would there be set-piece battles involving armies of angel enforcers fighting against the heathen nations? What would life be like in the kingdom of God once it was established? How would continuing human compliance with the divine will be secured once the kingdom was established? Did Jesus anticipate that there would still be illness, ageing, and death in the kingdom of God? Other contemporary Jewish apocalypses and heavenly redeemer traditions address these issues, sometimes in lurid detail. Jesus, it appears, bypassed them almost entirely.

We conclude that the concept of the kingship of God in Jewish thought at the time of Jesus functioned as a metaphor or a deeply rooted tensive symbol representing and evoking not one but whole a range of ideas and experiences. This explains how and why Jesus could speak about the kingdom of God in different ways at different times, flexibly deploying metaphors, parables, stories, riddles, and aphorisms according to the needs and circumstances of particular audiences. Despite this variety in approach, he evidently believed that in speaking of the kingdom of God he was speaking of a specific, already impacting, future reality. This underlying certainty explains the immediacy of much of his teaching and the way in which, in debate, he tended to go straight to the heart of the matter. Setting aside specific issues of historicity associated with individual stories and sayings, the tradition has surely here captured and preserved an essential aspect of the historical Jesus.

The Son of Man sayings

According to the writers of all four Gospels, Jesus repeatedly spoke of himself as the "Son of Man". In the Gospels and their underlying tradition, the term "Son of Man" functions effectively as a title used by Jesus of himself. He is represented as having used the term in connection with his present activity, in predictions of anticipated suffering and death, and in connection with the cataclysmic future coming in power and glory of the Son of Man. These sayings raise complex issues. It cannot be taken for granted that any particular saying or group of sayings is authentic.

The basic data can be summarized very briefly. The unusual Greek phrase translated into English as "the Son of Man" occurs more than sixty times in Matthew, Mark, and Luke, nine or ten times in John, once in the Acts of the Apostles, and twice (without the definite article) in the book of Revelation. It is present in the four commonly distinguished strands of the underlying synoptic tradition (Mark, Q, M, and L). Surprisingly, in the Gospels the term is never reported as having been uttered by anyone other than Jesus. Even more surprisingly, Jesus never explicitly calls himself "the Son of Man", nor does anyone ever refer to or address Jesus as "the Son of Man" (with the exception of Matthew 16:13–15, where it is implied that Jesus used the term as a reference to himself). There are no instances of statements having the form "I am the Son of Man" or "Jesus/he is the Son of Man".

These sayings have been debated by scholars for many years. The issues have never been settled and the debate is ongoing. Not only is there no consensus, there is not even any general agreement on the analytical framework within which the significance of the sayings may most appropriately be assessed. Fortunately, there is a more or less agreed starting point. So far as the authors of all four Gospels were concerned, the term "the Son of Man" refers unambiguously to Jesus. When Jesus is represented as speaking about the Son of Man, he is being represented as speaking about himself. The authors of the Gospels must also have believed that this was the general or even the universal understanding of those for whom they were writing, because they never, at any point, felt it necessary to explain to their readers what the term "the Son of Man" meant. It was taken for granted that everyone knew. Moreover, the identification of Jesus as "the Son of Man" is apparently very early indeed. Although the Acts of the Apostles was probably written after Luke, other than on certain specific issues its author is generally credited with having a sound historical sense. In his description of the martyrdom of Stephen—a prominent member of the earliest Greek-speaking Christian community in Jerusalem—Luke represents Stephen as having a vision of heaven open before him:

> But filled with the Holy Spirit, he [Stephen] gazed into heaven and saw the glory of God and Jesus standing at the right hand of God. "Look," he said, "I see the heavens opened and the Son of Man standing at the right hand of God!"
>
> *Acts 7:55–56*

The date of Stephen's death is not known, but it was early and apparently prior to the conversion of Paul. If Luke's testimony is to be trusted, even at this very early stage it was being taken for granted that the relationship between Jesus and the Son of Man was one of identity. Jesus was the Son of Man. The Son of Man was Jesus.

Nevertheless, the authors of the Gospels and the Acts of the Apostles were writing three or more decades after the events they purport to be describing, and they were writing in Greek. Jesus and his immediate entourage, on the other hand, spoke Aramaic. No one, so far as we know, kept any contemporaneous written record of Jesus' sayings. The sayings that we have were remembered and passed on as oral tradition within the community or communities of his followers prior to their being written down and, eventually, incorporated into the Gospels. In some cases, they underwent development and modification in the course of transmission, perhaps with the intention of clarifying their significance in the light of unfolding events. There is also the further possibility that some sayings actually originated within the early community of Jesus' followers after his death. This is not necessarily to imply conscious fabrication: there is some evidence to suggest that there were individuals who felt themselves inspired by the Spirit to utter what they believed to be genuine words or sayings of Jesus. Once assimilated into the oral tradition, such sayings would have become indistinguishable from authentic sayings of Jesus.

So far as the term "the Son of Man" itself is concerned, there is general agreement that behind the rather awkward Greek there lies an Aramaic phrase meaning "son of man" or "the son of man". The phrase in question can also signify "man" (as in "mankind") or "a man" (as in "a human being"). It may also signify "one" as in the expression, "One does not like to blow one's own trumpet." Some of the more mundane Son of Man sayings in the Gospels may have originated as Jesus' roundabout way of referring modestly to himself. In other words, they were circumlocutory self-references.

It is possible that the only authentic Son of Man sayings are those in which Jesus referred to himself in this roundabout way, and that all the other Son of Man sayings were created after his death, probably as a result of his disciples identifying the risen and exalted Jesus Christ with the heavenly being who is called the "one like a son of man" in Daniel's vision (Daniel 7:13–14). Some of the sayings about the suffering of the Son of Man also probably originated during Jesus' lifetime as sayings in which Jesus expressed confidence in his eventual vindication in rather general terms. These rather general expressions of confidence could have been "sharpened up" and rendered more explicit after his death by his followers who, by then, were identifying the risen and exalted Jesus with the Danielic Son of Man.

The Son of Man sayings can be categorized and analysed in various ways. One helpful way is to divide the sayings into three groups:

- sayings concerning the present activity on earth of the Son of Man,
- sayings concerning the expected suffering and subsequent vindication or rising of the Son of Man,
- and sayings regarding the future coming of the Son of Man.

An example of the first category is:

> "Foxes have holes, and birds of the air have nests; but the Son of Man has nowhere to lay his head."
>
> *Luke 9:58; Matthew 8:20*

An example of the second category is:

> Then he [Jesus] began to teach them that the Son of Man must undergo great suffering, and be rejected by the elders, the chief priests, and the scribes, and be killed, and after three days rise again.
>
> *Mark 8:31*

An example of the third category is:

> "Those who are ashamed of me and of my words in this adulterous and sinful generation, of them the Son of Man will also be ashamed when he comes in the glory of his Father with the holy angels."
>
> *Mark 8:38*

The salient feature of all the sayings in the third category is that they represent Jesus as having spoken in a highly significant way about the future coming of the Son of Man from heaven. In these sayings, we are told that the Son of Man will come suddenly and without warning. According to one saying (Matthew 24:34), he would come before the present generation had passed away. His coming would be attended with clouds of glory, and he would have with him angels ready to act on his command. The primary motif linking all the sayings about this future coming of the Son of Man from heaven is that the Son of Man will act as advocate and intercessor for those who have attached themselves to Jesus. In one of the key sayings, judgement takes place before a tribunal of angels, with the Son of Man acknowledging those who have acknowledged him and denying those who have denied him. The location—whether in heaven or on earth—is not specified, neither is the fate of those who have denied the Son of Man made explicit. Clearly it is not going to be pleasant. One of the sayings compares their fate with that of the inhabitants of Sodom, upon whom God rained down fire and brimstone.

The sayings in the synoptic tradition concerning the future coming of the Son of Man and the descriptions of the role and functions of that coming Son of Man are not entirely consistent, either in form or content. This may not be particularly significant. The sayings have reached the Gospel writers by various routes and are probably summaries of what Jesus said, rather than his actual words. Moreover, a comparison of duplicated and triplicated sayings shows creative modification of individual sayings. For instance, Matthew (or one of his sources) adds details enhancing the status of the Son of Man. A source used by Luke is more economical in matters of detail, but tends to lay special stress on the sovereignty of the Son of Man, and on the suddenness and high visibility of his coming.

John uses the concept of the Son of Man in a rather more complex and subtle way. For John, the Son of Man is not a figure who has gone from earth to heaven, and whose return now is awaited. The Son of Man is a heavenly being who has already decisively come from heaven to earth, and is exercising his function of judgement here and now in the present. Each of the Johannine Son of Man sayings has to be interpreted and understood in its own individual context.

A number of the sayings use imagery apparently drawn from the vision in Daniel 7:13–14 of "one like a son of man", who comes to God with the clouds of heaven and is awarded dominion and kingship over all the nations on earth. Although only two sayings (Mark 13:26 and 14:62) appear to be citing Daniel verbatim, a number of others more or less explicitly allude to the Danielic figure.

It is sometimes argued that the Son of Man sayings exhibiting Danielic influence must all be inauthentic, because Jesus (it is said) always taught on the basis of his own inherent authority, never buttressing or reinforcing his teaching with appeals to the Hebrew scriptures. This conclusion is too sweeping. One has to ask whether it is likely that the early followers of Jesus would have generated inauthentic Daniel-based sayings about the coming Son of Man and then retrojected them into the tradition, unless Jesus himself had said something to justify the creation and attribution of such sayings. Although the two sayings that quote Daniel 7 verbatim may not be authentic in the form that we now have them, Jesus could still have been using the Danielic term "one like a son of man" in a way that was sufficiently significant for it to point the early Christian exegetes towards Daniel 7:13–14. So the question remains, what, if anything, did Jesus say about the coming of the Son of Man? And if he did speak about the coming of the Son of Man, was he talking about himself or about someone else?

Jesus and the coming Son of Man

The problem with all the Son of Man sayings is not so much the shortage of data—although more data would be helpful—but rather that the data seem to point in several different directions at the same time. Some simplification is required. By eliminating evident duplications and triplications of the same saying, by setting aside sayings concerning the present activity of the Son of Man on earth, and by postponing for later consideration the suspiciously over-precise sayings concerning the impending crucifixion, death, and rising of the Son of Man, one arrives at the conclusion that the "pool" of probably or possibly authentic sayings concerning the "coming" of the Son of Man from heaven sayings comprises:

> "Those who are ashamed of me and of my words in this adulterous and sinful generation, of them the Son of Man will also be ashamed when he comes in the glory of his Father with the holy angels."
>
> *Mark 8:38*

> "And I tell you, everyone who acknowledges me before others, the Son of Man also will acknowledge before the angels of God; but whoever denies me before others will be denied before the angels of God."
>
> *Luke 12:8–9*

> "Everyone therefore who acknowledges me before others, I also will acknowledge before my Father in heaven; but whoever denies me before others, I also will deny before my Father in heaven."
>
> *Matthew 10:32*

> "For as the lightning flashes and lights up the sky from one side to the other, so will the Son of Man be in his day."
>
> *Luke 17:24; cf. Matthew 24:27*

> "Just as it was in the days of Noah, so too it will be in the days of the Son of Man . . . Likewise, just as it was in the days of Lot: they were eating and drinking, buying and selling, planting and building, but on the day that Lot left Sodom, it rained fire and sulphur from heaven and destroyed all of them—it will be like that on the day that the Son of Man is revealed."
>
> *Luke 17:26–30; cf. Matthew 24:37–39*

The second and third sayings are almost identical. They are generally agreed to be different versions of the same underlying saying, with Luke's version probably more accurately reflecting the original tradition. The phrase "Father in heaven" is a typical Matthean adjustment. Possibly more significant is the removal in Matthew's version of the reference to "the Son of Man" and the substitution of a direct reference to Jesus himself.

Other Son of Man sayings regarded as possibly authentic include:

> ". . . if the owner of the house had known in what part of the night the thief was coming, he would have stayed awake and would not have let his house be broken into. Therefore you also must be ready, for the Son of Man is coming at an unexpected hour."
>
> *Matthew 24:43–44*

> "For just as Jonah became a sign to the people of Nineveh, so the Son of Man will be to this generation."
>
> *Luke 11:30*

All these texts that speak directly or indirectly about the coming of the Son of Man share a number of important characteristics. The Son of Man is always spoken of as someone well known. The Son of Man is someone who is to come in the future, and his coming will be sudden, unexpected, and unmistakable. In this coming of the Son of Man, promise and threat are indissolubly linked. Nevertheless, the Son of Man will be the guarantor of salvation for those who confess Jesus. Although in these sayings the Son of Man is a transcendent, heavenly figure, there is little in the way of apocalyptic narrative, there is no description of the Son of Man's coming, and there are no descriptive details concerning his anticipated action. Most especially, in every instance Jesus appears to be speaking as if the Son of Man were someone other than himself. And yet the Gospel writers and their readers are evidently quite sure that Jesus himself is the Son of Man.

The kingdom of God and the Son of Man traditions

The fact that the sayings about the coming of the Son of Man found their way into the tradition and were accepted by the Gospel authors does not mean that they must be authentic sayings of Jesus. As we have seen, they could have originated in the early community of Jesus' followers after his death, as a result of exegesis of Daniel 7 and other passages in the Hebrew scriptures. If the primary thrust of Jesus' teaching was the imminence of the kingdom of God, which, even now, was already impacting on the present, is it likely that Jesus would also have been proclaiming the future coming from heaven either of himself or of some other heavenly being called the Son of Man? Possibly, possibly not. The real problem is that the concept of the coming of the Son of Man appears to be divorced from the concept of the kingdom of God in the Jesus tradition. The Gospels speak either about the kingdom of God or about the coming of the Son of Man, but never about both at the same time.

In addition, Jesus appears to have believed that the kingdom of God would come about as a result of God's own direct action. There is no suggestion of any role for an intermediary agent, human or divine. And when we look behind the texts, we find that apart from the two direct citations of Daniel 7:13 in Mark 13:26 and 14:62, sayings about the coming of the Son of Man appear only in the Q tradition or in material that is unique to Matthew. This suggests that sayings about the coming of the Son of Man and Jesus' teaching concerning the kingdom of God may originally have belonged to two different, independent streams of tradition. Sayings about the coming of the Son of Man could have originated after Jesus' death within the earliest community of his followers in Jerusalem and then been retrojected into one particular stream of Jesus tradition. This theory is compatible with understanding the historical Jesus to have been an eschatological preacher proclaiming the imminent coming of the kingdom of God rather than an apocalyptic figure predicting his own or another's future coming from heaven.

There have been weighty responses to this challenge. On the basis of a detailed analysis of the texts it can be shown that the separation of the kingdom of God and the coming Son of Man themes in the Gospel texts is more apparent than real. Both concepts are closely parallel in content and structure and they are connected by the motif of crisis. In both cases there is an interweaving of statements about the future and the present. In both there is a paring down and excision of descriptive detail as compared with other more or less contemporary apocalyptic traditions. Although the kingdom of God and Son of Man traditions are presented as separate elements in the synoptic tradition, both belong to the same complex of ideas. And, one has to ask, how could the two concepts have been joined together, either by Jesus or by the earliest followers of Jesus after his death, if they were believed to be incompatible?

Belief in God acting directly and belief in the Son of Man as an intermediary figure acting to bring about God's intention are not necessarily incompatible. In the Hebrew scriptures and other Jewish texts there are a number of passages that emphasize the directness and immediacy of God's saving action, even though the context makes it quite clear that human or angelic beings had given, or were expected to give, effect to God's purpose. For example, it is said that God delivered his people from bondage in Egypt. And yet, according to ancient tradition, it was Moses rather than God who brought Israel out of Egypt. There is no contradiction, because Moses was acting as God's agent of deliverance. Jesus undoubtedly spoke urgently and directly about the eschatological action of God as king and the bringing down of the kingdom of God from the future into the present. Why should he not also have spoken about the coming of the Son of Man (whether himself or another), if he believed this figure to be God's eschatological agent tasked with exercising delegated divine functions in connection with the establishment of God's rule or kingdom? Jesus' belief in the imminent coming of the kingdom of God does not automatically exclude the possibility that he may also have spoken about the future coming of the Son of Man, intending reference either to himself or to another as the agent through whom he expected God to act.

Conclusion

Jesus' passionate conviction concerning the imminent coming of the kingdom of God lies at the heart of his teaching about the future. Everything else revolves around this conviction. For Jesus, the kingdom of God was more than a metaphor. He believed the kingdom of God to be a future reality that was already making its impact on the present. It represented a challenge. It was an opportunity and a threat. Nevertheless, it was good news, especially for the poor and downtrodden. The coming of this kingdom of God was certain and irresistible. It would be established by God himself.

The Gospels also represent Jesus as having spoken about the future coming of a heavenly being called "the Son of Man". The sayings of Jesus about the Son of Man, and particularly the sayings about the future coming of the Son of Man, are a puzzle, but this does not mean that they are all inauthentic, or that they are incompatible with Jesus' teaching about the kingdom of God. If some of the sayings about the coming of the Son of Man are authentic sayings of Jesus—or based on authentic sayings of Jesus—these sayings will have major implications for understanding his teaching about the future. They will also raise fundamental questions about the identity of Jesus and his own self-understanding. We therefore need to shift the focus of inquiry from the teaching to the teacher. At the time when Jesus was teaching about the kingdom of God, what was believed about Jesus himself? Who or what was Jesus supposed to be? And, even more importantly, what did Jesus believe about himself? What were his own aims and intentions? We address these questions in the next chapter.

CHAPTER 6

Estimations of Jesus

The previous chapter focused on Jesus' direct and indirect teaching concerning the coming kingdom of God, and his reputed sayings concerning the future coming of "the Son of Man". In this matter the message and the messenger cannot be separated. To complete the task begun in the previous chapter, we therefore need to consider in greater detail how Jesus himself was regarded during his lifetime, both by ordinary people and also by the inner circle of his disciples. In particular, we want to know who and what Jesus believed himself to be, and what part he himself expected to play in bringing the anticipated future down into the present.

Jesus influenced his followers and opponents by what he said and taught, and also by the force of his personality and by what he was. The evidence suggests that both before and after his death he was variously estimated by his own followers and by others, and that they expressed their understandings of his significance in a variety of different ways. For example, during his lifetime Jesus was called a prophet, and he may have been identified with one particular prophet. After his death, he was acclaimed or invoked as heavenly Lord in the worship and prayer of the earliest communities of his followers. They held him to be the Messiah, the Son of God, and the Son of Man, titles and designations which were freighted with significance in first-century Judaism and which almost certainly had their roots in experience of Jesus during his lifetime.

Popular eschatological expectations

Jesus' teaching about the kingdom of God and his reputed sayings about the coming Son of Man must be set in the wider context of Second Temple Jewish eschatological expectations. These expectations reflect the turbulent social, political, and religious history of Judaea and Galilee. They were additionally fuelled by poverty, religious oppression, and alien occupation. There was widespread discontent and a yearning for change. Nor was this discontent and yearning confined to the poorest and least literate sectors of society. Large landholdings had been transferred by Herod the Great away from Jews into the hands of his own governing élite. There had been "knock-on" consequences all the way down to the lowest tenant farmers, many of whom had been dispossessed and impoverished. Religion, resentment, and a yearning for social reversal are combined in Jewish apocalyptic eschatology. One commentator speaks of hatred and malice burning their way into Jewish apocalyptic literature.

In its most extreme form, this social malaise found periodic expression in armed insurgency. The insurrectionary movements of the period fall into two groups having overlapping boundaries. First, there were armed insurrections of little or no religious significance. Such insurrections were typically led by a popularly acclaimed "king". There were three such rebellions at the time of Herod's death in 4 BCE. Similar insurrections occurred intermittently throughout the following decades, climaxing with the major rebellion and full-scale military campaign of Simon bar Giora in 68–69 CE. Secondly, there were rebellions or insurrections which, although possibly armed, were nevertheless primarily religiously motivated. Their leaders in some cases designated themselves "prophets" rather than "kings".

Josephus describes two religiously motivated rebellions occurring in the mid-first century CE, but he plays down their significance. Probably with an eye to pleasing his Roman patrons, he disparages the leaders, dismissing them as impostors and brigands. Nevertheless, these rebellions involved significant numbers of people, and in at least two cases there appears to have been a religious dimension. They all started with the leaders withdrawing into the desert with their followers. In the first instance, a man called Theudas led his followers—according to Josephus the "greater part of the population"—down to the river Jordan. Theudas was convinced that God would part the waters so that they could pass through, but no such miracle took place. Pursued by Roman horsemen, the rebels were scattered to the four winds. Theudas himself was caught and beheaded (*Antiquities* XX.97-98). In the second instance, a man known only as "the Egyptian"—presumably an Egyptian Jew—claimed to be a prophet. He led a large crowd of his followers—Josephus says thirty thousand—against Jerusalem. Halting on the Mount of Olives, the Egyptian and his followers waited for God to make the walls of Jerusalem collapse so that they could enter and take control of the city. They waited in vain. Most of the rebels were slaughtered, but "the Egyptian" evaded capture and disappeared without trace (*Wars* 2.261-262). There was a similar incident some years after Vespasian's conquest of Jerusalem and the destruction of the temple. A certain Jonathan of Cyrene led a large crowd of unarmed poor people out into the desert, promising them that God would show them signs and work wonders. These rebels also were quickly hunted down by the Romans and either killed or captured. Jonathan escaped (*Wars* 7.437-450).

The social and religious aspects of these uprisings are interesting, quite apart from any messianic implications. The uprisings all started in the desert, well away from the authorities. They all appear to have involved large numbers of desperate people willing to risk their livelihoods and their lives. Their leaders seem to have understood themselves to be prophets rather than kings, and the uprisings were all predicated on an expectation of decisive divine intervention and deliverance.

It is against this background of social unrest, reflected in popular insurrections rooted in biblical traditions of resistance to domination, and inspired by the ideal of a free and egalitarian society under the direct rule of God, that John the Baptist and Jesus must be assessed.

The Anointed One

In Second Temple Judaism the messianic hope was probably less widespread, and certainly less monolithic, than is generally supposed. It took various forms. One involved the expectation of an anointed, Davidic warrior-king, who would come to execute judgement once and for all on Israel's enemies and establish a new dynasty, ruling over a new, ongoing kingdom of peace and plenty. The Greek title "Christ"—meaning Messiah or Anointed One—is applied to Jesus so frequently in the earliest Christian texts that it appears almost to have been regarded as his proper name. This is puzzling, to say the least. Nowhere in the Jesus tradition featuring in the Gospels is there the slightest hint that Jesus and his followers ever contemplated any form of armed insurrection, or that Jesus ever envisaged himself as any kind of warrior-king, or that he intended to establish a dynasty. Indeed, it has been argued that Jesus himself never made any claim to messianic status.

However, there is evidence that Jesus' messiahship as represented in the Gospels is more than a retrojected motif. Especially towards the end of his ministry, an undercurrent of popular messianic expectation appears to have been attached to Jesus. It was almost certainly this that led to his arrest and execution. And although Jesus himself may have made no overt claim to be the Messiah, he nevertheless appears to have declined to repudiate the designation. Perhaps he felt that he could not deny the charge that he was the Messiah because to have done so would have been to put in question the final, eschatological validity of his message and ministry.

In addition to the anticipated coming of a dynasty-establishing, Davidic warrior-king, the messianic hope found expression in other ways. Some Messiahs were human figures, others were heavenly beings. For example, at Qumran there was a complex expectation involving two related figures, one a king-messiah and the other a priest-messiah. Additionally, as we have seen in Chapter 4, there were variously expressed beliefs concerning the figure of a mighty heavenly redeemer, an angelic being, sometimes explicitly called the Messiah, or otherwise depicted in terms that are clearly messianic. There was also a variant form of the messianic hope focusing on an anointed figure who would exercise the reputed Davidic functions of Spirit-inspired prophecy, teaching, and healing. It could be that it was in respect of these particular functions that the term Messiah was first considered to be appropriate for Jesus. This fits in well with Jesus' reputed quotation of Isaiah 61:1–2 at the outset of his ministry. According to Luke, Jesus went into the synagogue at Nazareth. In front of the congregation he opened the scroll and read:

> "The Spirit of the Lord is upon me,
> because he has anointed me to bring good news to the poor.
> He has sent me to proclaim release to the captives
> and recovery of sight to the blind,
> to let the oppressed go free,
> to proclaim the year of the Lord's favour."
>
> *Luke 4:18–19*

Then Jesus rolled up the scroll, handed it to the attendant, and sat down. The eyes of everyone in the synagogue, says Luke, were fixed on Jesus.

To go any further into the complex question of how and why, after his death, the title Messiah became so quickly and so universally attached to Jesus would be to deviate too far from the main thrust of the present argument. The key point for now is that it was widely believed that God was going to bring about a decisive change in the history of his people, and that God's power and continuing care would be mediated through a messianic figure. Whatever its form, the messianic hope is—by definition—an eschatological expectation. The function and purpose of the Messiah, regardless of whether he is a human warrior or priest, a Spirit-anointed prophet or a mighty, angelic, heavenly redeemer, is to redeem God's people and to preside over a new, ongoing era of peace and prosperity.

The Son of God

In Christian tradition, Jesus is referred to as "the Son of God". References to Jesus as the Son of God appear in all the principal strata of the Gospel tradition. In Mark, the earliest of the Gospels, one of the principal themes is the divine sonship of Jesus. It is reflected in the opening words of the Gospel:

> The beginning of the good news of Jesus Christ, the Son of God.
> *Mark 1:1*

It is announced by a voice from heaven when Jesus is baptized by John the Baptist:

> In those days Jesus came from Nazareth of Galilee and was baptized by John in the Jordan. And just as he was coming up out of the water, he saw the heavens torn apart and the Spirit descending like a dove on him. And a voice came from heaven, "You are my Son, the Beloved; with you I am well pleased."
> *Mark 1:9–11*

When Jesus exorcises evil spirits they cry out, "You are the Son of God!" (Mark 3:11). At the end of Jesus' life, the centurion who supervises his execution declares, "Truly this man was God's Son!" (Mark 15:39).

In Paul's letters, Jesus is referred to as "the Son of God", although not frequently. But the term was clearly in use in the early community of Jesus' followers. For example, Paul wrote to the Roman Christians in the mid-fifties CE describing the Christian message as:

> ... the gospel concerning his [i.e. God's] Son, who was descended from David according to the flesh and was declared to be Son of God with power according to the spirit of holiness by resurrection from the dead ...
> *Romans. 1:3–4*

In the Hellenistic world at the turn of the era, the term "son of god" was generally available. It could be used of specific figures sired by Zeus and of all men viewed as his offspring. Eminent persons, such as Alexander the Great, could be spoken of as a "son of god" and the term could also be used of especially righteous individuals. The term was actively promoted in the Roman emperor cult and appears in documents, in inscriptions, and on coins in daily circulation. The concept of divine sonship also occurs in Judaism. As we have seen, angels could be called "sons of God". The Jewish philosopher Philo frequently speaks of God as "Creator and Father". In one Hebrew biblical text God speaks of Israel as "my son" being called out of Egypt. This text (Hosea 11:1) later became significant for some Christians (Matthew 2:13–15).

Divine sonship is associated with kingship in Psalm 2, possibly with reference to a royal enthronement ceremony. It also appears in Psalm 89 in the context of a declaration of God's faithfulness to the anointed king David:

> I will tell of the decree of the LORD:
> He said to me, "You are my son;
> today I have begotten you."
>
> *Psalm 2:7*

> "I have found my servant David;
> with my holy oil I have anointed him;
> my hand shall always remain with him . . .
> He shall cry to me, 'You are my Father,
> my God, and the Rock of my salvation!'"
>
> *Psalm 89:20–21,26*

The term "son of God" is also used specifically of the Davidic king in key texts which subsequently played an important part in the emergence of understandings of Jesus after his death. Particularly important is the passage in 2 Samuel in which God, through the prophet Nathan, says to King David:

"... I will raise up your offspring after you, who shall come forth from your body, and I will establish his kingdom. He shall build a house for my name, and I will establish the throne of his kingdom for ever. I will be a father to him, and he shall be a son to me."

2 Samuel 7:12-14

The concept of divine sonship was further developed in intertestamental Judaism. In the wisdom literature, in the Pseudepigrapha, and in the Apocrypha there are repeated references to Israel as God's son, and to the people of Israel as sons or children of God. Significantly, the term is also applied to especially righteous individuals and martyrs. In the Wisdom of Solomon, persecuted and suffering righteous men are described as "children of God".[66] A righteous man is admonished by God as "a beloved son" in the Psalms of Solomon.[67] Martyrs are described as "children of heaven" in 2 Maccabees.[68] The first book of Enoch also has references to the "children of heaven" and "children of the angels". In the Qumran scrolls, the possibly transcendent figure in scroll 4Q246 is called "Son of God". The Messianic Rule scroll (1QSa) speaks of God "engendering" the Messiah.[69] These examples are important, not just because they indicate that the term "Son of God" could be a title for the Messiah, but because they show that Christians almost certainly inherited rather than invented this understanding. They also show that, even before the time of Jesus, the term "Son of God" could be used of an exalted heavenly being, either designated "the Messiah" or apparently possessing messianic functions. The cumulative evidence of the Hebrew scriptures, intertestamental writings, and the Dead Sea scrolls points clearly to divine sonship having been a readily available but rather elastic concept within Judaism at the turn of the era, just as it was in the Hellenistic world. It denoted not divinity as such, but rather exceptional status and a relationship involving significant closeness to God.

Although the four Gospels explicitly present Jesus as "the Son of God", there is scant evidence of his disciples having used this designation of Jesus during his lifetime, or of Jesus having used the term of himself. The only instances of the disciples having addressed Jesus as "Son of God" occur in Matthew in connection with the story of Jesus walking on the lake, and a little later in the same Gospel when Peter is represented as saying to Jesus, "You are the Messiah, the Son of the living God" (Matthew 16:16; cf. 14:33). Mark's simpler version of the same incidents make no reference to Jesus being spoken of as the "Son of God"; it appears that Matthew is adding his own secondary gloss.

The Gospels have just four instances in which Jesus is represented as speaking of himself as the Son of God. One is at the end of Matthew, where the risen Jesus commissions his disciples to make disciples of all nations and to baptize them "in the name of the Father and of the Son and of the Holy Spirit" (Matthew 28:19). This saying is almost universally agreed not to be authentic; the triadic formula marks it out as a later construction of the early Church. The second instance is a saying in which Jesus speaks of no one knowing when the Son of Man will come in power:

> "But about that day or hour no one knows, neither the angels in heaven, nor the Son, but only the Father."
>
> *Mark 13:32; cf. Matthew 24:36*

The context of the saying is an apocalyptic discourse, which is clearly composite and probably includes part of a pre-existing Jewish apocalypse. In its present form, Mark 13:32 is unlikely to be an authentic saying of Jesus. The phrase "nor the Son, but only the Father" has probably been added to a saying originally concluding with the words "... about that day no one knows."

The third instance is the parable of the wicked tenants. Mark represents Jesus as telling a story about a man who first planted and then leased out a vineyard (Mark 12:1-9). The tenants withhold the rent due to the owner of the vineyard. A succession of messengers (the prophets) are sent by the owner to collect the rent, but one after another, these messengers are beaten and killed. Eventually the owner sends his own beloved son, believing that he at least will be respected; but the son too is murdered by the tenants. Therefore, we are told, the owner is going to come and destroy the wicked tenants. Mark clearly believed that Jesus was speaking about himself as the about-to-be-murdered Son of God. The authenticity of the story is often questioned, but in this instance scepticism may be unwarranted. The veiled passion prediction is couched only in very general terms, and the son–prophet contrast is capable of interpretation in terms of the story's own inner dynamic. Also, the term "son" is used in a way that is compatible with Jesus' distinctive "Abba-experience" and his associated sense of the filial obedience due to his heavenly Father (see below). Anticipating opposition and rejection, Jesus could have intentionally cast himself as the pivotal figure in the story. By allowing himself to be shaped and driven by the impending reign of God, he could have tacitly considered himself to be the Son of God, but without making this claim the burden of his message.

The fourth and final instance is a saying attributed to Jesus in the Q tradition. The saying is unlike anything else in Q, but similar to much of the Christology in the Gospel and letters of John:

> "All things have been handed over to me by my Father; and no one knows who the Son is except the Father, or who the Father is except the Son and anyone to whom the Son chooses to reveal him."
>
> *Luke 10:22; cf. Matthew 11:27*

The authenticity of this saying is questionable. The generally accepted view is that the absolute nature of the relationship depicted between Jesus and God is out of character with the rest of Jesus' sayings about himself in the synoptic tradition. The saying probably originated in the post-Easter community, with the absolute terms "the Son" and "the Father" possibly reflecting an early tradition that contributed to the formation of Johannine theology. On the other hand, the saying could just possibly be authentic. Jesus may have been elaborating his own consciousness of mission and his own understanding of the distinctive and intimate relationship at the heart of his "Abba-experience". There are a number of possible parallels to this Q saying in the wisdom literature. Jesus could have regarded himself as a recipient of divine revelation and as a specially appointed channel of divine wisdom.

From all this evidence we can see that Jesus' own beliefs, and those of others, concerning his divine sonship seem directly or indirectly to be reflecting his strong sense of a relationship with God which, if not unique, was nevertheless highly distinctive. Although the instances are not numerous, there are examples of Jesus addressing God as *Abba* (the

Aramaic term for "father") in all the different strands of the Gospel tradition. With only one exception, this form of address is used in all his recorded prayers. That Jesus did consistently address God in prayer as *Abba*, and that this practice was sufficiently distinctive and significant for the memory of it to have been carried over after his death into the usage of the early community of believers, is confirmed by Paul. For example:

> ... When we cry "Abba! Father!" it is that very Spirit bearing witness with our spirit that we are children of God ...
>
> *Romans 8:15–16*

> And because you are children, God has sent the Spirit of his Son into our hearts, crying, "Abba! Father!"
>
> *Galatians 4:6*

It may also be significant that in the three synoptic Gospels, Jesus' references to God as "Father" (other than in prayer) are always references to "*my* Father", or "*your* Father", rather than "*our* Father". This suggests that Jesus may have been deliberately differentiating his own intense conviction of divine sonship from any parallel or derivative convictions on the part of his disciples.

Jesus' use of the term *Abba* is highly distinctive and almost unprecedented in the Judaism of the period. It seems to indicate that he understood the Fatherhood of God to be a definitive experience of relationship, involving absolute filial obedience, rather than a matter of abstract belief or religious conviction. Even though the term "Son of God" was almost certainly never used as a title during his lifetime, Jesus' commitment and obedience to what he perceived to be the will and purpose of his heavenly Father must have strongly implied to others that he was distinctively or even uniquely a "son of God". In due course we shall argue that the memory of Jesus, defined by his absolute obedience to what he perceived to be the will of his heavenly Father—and also by his teaching concerning the imminently coming kingdom of God—was one of the major factors contributing to the emergence of resurrection faith.

The Lord

In the Greek of late antiquity, the term *kyrios* (meaning "lord") could be used in various ways. Its primary reference was to someone in a position of legitimate authority or rightful ownership over someone else, as in the case of the master of a slave. To call someone "lord" was to acknowledge their superiority, accept their authority, and concede their entitlement to one's personal obedience. In the Hellenistic milieu, the term *kyrios* had also acquired significant religious connotations. In particular, it was used in the cultic veneration of rulers, especially in the increasingly popular Roman emperor cult. In the first century CE, the terms *kyrios* and *kyria* (lady) were also used in reverential references to local deities in the religions of Asia Minor, Egypt, and Syria, and possibly in mystery cults such as those of Serapis, Osiris, and Isis.

The Gospels represent Jesus as having been addressed during his lifetime, at different times and in different settings, as "lord", "rabbi", or "teacher", the three terms apparently having more or less the same significance. In most instances, the Greek term for "lord" is used in its conventional sense. It emphasizes Jesus' inherent human authority and status, but it appears not to be a title and not to have any connotations of divinity. In the few instances where the term does seem to be functioning as a title or to have connotations of divinity, it is probably reflecting later understandings retrojected into the tradition. For example, other than in Matthew the three terms are used of Jesus indiscriminately by outsiders, opponents, and disciples alike. The author of Matthew, however, seems to think that only true followers may address Jesus as "lord". In effect, Matthew is retrojecting into the tradition a later, more developed understanding concerning Jesus' heavenly lordship. The same process of retrojection can be observed in John's Gospel. In John there are three instances in which the term "Lord" seems clearly to be reflecting a post-resurrection understanding of Jesus' exalted lordship. One instance is the story of Jesus washing his disciples' feet, in which Jesus says that his disciples rightly call him "Teacher and Lord", because that is what he is (John 13:12–15). The other two instances occur in connection with the stories of the feeding of the five thousand (John 6:23), and of Jesus raising Lazarus from the dead (John 11:27). In all three stories, the term "Lord" gives expression to John's belief that Jesus' actions have sacramental significance; they are specific local instances or outcroppings of an underlying, universal act of redemption. We conclude that during his lifetime Jesus probably was spoken of as "the lord". The actual word that was used was probably *mar*, the Aramaic equivalent of the Greek *kyrios*.

However, at a very early stage after Jesus' death, his followers began to identify him as their heavenly Lord. This identification took place during the period in which the oral Jesus tradition was taking shape, long before even the first of the Gospels was written. The early identification of Jesus as heavenly Lord is closely connected with the emergence of belief in Jesus' resurrection and heavenly exaltation. It contributed significantly to the emergence of cultic worship of Jesus, not least because it enabled the transfer to Jesus of understandings associated with God, who was referred to as Lord in both the Hebrew scriptures and their Greek translation.

This transfer was facilitated by the multilingual environment. Most Jews in Palestine, including Jesus and his immediate entourage, spoke Aramaic. Many Jews, especially the educated and those in the mercantile classes, also spoke Greek with varying degrees of fluency. The scriptures, however, were transmitted in the form of scrolls written in Hebrew. When the scrolls were read aloud in synagogues, they were read in Hebrew, usually with parallel oral translation and commentary in Aramaic or Greek. In reading, it was the practice never to speak aloud the divine name Yhwh, so when the reader encountered the word Yhwh in the scroll, he would utter the Hebrew word *adonai,* meaning "lord". In the Greek version of the Hebrew scriptures known as the Septuagint (the LXX), the Greek word for "lord", *kyrios*, was actually written into the text as a substitute for the divine name Yhwh. There is also some evidence that in everyday speaking about God, the Aramaic term *mar* was sometimes used rather than the Hebrew *adonai*. The three terms *adonai, mar,* and *kyrios* seem to have functioned as translation equivalents.

The Jerusalem-based community of Jesus' earliest followers comprised two associated groups. One group, known as "the Hebrews", were Aramaic speakers; the other group, known as "the Hellenists", were Greek speakers (Acts 6:1). The members of both linguistic groups were mainly Jews, but there were probably some Gentiles as well, particularly in the Greek-speaking group. Most members of both groups would have been familiar with the scriptures in Hebrew, and some would have been bilingual in Aramaic and Greek. The Aramaic speakers seem probably to have used the term *mar* when speaking of Jesus as Lord, whereas the Greek speakers used the term *kyrios*. The three terms *adonai, mar,* and *kyrios* enabled the transfer to Jesus of what in the Hebrew scriptures and Septuagint were references to functions and attributes of God. In effect, the concept of Jesus' lordship served as a vector for the transfer of divine significance from God to Jesus. For example:

> For thus says the LORD [God],
> who created the heavens . . .
> "To me every knee shall bow,
> every tongue shall swear."
>
> *Isaiah 45:18,23*

In the probably very early christological hymn in Philippians 2:5–11, this text becomes an eschatological acclamation of Jesus Christ as supremely exalted heavenly Lord:

> Therefore God also highly exalted him
> and gave him the name
> that is above every name,
> so that at the name of Jesus
> every knee should bend,
> in heaven and on earth and under the earth,
> and every tongue should confess
> that Jesus Christ is Lord,
> to the glory of God the Father.
>
> *Philippians 2:9–11*

An eschatological prophet

Although Jesus appears never to have defined himself in terms of dynastic Davidic messiahship or to have called himself the Son of God or Lord, there is evidence that he claimed to be a prophet, and that he was regarded as such both by his own followers and by the wider public. That Jesus was seen as a prophet is evident in Mark's story of a debate concerning the identity of Jesus. Various views were being canvassed:

> Some were saying, "John the baptizer has been raised from the dead; and for this reason these powers are at work in him [Jesus]." But others said, "It is Elijah." And others said, "It is a prophet, like one of the prophets of old."
>
> *Mark 6:14–15*

That Jesus also regarded himself as being in some sense a prophet of the coming kingdom of God seems equally certain. A few examples will suffice. Mark has a story about Jesus teaching in the synagogue at Nazareth, his hometown. The response of those who heard him was dismissive. Jesus commented:

> "Prophets are not without honour, except in their hometown, and among their own kin, and in their own house."
>
> *Mark 6:4; cf. Matthew 13:57*

Luke has a story about Jesus being warned that Herod was seeking to kill him. Jesus' defiant reply concludes with the enigmatic statement:

> ". . . I must be on my way, because it is impossible for a prophet to be killed away from Jerusalem."
>
> *Luke 13:33*

Both sayings suggest that Jesus understood himself to be a prophet. This accords with his pronounced sense of calling and mission. Likewise, Luke's account, referred to earlier in this chapter, of Jesus reading the

Isaiah scroll in the synagogue at Nazareth, affords a significant insight into Jesus' self-understanding:

> "The Spirit of the Lord is upon me,
>   because he has anointed me to bring good news to the poor.
> He has sent me to proclaim release to the captives
>   and recovery of sight to the blind,
> to let the oppressed go free,
>   to proclaim the year of the Lord's favour."
>
> *Luke 4:18–19*

In effect, Jesus is using Isaiah 61:1 as a programmatic statement of his prophetic mission. His ministry to the poor, the sick, and the needy reflects classic prophetic priorities. Taken together with his repeated references to his having been "sent" or "called" by his Father, the evidence clearly suggests that Jesus regarded himself as a prophet.

The synoptic tradition also suggests that Jesus considered himself to be not just any prophet, but an eschatological prophet of the coming kingdom or rule of God. In a Q saying, Jesus bitterly declares woes against the scribes and Pharisees. They are accused of blood-guilt for the deaths of all the prophets sent by God's Wisdom since the world began. Now, says Jesus, they are facing the final reckoning:

> "Woe to you! For you build the tombs of the prophets whom your ancestors killed. So you are witnesses and approve of the deeds of your ancestors; for they killed them, and you build their tombs. Therefore also the Wisdom of God said, 'I will send them prophets and apostles, some of whom they will kill and persecute', so that this generation may be charged with the blood of all the prophets shed since the foundation of the world . . ."
>
> *Luke 11:47–50; cf. Matthew 23:34–36*

The same idea appears in the first letter to the Thessalonians. Speaking of the ongoing persecution of believers in Judaea by hostile Jews, Paul brackets Jesus with the prophets when he speaks of those:

> ... who killed both the Lord Jesus and the prophets, and drove us out; ... but God's wrath has overtaken them at last.
>
> *1 Thessalonians 2:15–16*

There are other indications that Jesus considered himself to be an eschatological prophet. Earlier in this chapter, reference was made to the parable of the wicked tenants who withheld the rent due to the owner of a vineyard. They abused the owner's messengers and eventually murdered his son. This parable can be interpreted as an expression of Jesus' conviction that his ministry constituted the final crisis for God's people. Jesus, by implication, is the last and most important in the long line of rejected prophets.

The authority assumed by Jesus in his teaching and implicit in his significant actions, including his exorcisms and healings, also implies an eschatological as well as a prophetic role. Jesus' reply to John the Baptist's messengers is significant: when they ask him whether he is "the one who is to come", Jesus replies obliquely, using phrases drawn from several different texts in Isaiah:

> "Go and tell John what you have seen and heard: the blind receive their sight, the lame walk, the lepers are cleansed, the deaf hear, the dead are raised, the poor have good news brought to them. And blessed is anyone who takes no offence at me."
>
> *Luke 7:22–23; cf. Matthew 11:4–6*

Significantly, the only other example we have of this particular combination of citations or allusions is in a fragment of a scroll from Qumran (4Q521) sometimes called the "Resurrection Fragment", where the same or very similar functions are explicitly linked to messiahship. The heavens and the earth, we are told, will listen to God's Messiah, who will liberate captives, give sight to the blind, heal the sick, revive the dead, and bring good news to the poor.[70]

This similarity between Qumran scroll 4Q521 and the Q tradition in the verses from Luke 7 and Matthew 11 does not necessarily mean that the Q tradition is directly dependent on the Qumran document, but it does suggest that by the time of Jesus this particular combination of motifs was already associated with messianic expectation. If Jesus' reply to John the Baptist's messengers is authentic, Jesus was unambiguously defining his own eschatological messianic significance in terms of the reputed messianic functions of Spirit-anointed prophecy, teaching, and healing.

Taken as a whole, the evidence supports the conclusion that during his lifetime Jesus regarded himself, and was regarded by others, as God's final eschatological emissary and envoy to his people Israel, and that in Jesus' ministry the eschatological kingdom of God was drawing near and impinging on the present. The end of the age was at hand. The final realization of the kingdom of God would not be long delayed. This sense of urgency and imminence is well captured in the Gospel of Mark, in what may be two different versions of the same saying:

> "Truly I tell you, there are some standing here who will not taste death until they see that the kingdom of God has come with power."
>
> *Mark 9:1*

> "Truly I tell you, this generation will not pass away until all these things have taken place."
>
> *Mark 13:30*

A specific person

The conclusion that Jesus regarded himself, and was regarded by others, as an eschatological prophet of the imminently coming kingdom of God raises a further question. Was Jesus regarded by others or by himself as a specific prophet or a specific figure whose role and functions were already to some extent defined? During Jesus' lifetime, there appear to have been various conjectures concerning his identity. There was speculation that he might be the dead John the Baptist returned to life, or alternatively, that he was the prophet Elijah (Mark 6:14–16). In the Q tradition, John the Baptist's messengers ask Jesus whether he is "the one who is to come" (Luke 7:20; Matthew 11:2). It was this question that elicited

Jesus' Isaiah-based reply, with its possibly messianic implications (see above). In Mark 8:28 there is a second reference to the speculations first reported in Mark 6. This time it is Jesus himself who raises the question of his identity:

> "Who do people say that I am?" And they answered him, "John the Baptist; and others, Elijah; and still others, one of the prophets."
>
> *Mark 8:27-28*

If Jesus did regard himself as a specific figure, or if he saw himself exercising the functions of a specific figure, there are three principal candidates for consideration. The first is the figure of the "prophet like Moses". In the book of Deuteronomy, God promises Moses:

> "I will raise up for them [the people of Israel] a prophet like you [Moses] from among their own people; I will put my words in the mouth of the prophet, who shall speak to them everything that I command. Anyone who does not heed the words that the prophet shall speak in my name, I myself will hold accountable."
>
> *Deuteronomy 18:18-19*

The two salient characteristics of this prophet that might be applied to Jesus are, firstly, that his words are God's words, and secondly, that he must therefore be heeded and obeyed. Anyone who does not obey this prophet will be held accountable by God himself. The inclusion of this passage from Deuteronomy in a short miscellany of messianic proof-texts in one of the Qumran scrolls (4Q175), indicates that in at least some circles in Second Temple Judaism the figure of the "prophet like Moses" had messianic significance.[71] There is no evidence that Jesus ever specifically identified himself with this figure, but it may be significant that it is Moses who appears alongside Elijah in the important account of Jesus' Transfiguration (Mark 9:2-8). It may also be significant that the voice of God speaking from the cloud explicitly commands Peter, James, and John to take heed of what Jesus says:

> Then a cloud overshadowed them, and from the cloud there came a voice, "This is my Son, the Beloved; listen to him!"
>
> *Mark 9:7*

The Deuteronomic prediction of a future prophet like Moses did not escape the attention of Jesus' followers. In the Acts of the Apostles, Peter is represented as preaching shortly after the death of Jesus to a crowd assembled at Solomon's Porch on the Temple Mount. Peter quotes Deuteronomy 18:18–19 verbatim, but with added emphasis. He reminds his hearers:

> "Moses said, 'The Lord your God will raise up for you from your own people a prophet like me. You must listen to whatever he tells you. And it will be that everyone who does not listen to that prophet will be utterly rooted out from the people.'... When God raised up his servant [i.e. Jesus], he sent him first to you [i.e. not to the Gentiles], to bless you by turning each of you from your wicked ways."
>
> *Acts 3:22–26*

The implication is unmistakable. Jesus is to be regarded as the expected prophet like Moses, at least in respect of his exceptional authority and the absolute necessity for what he says to be heeded. How general this understanding of Jesus was, and where and when and in what circumstances it first emerged, is not known.

The second candidate for consideration is that of the anonymous eschatological prophet who appears in the Gospel of John. John the Baptist was questioned about his identity. His reply to the questioners indicates that the possibilities being considered included the Messiah, the prophet Elijah and an anonymous figure called "the prophet":

> This is the testimony given by John [the Baptist] when the Jews sent priests and Levites from Jerusalem to ask him, "Who are you?" He confessed and did not deny it, but confessed, "I am not

the Messiah." And they asked him, "What then? Are you Elijah?" He said, "I am not." "Are you the prophet?" He answered, "No."

John 1:19–21

This figure of the anonymous prophet appears again at the end of the story of the feeding of the five thousand on a mountainside in Galilee. Afterwards the astonished spectators say of Jesus, "This is indeed the prophet who is to come into the world" (John 6:14). A little later, in Jerusalem on the final day of the festival of *Sukkot* (Tabernacles), a crowd was again debating the question of Jesus' identity. Some were saying, "This is really the prophet." Others were saying, "This is the Messiah" (John 7:40–41). Alongside its well-known reference to the two messiahs of Aaron and Israel, the Qumran Community Rule refers to the anticipated future coming of an eschatological prophet (1QS 9:11).[72] Whether the Johannine figure and the figure in the Community Rule are related and whether either of them has any connection with the figure of the Deuteronomic "prophet like Moses" is not known.

The third candidate for identification with Jesus is the prophet Elijah. According to the book of Malachi, Elijah was expected to return from heaven to earth to prepare for the coming of the Messiah:

> Lo, I will send you the prophet Elijah before the great and terrible day of the LORD comes. He will turn the hearts of parents to their children and the hearts of children to their parents . . .
>
> *Malachi 4:5–6*

This traditional belief receives explicit mention three times in the Gospel of Mark. It also appears in parallel passages in Matthew and Luke. Despite the popular speculations about Jesus' identity, nowhere in the Jesus tradition is there any suggestion that his followers ever identified him with Elijah, or that Jesus so identified himself. In the account of the Transfiguration, Jesus, Elijah, and Moses are separate individuals (Mark 9:2–8). On the other hand, there is evidence that John the Baptist was identified with Elijah, presumably in circles where the John 1:19–21 tradition (that John the Baptist was not Elijah) was either unknown or disregarded. For example, in the Gospel of Mark, Jesus apparently refers to John the Baptist when he says:

> "I tell you that Elijah has come, and they did to him whatever they pleased, as it is written about him."
>
> *Mark 9:13; cf. Matthew 11:11–14*

In the Lucan infancy narrative, this identification is given particular prominence. The Gospel opens with an account of an angel appearing to a righteous priest called Zechariah. The story, which is clearly modelled on the appearance of the angels to Abraham and Sarah (Genesis 18:1–15), echoes the Elijah prophecy in Malachi 4. Zechariah is told by the angel that he and his barren wife Elizabeth will have a son (John the Baptist) who will be great in the sight of the Lord and filled with the Holy Spirit:

> "He will turn many of the people of Israel to the Lord their God. With the spirit and power of Elijah he will go before him, to turn the hearts of parents to their children . . . to make ready a people prepared for the Lord."
>
> *Luke 1:16–17*

Whether this means that the author believed Zechariah and Elizabeth's child would actually be Elijah or that the functions of Elijah were to be remitted to him is unclear. What is apparent is that in the early Jesus tradition, other than in circles where the John 1:19–21 tradition was known and accepted, it was John the Baptist rather than Jesus who was held to be Elijah, or held to be exercising the functions of Elijah.

The traditions bearing on the popular estimations of both Jesus and John are confused and inconsistent, as are the traditions concerning their estimation of each other. There is no convincing evidence that during his lifetime Jesus believed himself to be either the anonymous prophet referred to in the Gospel of John, or the "prophet like Moses" of Deuteronomy 18, although after his death the latter understanding was applied to him. Nevertheless, many of his sayings, much of his teaching, and a number of highly significant actions suggest that prophetic traditions contributed to shaping Jesus' own understanding of his ministry and message. That Jesus identified himself with any specific eschatological figure anyway seems unlikely. He probably felt intuitively that the eschatological significance of his mission and ministry transcended existing prophetic categories.

The coming Son of Man

If Jesus made no explicit claim to messiahship, if he never called himself the Son of God, and if he never allowed himself to be called Lord other than in a conventional sense, what do we make of the sayings in which the Gospel writers understand him to be referring to himself as the Son of Man—a majestic, heavenly being expected to come suddenly in glory with angels in attendance to execute judgement on the ungodly and to make safe the faithful? The basic data concerning the Son of Man sayings were summarized in the previous chapter. Even if these sayings about the future coming of the Son of Man are not authentic, they are important because, from a very early stage after Jesus' death, his followers undoubtedly did believe in the future coming of "the Son of Man", whom they believed to be Jesus. If the sayings are authentic, they are even more important because they bear directly on the question of the estimation of Jesus by others and on his own self-understanding.

Some scholars conclude that Jesus was referring to someone other than himself when he spoke about the future "coming" of the Son of Man. This conclusion depends on the authenticity and interpretation of two sayings in particular. These two sayings, noted in the previous chapter, require further scrutiny. The first appears in Mark, whence it has been copied by the authors of Matthew and Luke. In this saying the future "coming" of the Son of Man is explicit. The second saying is derived from the Q tradition, and appears in variant forms in Luke and Matthew, with Luke's version generally thought to be closer than Matthew's to what Jesus actually said. In this second saying the future coming of the Son of Man is implicit rather than explicit.

The Marcan saying reads:

> "Those who are ashamed of me and of my words in this adulterous and sinful generation, of them the Son of Man will

also be ashamed when he comes in the glory of his Father with the holy angels."

Mark 8:38; cf. Luke 9:26, Matthew 16:27-28

The Q-tradition saying is:

> "And I tell you, everyone who acknowledges me before others, the Son of Man also will acknowledge before the angels of God; but whoever denies me before others will be denied before the angels of God."
>
> Luke 12:8-9; cf. Matthew 10:32-33

Matthew's version of the second saying differs slightly from Luke's. In Luke, believers will be acknowledged "by the Son of Man before the angels of God". In Matthew, Jesus himself acknowledges believers "before my Father in heaven". Matthew's version of the saying must have been adjusted to reflect the primitive community's post-Easter identification of the exalted Jesus with the heavenly Son of Man.

On the question of the authenticity or otherwise of the underlying sayings or saying, one has to ask whether it is really very likely, once the early and important post-Easter identification of Jesus with the Son of Man had been made, that anyone would have wanted to invent sayings like Mark 8:38, Luke 12:8-9, and their parallels—sayings that leave the question of this identification hanging open. This consideration tends to support the argument that the underlying saying or sayings may well be authentic.

These sayings constitute a clear warning that confessing Jesus and accepting his words cannot be reconciled with the competing claims of "this sinful generation". The status and sovereignty assigned to Jesus and to the Son of Man are extraordinarily exalted. Attachment to Jesus on earth apparently involves a binding fellowship and commitment which will be confirmed at the coming of the Son of Man from heaven. As we have seen, the sayings can be interpreted in various ways. Jesus could have been speaking about his own future coming in power and glory as the Son of Man. Or he could have been speaking about the coming of the Son of Man, intending thereby reference to a mighty heavenly being, someone other than himself. The third possibility is that the sayings are entirely the creation of the post-Easter community of Jesus' followers.

Those who want to go down this third road have to explain how and why sayings about the coming Son of Man came into being, and how they found their way into the tradition. The explanation generally advanced is that there was a process involving a number of distinct steps or stages. First of all, it is assumed that the figure of the "one like a son of man" who is seen "coming to God with the clouds of heaven" in Daniel 7:13–14 was probably already understood by Jesus' followers to be a symbol for God's suffering but eventually vindicated people of Israel. Then, towards the end of his life, Jesus realized that he was likely to suffer and that he might even be killed before the kingdom of God had come in power. Nevertheless, he let it be known that he was convinced that in some unspecified way he would be vindicated by God. This was the second stage. The third stage was the emergence, after Jesus' death, of his followers' conviction that he must necessarily already have been vindicated by resurrection and heavenly exaltation. The fourth and all-important development was his followers giving expression to their conviction by latching on to what they believed to be the implications of Daniel 7:13–14. That is, that Jesus—like the figure in Daniel 7—had been vindicated by "coming to God" in glory. Indeed, the figure of the "one like a son of man" whom they had previously supposed to be a symbol for the persecuted and vindicated people of God was in fact Jesus himself. The final stage in the process was the morphing of understandings about Jesus coming to God in glory into sayings about Jesus the Son of Man *returning to earth in glory to exercise universal dominion*. These sayings were then retrojected into the ongoing Jesus tradition, whence they eventually found their way into the Gospels.

Two sayings in Mark may possibly reflect the all-important fourth stage, that is, the early idea of heavenly vindication expressed in terms of Jesus' "coming to God". Both are clear allusions to Daniel 7:13. One is the conclusion of the Marcan apocalyptic discourse:

> "Then they will see 'the Son of Man coming in clouds' with great power and glory. Then he will send out the angels, and gather

his elect from the four winds, from the ends of the earth to the ends of heaven."

Mark 13:26–27

The other is Jesus' reputed reply to the High Priest at the time of his trial. The High Priest asks Jesus whether he is the Messiah. Jesus replies:

"I am; and 'you will see the Son of Man seated at the right hand of the Power', and 'coming with the clouds of heaven.'

Mark 14:62

What this shows is that all the sayings about the "coming" of the Son of Man could have originated after Jesus' death. In which case, the apocalyptic eschatology implicit in these sayings, as we now have them in the Gospels, originated not with Jesus but within the early post-Easter community of his followers. This understanding is compatible with Jesus' own estimation of himself as God's final, prophetic envoy of the imminently coming kingdom of God. That is to say, Jesus' message was eschatological but not necessarily apocalyptic.

A variant form of the same basic argument is that it was Jesus, during his lifetime, who applied the term "Son of Man" to himself, as a means of giving expression to his expectation that he would eventually be vindicated, even after suffering and possible death. In other words, Jesus himself understood the Danielic figure to be a symbol for the suffering and eventually vindicated people of God. By speaking of the Son of Man "coming to God in glory", Jesus was giving cryptic expression to his personal conviction of his own eventual vindication after anticipated suffering. If this is what happened, Mark 13:26–27 and 14:62 (see above) could have originated as genuine sayings of Jesus about his "coming" to God. Then, after Jesus' death, these sayings—or their precursors—would have been adapted by his followers to become sayings about Jesus coming back to earth as a mighty heavenly being.

This theory is attractive because it allows the key understandings to have their origins in the authentic teaching of Jesus. Nevertheless, it is open to challenge. In particular, it depends on the "symbolic" interpretation of the figure in Daniel 7:13–14. The problem is that the internal evidence of Daniel 7 suggests that the figure described as "one like a son of man" is an individual being, not a symbol for the suffering and vindicated people of God. In Daniel 7 there is no suggestion that this heavenly being has suffered or could ever suffer. Moreover, in every other instance in which more or less contemporary Jewish exegetes have made use of this same Danielic tradition, the figure is never symbolic. On the contrary, it is always understood to be that of a majestic, individual, heavenly being, God's vice-regent and/or Israel's heavenly representative and champion.

Partner to a heavenly being

The remaining possibility is that when Jesus spoke about the "coming" Son of Man he was referring not to himself but to someone else. That is to say, Jesus, like other contemporary eschatological and apocalyptic Jewish exegetes of Daniel 7, was speaking about the future coming from heaven to earth of a specific individual figure, someone he referred to as "the Son of Man". This "Son of Man" was an individual, heavenly being. He would intervene decisively on earth. He would keep the righteous safe, execute judgement on the wicked, and preside over a new, ongoing kingdom of peace and blessedness.

Two major objections have been advanced against this interpretation. First, it is argued that Jesus' kingdom of God sayings and his Son of Man sayings reflect two different, mutually exclusive streams of tradition, only one of which can be authentic. We have seen in the previous chapter that this objection is not fatal. Second, it is objected that there is no evidence that there was an ongoing pre-Christian heavenly redeemer tradition in Second Temple Judaism. This objection, too, is not fatal. Strictly speaking, there may not have been a heavenly redeemer tradition as such. Nevertheless, we have seen that there are repeated instances of authors using the figure in Daniel 7:13–14 as the basis for giving expression to their own individual convictions concerning the coming of an anticipated heavenly redeemer. So although there may not be one continuous stream of tradition, there does seem to be a very definite tradition of repeatedly interpreting the Daniel figure in terms of a hoped-for heavenly redeemer.

The possibility that Jesus believed the "coming" Son of Man to be someone other than himself receives indirect support from the way in which, after his death, the process of forming the tradition rapidly "closed ranks" around the understanding that Jesus was himself was the Son of Man. This may seem paradoxical, but consider what appears to have happened. Whatever Jesus had actually said about the Son of Man during his lifetime, after his death his earliest followers very quickly concluded that he had been speaking about himself. That is, they identified him with the heavenly Son of Man. Once this identification had taken place, there would have been no conceivable incentive to create and retrospectively attribute to Jesus sayings in which he appears to speak of the Son of Man as someone other than himself. This suggests that the saying or sayings underlying Mark 8:38 and Luke 12:8–9 may well be authentic. In which case, the basic line of development becomes clear. Jesus believed that a heavenly being called the Son of Man was about to come from heaven to redeem, to judge, and to establish the kingdom of God. Immediately after Jesus' unexpected death, in parallel with the emergence of belief in his resurrection and exaltation, his followers came very quickly to the conclusion that Jesus himself was the Son of Man of whose coming he had spoken. This understanding was then retrojected into the tradition via the exegesis of Daniel 7:13, and this is what we see reflected in sayings such as Mark 13:26–27 and Mark 14:62.

But if Jesus spoke of the Son of Man as someone other than himself, important questions arise concerning Jesus' relationship with the Son of Man. Before we can address these questions, we need to backtrack slightly and consider another strand of evidence. That Jesus was widely regarded by others as an eschatological prophet, and that he regarded himself in the same light, seems certain. It is implicit in his words and deeds, and especially in the urgency of his proclamation. This sense of urgency is evident in his acts of exorcism, which he understood to be revealing the powerlessness of Satan in the face of the already impinging kingdom of God. For example, after an act of exorcism, onlookers questioned the source of Jesus' authority. Jesus is reputed to have replied:

> "But if it is by the finger of God that I cast out the demons, then the kingdom of God has come to you. When a strong man, fully

armed, guards his castle, his property is safe. But when one stronger than he attacks him and overpowers him, he takes away his armour in which he trusted and divides his plunder."

Luke 11:20-22; cf. Matthew 12:28-29

This saying is particularly significant because Jesus is implicitly claiming to be *more* than a prophet of the coming kingdom of God. He is implicitly representing himself to be the conduit through which the power and the presence of God's kingdom is entering into present time. Similarly significant are the immediacy of his teaching, and the authority implicit in his teaching and explicit in his calling of others to discipleship. Consider, for example, the implications of his unilateral appointment of twelve of his followers to be the nucleus of the new people of God:

"... I confer on you, just as my Father has conferred on me, a kingdom, so that you may eat and drink at my table in my kingdom, and you will sit on thrones judging the twelve tribes of Israel."

Luke 22:29-30; cf. Matthew 19:28

The reference to "eating and drinking at my table" is an allusion to the anticipated eschatological banquet referred to in Isaiah 25:6-8 and elsewhere. The eschatological banquet was expected to be hosted by God himself to celebrate his final victory over Israel's enemies and the inauguration of the new, everlasting kingdom of peace and plenty. Taken in the context of this expectation, Jesus' references to "my kingdom", "my table", and his statement that the twelve "will sit on thrones" are altogether extraordinary. The authenticity of this particular saying is questionable, but whether authentic or not it alerts us to the remarkable authority implicit in the act of selecting and appointing "the twelve". Jesus seems to have intended to present "the twelve" as the nucleus of the new Israel, but who gave him the right to make such extraordinary appointments? What does this say about who Jesus thought he was? As the proleptic point of presence of the coming kingdom of God, the focal point of the righteous people of God, Jesus seems to be believing himself to be God's agent, actively participating in the bringing-down of the future into the present.

If this is a correct understanding of Jesus' estimation of his own significance, and if Jesus understood the Son of Man to be a real, individual heavenly being, someone other than himself, how are we to understand the relationship of Jesus with this coming heavenly Son of Man? One suggestion is that Jesus understood his relationship with this figure to be a partnership of purpose akin to the partnership apparently depicted between the messianic heavenly redeemer Michael-Melchizedek and his associated earthly herald in Qumran scroll 11Q13. Jesus may have regarded himself and the coming Son of Man as separate but nevertheless indissolubly linked partners, one on earth and the other in heaven.

This hypothesis has been expanded by some scholars to include the further suggestion that the figure of the "one like a son of man" in Daniel 7:13–14 is Michael, or Michael-Melchizedek, the great angel of Israel. If Jesus regarded himself as the earthly partner of the heavenly archangel Michael-Melchizedek, he probably also believed Michael-Melchizedek to be his own personal guardian angel or alter ego. This would explain how he could regard himself as the nucleus of the new Israel and the point of presence of the coming kingdom of God. It is even possible that the two identities—Jesus the earthly herald and the heavenly Son of Man, his partner and alter ego—became blurred to such an extent that the authority of the latter became assumed into the identity of the former. It might also explain how Jesus could speak *as* the Son of Man *of* the Son of Man.

These suggestions are interesting, but speculative. They rest on the unprovable assumption that Jesus did in fact speak of the Son of Man as a real being, someone other than himself. Debate is ongoing because the historical data are insufficient to provide a basis for deciding between the three possibilities outlined above. This is disappointing, but probably does not matter. It will be argued in the next chapter that understandings arising *during Jesus' lifetime* concerning the identity of the coming Son of Man had only a relatively minor bearing on the events and processes involved in the emergence of resurrection faith. What is important is that Jesus appears to have regarded himself—and to have been regarded by others—as the last and greatest of the prophets. He was an eschatological prophet whose role and function was to be God's final envoy and agent to his people Israel. Moreover, he himself was the proleptic or anticipatory point of presence of the coming kingdom of God. He was actively participating in what he was proclaiming.

An angelomorphic being

The hypothesis that Jesus spoke about the Son of Man as a heavenly being other than himself, and that he regarded himself as the earthly partner of this heavenly Son of Man, would be reinforced if it could be shown that that Jesus' followers had already sensed during his lifetime that he possessed some sort of foothold in the heavenly realm. Discussion of this possibility revolves primarily around the puzzling story of the Transfiguration of Jesus, which on account of its oddity has sometimes been considered to be a misplaced resurrection story. The story of the Transfiguration is heavily freighted with theological significance. The earliest version tells how Jesus took Peter, James, and John up a high mountain:

> ... And he [Jesus] was transfigured before them, and his clothes became dazzling white, such as no one on earth could bleach them. And there appeared to them Elijah with Moses, who were talking with Jesus... Then a cloud overshadowed them, and from the cloud there came a voice, "This is my Son, the Beloved; listen to him!" Suddenly when they looked around, they saw no one with them any more, but only Jesus.
>
> Mark 9:2–8; cf. Matthew 17:1–9, Luke 9:28–36

Entangled in this story are a rich profusion of motifs drawn from the Hebrew scriptures and other related texts. These include the motif of angelomorphic transformation and heavenly ascent; the belief that exceptionally righteous heroes of faith could bypass *Sheol* and go straight to heaven; belief in Moses as the greatest of the prophets; belief in Elijah as the forerunner of the Messiah; the idea of Jesus as the "prophet like Moses" in Deuteronomy 18:18–19; the understanding that Elijah had ascended into heaven whilst still alive; and the extra-biblical tradition that Moses also had ascended directly into heaven. In the Lucan version of the Transfiguration story there is the added motif of Jesus' impending "departure" or "exodus", which has the effect of strengthening the forward-looking, resurrection-related implications of the story. In both Matthew and Luke, there is also the additional detail that Jesus' face was shining, like the face of Moses on Mount Sinai. The implied location of the Transfiguration event is ambiguous; whether it is supposed to have taken place on earth, in heaven, or at the interface between heaven and earth is unclear. If the interface between earth and heaven is intended, then there are further parallels with the Apocalypse of Zephaniah, where the seer, arriving at the frontier between *Sheol* and heaven, sees Abraham, Isaac, Jacob, Enoch, Elijah, and David, all of whom are already inhabitants of heaven.

For present purposes, the most significant aspect of the story of the Transfiguration is that Jesus' disciples are represented as not yet fully understanding the true purpose and deeper significance of Jesus. When Jesus was baptized by John in the river Jordan, the voice from heaven had declared him to be the Son of God. According to Mark, those around Jesus either did not hear or did not understand. At the Transfiguration, Jesus' chosen inner circle of disciples again hear the voice from heaven. It delivers the same message, and they see Jesus transformed into a heavenly being. Still they do not understand. The circumstantial details wrapped around the story are almost certainly artificial. What actually happened, if anything, we have no way of knowing. Nevertheless, the point that Mark is making could well be historical. Throughout Jesus' ministry, his disciples seem always to have been struggling to come to terms with the implications of his convictions and message. The Transfiguration story suggests that there may have been a moment when some of the key members of Jesus' inner circle sensed for the first time that he was more than a prophet and, possibly, more even than a merely human agent of God's purpose. The Transfiguration is almost certainly not a misplaced resurrection story, but it does reflect a dawning awareness that there might be a dimension of cosmic significance associated with Jesus.

The Transfiguration needs also to be set in the wider context of the part played by visions in the ministry of Jesus and in the life of the early Church A few examples must suffice. The Gospel of Mark opens with Jesus' vision of the heavens torn asunder and of the Spirit of God descending in the form of a dove. Later, Jesus appoints seventy missionaries to go through the villages of Galilee. When they return, enthused by their success, Jesus has a vision in which he sees Satan falling from heaven like a flash of lightning (Luke 10:18). We shall show that the earliest evidence points to the resurrection appearances also having been visionary experiences. Visions and dreams continue to be significant in the early Church. The Acts of the Apostles includes a description of a collective vision in which divided tongues of fire-like flame were seen to be resting on each of the twelve apostles (Acts 2:1–3). Just before Stephen is murdered, he looks upwards and has a vision of the heavens opened and the Son of Man standing at the right hand of God (Acts 7:55–56). A disciple in Damascus called Ananias has a vision in which he is commanded by God to go to a particular house where he will find the newly converted Paul (Acts 9.10–12). Peter falls into a trance in which he sees heaven opened and all manner of animals being lowered to the ground. A voice from heaven commands him to kill and eat, but he refuses. The voice rebukes him: "What God has made clean, you must not call profane" (Acts 10:9–16). Paul has an experience of rapture in which he believes he was taken up "to the third heaven", where he heard "things that are not to be told, that no mortal is permitted to repeat" (2 Corinthians 12:1–4). There is a turning point in Paul's mission when he was perplexed as to where to go next. In a vision, a man begs him to come and proclaim the good news in Macedonia (Acts 16:7–10). The book of Revelation contains an extended account of a series of visionary experiences which draw together fundamental convictions about God, Christ, and history. The "truth" or otherwise of these visionary experiences is not the issue. Collectively they testify to the conviction that in the life of Jesus, and in the ongoing mission of the community of his followers, the heavenly and earthly realms are closely intertwined.

Conclusion

Jesus almost certainly never made any claim to be the Messiah, at least not in the sense of a dynasty-establishing, Davidic warrior-king. There is evidence of a contemporary belief in an anointed figure who would exercise the reputed Davidic functions of Spirit-inspired prophecy, teaching, and healing. It may be that it was in respect of these functions that the term Messiah was first considered to be appropriate for Jesus. Nevertheless, it seems that messiahship was a significant issue during Jesus' lifetime and that Jesus was probably crucified as some sort of messianic pretender. He may have felt it impossible to repudiate the title of Messiah, even though he understood himself to be a Spirit-anointed prophet rather than a putative warrior-king.

It seems unlikely that, during his lifetime, Jesus' disciples ever regarded him as "the Son of God", or that Jesus himself ever made any claim to such a title. Nevertheless, an intense relationship involving filial obedience to God as Father appears to lie at the heart of Jesus' teaching and ministry. Also, those who address God as Father are implicitly claiming to be sons and daughters of God. Even though Jesus and his disciples may have made little use of the term "Son of God", and even though it was almost certainly never used as a title during his lifetime, Jesus' commitment and obedience to what he perceived to be the will and purpose of his heavenly Father suggest that the duty of obedience associated with sonship was an integral part of his self-understanding.

During Jesus' lifetime the use of the word "lord" in addressing Jesus and speaking of him appears to have been little more than his disciples' way of acknowledging the claim laid on them by his teaching and by the seriousness of his purpose. As probably used of Jesus during his lifetime, the Aramaic word *mar* (lord) does not appear to have had any specific connotations of divinity. Nevertheless, there is evidence that after Jesus' death the equivalent Greek word, *kyrios*, functioned as an important vector facilitating the transfer of attributes of divinity from Y{\small HWH} in the Hebrew scriptures, via the Greek Septuagint, to Jesus as heavenly Lord.

There is no convincing evidence that Jesus ever identified himself with any specific historical figure. Nevertheless, it seems clear that he regarded himself, and was regarded by others, as an eschatological prophet. Jesus believed that the kingdom of God was drawing near, and that in his ministry it was already impinging on the present. The end of the age was at hand. Jesus believed himself to be God's final envoy and eschatological agent, not just proclaiming but actively participating in the bringing in of the coming kingdom of God.

Finally, there are Jesus' reputed sayings about the "coming" of the Son of Man. Three possibilities have been identified. One is that Jesus' followers created all these sayings after his death. The second is that Jesus did speak about the "coming" of the Son of Man and that he was using the term as a coded reference to his own expectation that he would be vindicated after his death by "coming" to God. The third possibility is that Jesus spoke about the Son of Man coming suddenly to earth in judgement, and that he intended reference not to himself, but to the future coming of a mighty heavenly redeemer, an angelic power called the Son of Man. If Jesus spoke about the coming Son of Man as someone other than himself, a further possibility is that he thought of himself as the earthly herald of this heavenly power, who was his own and Israel's correspondent angelic being. There could even have been a sense of overlapping or dual identities.

Armed with these understandings, we can now begin to investigate the emergence of belief in the resurrection and heavenly exaltation of Jesus. In the first instance, we focus on the very earliest available testimony, leaving the relatively late empty-tomb traditions and appearance stories of the Gospels for later consideration. The evidence is fragmentary and has to be carefully disentangled from the later documents in which it is embedded. Nevertheless, in many respects its quality is outstanding. Although lacking in circumstantial details, the picture that will emerge is clearly defined and markedly different from the traditions in the Gospels which for many centuries have been regarded as normative.

CHAPTER 7

The Earliest Resurrection Testimony

To investigate the earliest form and content of emergent belief in the resurrection and heavenly exaltation of Jesus may seem an ambitious undertaking, given that he apparently died in 30 or 33 CE and that the earliest of the four Gospels—none of whose authors were eye-witnesses of the events they describe—was probably not written until sometime around 70 CE. (The other Gospels were written towards the end of the first century, although they contain earlier traditions.)

The earliest historical testimony that we have is embedded in the letters of Paul, the first of which was written in 50–51 CE, some seventeen years after Jesus' death and some twenty years before the earliest of the Gospels. This embedded material includes what appear to be early hymns or hymnic fragments and brief formulae (possibly primitive creeds and confessions of faith) apparently antedating the documents in which they are now located. Some of these fragments can be identified with reasonable certainty. We also have information bearing on the early worship practices of Jesus' followers. When this evidence is set alongside first-hand, personal testimony referring to experiences almost contemporaneous with the death of Jesus, significant conclusions emerge.

Resurrection formulae

Scattered throughout Paul's letters and the works of later New Testament writers are brief formulae or affirmations which appear to have been part of the preaching and tradition of the earliest Jewish followers of Jesus after his death (at this stage they were not yet called Christians). These formulae and affirmations are of two basic types. Statements of the first type make no mention of Jesus' death; they refer only to his resurrection. Statements of the second type are based on an explicit antithesis of Jesus' death and resurrection. Examples of the first type include:

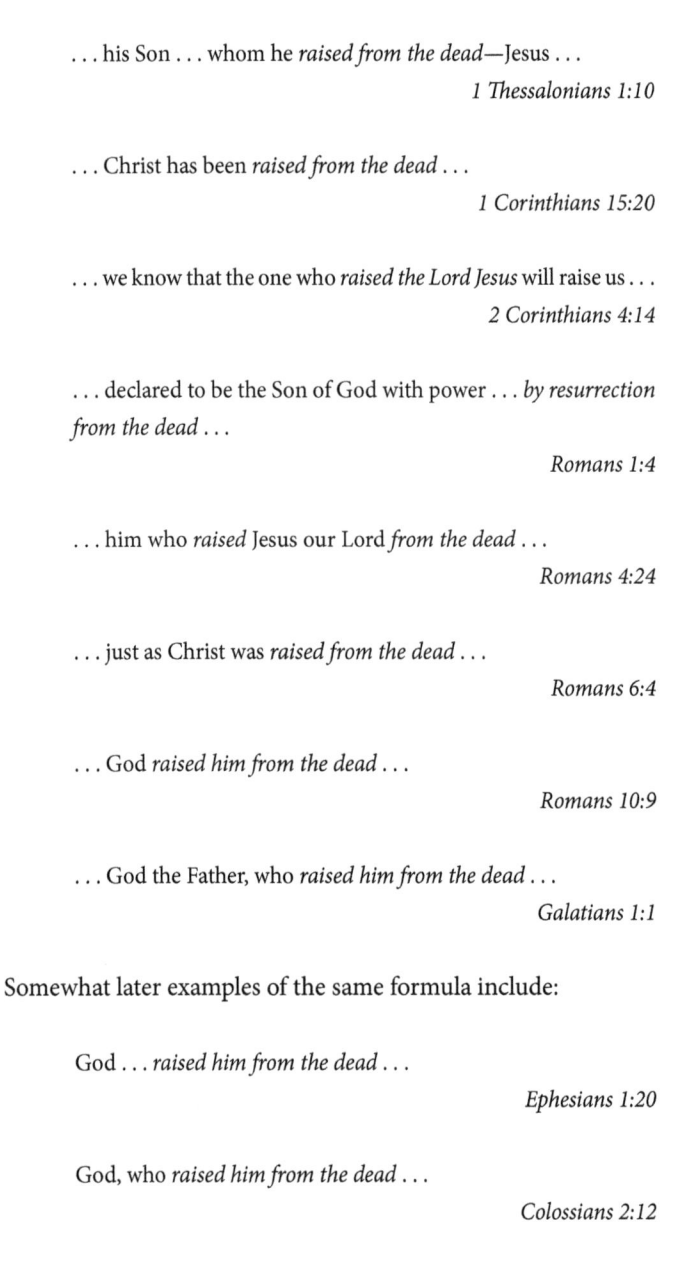

> ... his Son ... whom he *raised from the dead*—Jesus ...
>
> 1 Thessalonians 1:10

> ... Christ has been *raised from the dead* ...
>
> 1 Corinthians 15:20

> ... we know that the one who *raised the Lord Jesus* will raise us ...
>
> 2 Corinthians 4:14

> ... declared to be the Son of God with power ... *by resurrection from the dead* ...
>
> Romans 1:4

> ... him who *raised* Jesus our Lord *from the dead* ...
>
> Romans 4:24

> ... just as Christ was *raised from the dead* ...
>
> Romans 6:4

> ... God *raised him from the dead* ...
>
> Romans 10:9

> ... God the Father, who *raised him from the dead* ...
>
> Galatians 1:1

Somewhat later examples of the same formula include:

> God ... *raised him from the dead* ...
>
> Ephesians 1:20

> God, who *raised him from the dead* ...
>
> Colossians 2:12

> Remember Jesus Christ, *raised from the dead* . . .
>
> 2 Timothy 2:8

> God, who *raised him from the dead* . . .
>
> 1 Peter 1:21

Similar formulaic statements later appear in the Acts of the Apostles in sermons which Peter and Paul are represented as having preached at a very early date, in the first instance only a few weeks after the death of Jesus:

> ". . . God *raised him up*, having freed him *from death* . . ."
>
> Acts 2:24

> ". . . the Author of life, whom God *raised from the dead.*"
>
> Acts 3:15

> ". . . by *raising him from the dead.*"
>
> Acts 17:31

Early examples of the type of saying in which Jesus' death and resurrection are explicitly opposed include:

> . . . we believe that Jesus *died and rose again* . . .
>
> 1 Thessalonians 4:14

> Christ *died* . . . and . . . *was raised* . . .
>
> 1 Corinthians 15:3–4

> [Jesus] . . . was *handed over to death* . . . *and was raised* . . .
>
> Romans 4:25

> . . . Christ *died and lived again* . . .
>
> Romans 14:9

> It is Christ Jesus, who *died, yes, who was raised* ...
>
> Romans 8:34

Taken as a whole, the evidence suggests that statements such as "God raised Jesus from the dead." were used by the followers of Jesus as summary affirmations of belief—or "faith statements"—at a very early stage. They were in existence before Paul wrote any of his letters, and they almost certainly originated in the forties or even the thirties of the Common Era. These brief, formulaic statements are the earliest evidence we have, not just for belief in the resurrection of Jesus, but for the existence of Jesus himself as a historical, human figure.

The origin and purpose of these sayings is uncertain. One possibility is that they originated in a liturgical or worship setting. The titles given to Jesus in sayings of this type—"Christ", "Lord", and "Son of God"—are now almost certainly significant, but a distinction has to be made between titles applied to Jesus in the underlying tradition and titles that may have been added to a saying by the author of the letter in which the formula appears. Analysis suggests that in the basic formula it was always "Christ" or "Jesus Christ" who was said to have died and been raised.

As indicated in the previous chapter, there are complex issues surrounding the attribution of the Hebrew title "Messiah" (*Christos* in Greek) to Jesus during his lifetime. Nevertheless, Jesus was undoubtedly regarded as "Messiah" by his followers at a very early stage following his death and the initial emergence of resurrection faith. The fact that the title would have had its full relevance only in a Jewish rather than a Hellenistic environment suggests that the resurrection "faith formula" originated among the earliest Aramaic-speaking Jewish followers of Jesus, probably in the form of a sentence such as "God raised Jesus from the dead," perhaps coupled with the declaration that "Jesus is the Messiah." It was probably among the Greek-speaking Jewish followers of Jesus (the "Hellenists" of Acts 6:1) that the two clauses first became amalgamated, thereby creating statements such as "God raised Jesus Christ from the dead." These basic statements became freighted at an early stage with additional understandings, including the understanding that the death and resurrection of Jesus were "for us" and "in accordance with the scriptures".

The uncertainty concerning the precise circumstances in which the designations "Christ", "Son of God", and "Lord" first became attached to Jesus is less important than was once supposed. It is now clear that the relevant concepts and usages were available—and possibly linked with one another—in some circles within late Second Temple Aramaic-speaking Judaism. The concept of a supreme, quasi-divine being having lordship over all other heavenly powers was already available. In the Qumran scrolls there are examples of the Aramaic term *mar* functioning as a substitute for the divine name YHWH in much the same way as the equivalent Greek word *kyrios* substitutes for the name YHWH in the Septuagint. There is also evidence in the Qumran scrolls and in 4 Ezra suggesting that the concepts of the Messiah, Lordship, and the Son of God were already connected in Jewish exegesis of 2 Samuel 7:14, Psalm 2:7, and—possibly—Psalm 110:1. Another Qumran scroll apparently depicts the figure of an exalted human or heavenly warrior-king who exercises messianic functions and is designated "Son of God" (see Chapter 4 above). Although the worship of Jesus as supremely exalted cosmic Lord may have reached its full fruition only later in the Greek-speaking Gentile church, the acclamation, invocation, and veneration of Jesus as risen and exalted Lord appears to have been a feature of the devotional life of the early Aramaic-speaking Jewish Christians just as much as it was of Paul's later Hellenistic Gentile churches.

Christological hymns

In addition to the basic, formulaic assertion that God has raised Jesus Christ from the dead, embedded in several New Testament texts are a number of probably pre-Pauline, Christian hymns, or hymnic fragments. These focus not on the resurrection of Jesus but on his heavenly exaltation. A number of criteria have been proposed for the identification of these pieces. They include the use of a rhythmical style, a vocabulary differing significantly from that of the context in which the piece is set, and the presence of christological reflection expressed in exalted and liturgical language. A number of these early hymns and hymn-like fragments have been identified in the letters (sometimes called epistles) known as

Philippians, Colossians, Hebrews, and 1 Timothy. The prologue to the Gospel of John may also be an early Christian (or even pre-Christian) hymn. Because these fragments almost certainly antedate their present settings, they provide important information concerning the formation and development of early Christian thinking, including resurrection belief, Christology, and worship practices.

The most important of these hymns and fragments is located in the letter to the Philippians. Paul is exhorting his readers not to be selfish. They are to put the interests of others before their own. He quotes the example of Jesus:

> who, though he was in the form of God,
> did not regard equality with God as something to be exploited,
> but emptied himself,
> taking the form of a slave,
> being born in human likeness.
> And being found in human form,
> he humbled himself
> and became obedient to the point of death—
> even death on a cross.
> Therefore God also highly exalted him
> and gave him the name that is above every name,
> so that at the name of Jesus
> every knee should bend,
> in heaven and on earth and under the earth,
> and every tongue should confess
> that Jesus Christ is Lord,
> to the glory of God the Father.
>
> *Philippians 2:6–11*

There are a number of reconstructions based on different arrangements of lines and verses. Some allow for the possibility that the phrases "even death on a cross", "in heaven, on earth, and under the earth" and "to the glory of God the Father" may be Paul's own additions. One suggestion is that the hymn originally comprised three strophes (or distinct, balanced sections) and that it might have been sung or recited in early Christian worship. For example:

> Who being in the form of God
> Did not claim godly treatment
> But he emptied himself
> Taking the form of a servant.
> Being born in the likeness of men
> And being found in shape as a man
> He humbled himself
> Becoming obedient unto death.
> Therefore God super-exalted him
> And gave him the supreme name
> So that at Jesus' name every knee should bow
> And every tongue confess "Jesus Christ is Lord".[73]

Philippians 2:6–11 has generated an enormous specialist literature. There are complex stylistic and linguistic and interpretive issues, including the unresolved question of whether there was an Aramaic original underlying the present Greek text. Reasons given for regarding the passage as a self-contained entity include: the logical structure proceeding step by step to the eventual climax; the parallelism; and other linguistic and stylistic features. There are a number of problems associated with the translation and interpretation of the hymn. The meanings of the Greek phrases translated into English as "in the form of God", "equality with God as a thing to be exploited", "taking the form of a slave", and "being found in human form" are all disputed. The Greek term *harpagmon*, translated as "exploited", "grasped", or "claimed", poses particularly thorny questions.

The hymn's apparent attribution of pre-existence to Jesus is striking. It seems to be implied that Jesus already existed in heaven prior to his birth as a human being. Although he was a pre-existent heavenly being, Jesus then declined to cling on to his heavenly status. He willingly emptied himself of his heavenly attributes and assumed human form and human likeness, with all that this implies in terms of contingent being.

There is an alternative interpretation of the hymn that avoids the idea of pre-existence. The premise is that from the outset the hymn is talking about Jesus as a human being here on earth, albeit a man of unique godliness, destined for immortality. According to this alternative interpretation, Jesus voluntarily emptied himself not by coming from heaven to earth, but here on earth by embracing servitude, suffering, and death, prior to his eventual vindication by heavenly hyper-exaltation. The hymn, it is suggested, is a theological story, the central theme of which is the vindication of a righteous man who has suffered unjustly. Jesus is a kind of Adam-in-reverse. Both Adam and Jesus are made in the image of God. But whereas Adam was disobedient and sought to exalt himself, Jesus was obedient, even though his obedience led to his death. Adam's disobedience resulted in his disgrace. Jesus by his obedience has been hyper-exalted in heaven.

On either interpretation, the primary significance of the story is its depiction of Jesus' post-mortem exaltation. Jesus died, and yet he is now alive with God in heaven, highly exalted and appointed to be universal Lord of all. Other notable features of the story include the lack of any mention of resurrection, the absence of any eschatological perspective, and the awarding to Jesus of the "name that is above every name".

The hymn refers to Christ Jesus being "in the form of God", but it offers no explanation as to what this might mean. Another early christological hymn embedded in the letter to the Colossians is much more explicit, both in its declaration of pre-existence and in its explanation of the relationship between Jesus and God. The author reminds his readers that God has rescued them from the power of darkness and brought them into the kingdom of his beloved Son. He goes on to say of Jesus:

> He is the image of the invisible God, the
>   firstborn of all creation;
> for in him all things in heaven and on earth were created,
> things visible and invisible,
> whether thrones or dominions or rulers or powers—
> all things have been created through him and for him.
> He himself is before all things,
> and in him all things hold together.
> He is the head of the body, the church;
> he is the beginning, the firstborn from the dead,
> so that he might come to have first place in everything.
> For in him all the fullness of God was pleased to dwell,

and through him God was pleased to
  reconcile to himself all things,
whether on earth or in heaven,
by making peace through the blood of his cross.

Colossians 1:15–20

Much of the language and imagery of this hymn reflects the Jewish wisdom tradition. In Proverbs, in the Wisdom of Solomon, and in Ecclesiasticus the personified Wisdom of God is spoken of as having existed before the creation of the heavens and the earth. The Wisdom of God is also said to have been active in creation and in re-creation. Wisdom has this ability:

> For she is a breath of the power of God,
> and a pure emanation of the glory of the Almighty;
> therefore nothing defiled gains entrance into her.
> For she is a reflection of eternal light,
> a spotless mirror of the working of God,
> and an image of his goodness.
> Although she is but one, she can do all things,
> and while remaining in herself, she renews all things . . .

Wisdom of Solomon 7:25–27

The Colossians hymn is therefore drawing on motifs already existing in Jewish wisdom literature, and applying them to the heavenly Lord Jesus Christ. Even the reconciliation soteriology in the third stanza of the hymn has parallels in the Jewish wisdom tradition because Wisdom "renews all things" (see above). If, as many scholars believe, the references to "the church" and "the blood of the cross" are later additions, the Colossians hymn's only explicit reference to the historical Jesus is the allusion to the resurrection implicit in the phrase "firstborn from the dead". Taken as a whole, the hymn appears to be a theological statement implying that the creative activity of the Wisdom of God has been fulfilled in Christ. Resurrection, envisaged as exaltation, connects divine Wisdom with salvation envisaged as reconciliation.

The opening verses of the (much later) letter to the Hebrews are clearly an integral part of the letter's text, but they also contain hymnic language and a series of clauses expanding the affirmation of the Son's status as heir of all things. There are significant parallels with the christological hymns in Philippians and Colossians. The author begins by declaring that God, who spoke in former times through the prophets, has now spoken again in "these last days" not through a prophet but through his Son:

> . . . whom he appointed heir of all things,
> through whom he also created the worlds.
> He is the reflection of God's glory
> and the exact imprint of God's very being,
> and he sustains all things by his powerful word.
> When he had made purification for sins,
> he sat down at the right hand of the Majesty on high . . .
>
> *Hebrews 1:2b–3*

As in the Colossians hymn, the wisdom motifs of pre-existence, participation in creation, the bearing (or impression) of God's image, the reflection of God's glory, and the ongoing sustaining of creation are brought into association with a declaration of the soteriological activity of the Son, who has made "purification for sins". Step by step the clauses build up to the climactic declaration that the Son, who is the reflection of God's glory, has been exalted to the place of highest possible honour, seated at the right hand of God himself. There is no explicit reference either to the death or to the resurrection of Jesus. His death is implicit, but the concept of resurrection is either absent or subsumed in the concept of exaltation.

Finally, embedded in the first epistle to Timothy there is another brief and epigrammatic example of an early Christian hymn. Of Christ Jesus it says:

> He was revealed in flesh,
> vindicated in spirit,
> seen by angels,
> proclaimed among Gentiles,

believed in throughout the world,
taken up in glory.

1 Timothy 3:16

The hymn's structure, with its slightly odd chronology, is chiastic—a form well known in classical antiquity. The first and last lines function as contrasting parentheses, initial action on earth being contrasted with concluding action in heaven. The second and third lines are paired; both speak of action in heaven. The contrasting fourth and fifth lines are likewise paired, both speaking of action on earth. There are a number of other noteworthy features. Christ Jesus is said to have been "revealed in flesh". The implication is that he existed prior to his human birth, either as a being in heaven, or hidden in the intention of God. The phrase "vindicated in spirit" reflects the wisdom motif of the post-mortem vindication of the righteous man. There is no reference at all to Jesus' death and resurrection. If the hymn were detached from its context, it might be supposed that Jesus had been taken up to heaven whilst still alive, like Elijah or Enoch. The reference to Jesus having been "seen by angels" may reflect the influence of heavenly-ascent traditions. On the other hand, the statement that he was "proclaimed among Gentiles and believed in throughout the world" connects theology to history more explicitly than do any of the other hymns and fragments so far considered. Taken as a whole, the hymn functions as a concise theological account of the action of God in Christ.

Drawing the threads together, a number of conclusions stand out. The first is that many of the concepts and ideas in these hymns and fragments reflect the influence of Jewish wisdom traditions. Secondly, none of them make any explicit mention of resurrection. Jesus Christ is vindicated by exaltation rather than resurrection, and exaltation involves heavenly glory and a place of supreme honour in the presence of God. Thirdly, there is little if anything in the way of eschatology. Insofar as there is a narrative, the exaltation of Jesus Christ to glory in heaven appears to be the end of the matter. Salvation is reconciliation, and reconciliation is collective rather than individual. Finally, and most remarkably, these hymns and hymnic fragments contain very little that connects them with history. There are hardly any biographical details. Jesus' birth receives no explicit mention and his death is referred to only in the Philippians and Colossians hymns. We infer that he was a human being because he was "revealed in flesh", had "human form and likeness", died and was "firstborn of the dead". Nevertheless, the Jesus of the hymns could be a heavenly entity who merely appeared to be human whilst on earth.

The interpretation of these christological hymns has been debated intensively for almost a hundred years. The New Testament documents taken as a whole undoubtedly present a picture of Jesus as a fully human being, albeit a human being having a highly distinctive relationship with God. This was probably also the understanding of the authors of these early christological hymns and fragments. Nevertheless, given that they are some of the earliest evidence we have for the existence of Jesus, difficult questions have to be asked. Taken at face value, the hymns speak of Jesus Christ as a pre-existent, heavenly being far more confidently and at much greater length than they speak of him as a historical and genuinely human being. Given that in Second Temple Judaism, more or less at the time of Jesus, there are a number of other examples of belief in similar heavenly beings, the possibility that there is a relationship between these figures and the heavenly Jesus Christ has to be taken seriously. We shall return to this matter in the next chapter when all the relevant evidence has been assembled. For the moment, we focus on the beliefs and practices of the first post-Easter believers, to see whether they shed further light on the emergence of resurrection faith.

The invocation or acclamation of Jesus as Lord

Some twenty years after the death of Jesus, Paul wrote in Greek to the Greek-speaking church in Corinth. The letter was apparently dictated to an amanuensis, but at its conclusion Paul added his own personal farewell:

> I, Paul, write this greeting with my own hand. Let anyone be accursed who has no love for the Lord. Our Lord, come! (*Marana tha*). The grace of the Lord Jesus be with you. My love be with all of you in Christ Jesus.
>
> *1 Corinthians 16:21–24*

The form and meaning of the Aramaic phrase *maranatha* embedded in this farewell inscription is disputed. The problem is that *maranatha* is a combination of two words. The words could be *marana* followed by *tha* (as assumed by the NRSV English translation above) or they could be *maran* followed by *atha*. These two possibilities make translation problematic. *Marana tha* is an imperative prayer addressed to the heavenly Jesus, meaning "Our Lord, come!" (cf. Revelation 22:20). *Maran atha*, on the other hand, is a statement of faith in the perfect tense, meaning "Our Lord has come." The modern view is that the term used by Paul was *marana tha*, signifying the imperative prayer or invocation, "Our Lord, come!"

There is an important issue here. Why should Paul, who was in Ephesus at the time, use a minority language like Aramaic when he was addressing a community of Greek-speaking Christians more than five hundred miles away from Judaea? He would scarcely have used the Aramaic phrase *maranatha* without translation or explanation unless its meaning was well known to those to whom he was writing. We must therefore assume that this prayer or invocation was particularly important, and that it was used regularly by both Aramaic-speaking and Greek-speaking Christians in the 40s of the Common Era, or possibly even earlier. The question is, does this use of the Aramaic word *mar* (lord) in a Greek milieu tell us something significant about the origins of post-Easter belief in Jesus' heavenly lordship?

The answer is that it does. Although belief in Jesus actively ruling from heaven as cosmic Lord of all creation probably only reached its full and final fruition at a relatively late stage in a Greek-speaking, Jewish-Christian environment, the basic idea of lordship associated with Jesus' heavenly exaltation was very early. Almost from the outset, it seems to have found expression in the parallel use of the terms *mar* and *kyrios* by his Aramaic-speaking and Greek-speaking Jewish followers. We know that at an early stage there emerged in Jerusalem separately administered but interconnected communities of Greek-speaking and Aramaic-speaking followers of Jesus. Significant understandings arrived at in one linguistic community would almost certainly have been shared more or less immediately with the other. Even if important understandings originated elsewhere (for example, in Galilee), we can safely assume that they would have quickly found their way back to the leaders of both Jerusalem communities. The evidence suggests that the word *mar* carried much the same significance in the Aramaic-speaking community of Jesus' followers as did the word *kyrios* in the parallel Greek-speaking community, particularly when used in connection with the invocation of Jesus as Lord by virtue of his heavenly exaltation. Paul's use of the Aramaic invocation *marana tha* in his letter to Greek-speaking Christians in faraway Corinth reinforces this conclusion.

We conclude that key understandings concerning Jesus' fate after his death probably emerged more or less in parallel in both the Aramaic-speaking and the Greek-speaking communities of his followers. In particular, the use by Greek-speaking worshippers of the imperative invocation *marana tha* must mean that the understanding of Jesus as the exalted heavenly Lord, expected to return from heaven in power and glory, was a very early development shared by both communities of Jesus' followers, whether Aramaic or Greek-speaking.

The earliest resurrection-appearances tradition

Conspicuously lacking in the evidence so far examined are references to appearances of the risen Jesus Christ. This deficiency is made good in a letter written by Paul in the early fifties. Writing to the believers in Corinth, he says:

> For I handed on to you as of first importance what I in turn had received: that Christ died for our sins in accordance with the scriptures, and that he was buried, and that he was raised on the third day in accordance with the scriptures, and that he appeared to Cephas [Peter], then to the twelve. Then he appeared to more than five hundred brothers and sisters at one time, most of whom are still alive, though some have died. Then he appeared to James, then to all the apostles. Last of all, as to someone untimely born, he appeared also to me.
>
> *1 Corinthians 15:3–8*

As the earliest written evidence bearing on specific events accessible to historical analysis and evaluation, this is a pivotal passage. Paul's statement is brief and there is a certain formality in the way in which he speaks of handing on a tradition which he has himself received. The phrases "according to the scriptures" and "for our sins" appear to be secondary additions qualifying the statements about the death and the resurrection. The assertion of the resurrection has also been rendered more specific by the addition of "on the third day". Setting this aside, an underlying threefold structure is apparent. What we have is a slightly expanded tripartite version of the early faith formula:

1. Christ died...	for our sins		according to the scriptures
2. was buried...			
3. was raised...		on the third day	according to the scriptures

The list that follows comprises a series of carefully crafted statements to the effect that Christ appeared sequentially to:

1. Cephas [i.e. Peter]
2. "the twelve"
3. "more than five hundred brothers and sisters at one time"
4. James
5. "all the apostles"

This list, which seems to be a traditional formula, may reflect the merger of two separate, earlier appearance traditions, possibly reflecting rivalry associated with a shift in leadership of the Jerusalem community from Peter to James. The implications of the additional phrase "and then to all the apostles" are not entirely clear. Paul appends to the traditional list his own statement that "Last of all .... [Christ] appeared also to me." Apostleship was clearly an issue for Paul (see 1 Corinthians 9:1). He seeks here to strengthen his claim to apostolic status by emphasizing that his own experience of encounter with the risen Christ matches that of

James and the others. (James's experience would have been particularly significant for Paul, because both he and James had experienced visions of the risen Christ, even though neither of them had been members of the inner circle of "the twelve".) Nevertheless, it is unlikely that Paul was intending to define apostleship simply in terms of having seen the risen Christ. Elsewhere (for example in 1 Corinthians 9:1 and 15:9–10) he justifies his claim to apostolic status by drawing attention to the evident working of God's grace through him, an argument which would be redundant if seeing the risen Christ sufficed to confer apostolic status.

The original purpose of the earliest resurrection-appearances tradition is unknown, but it may have been used in the instruction of new converts. In its present form, it testifies to happenings and dictates their meaning, but we do not know whether it includes all the then known appearances of the risen Christ. Setting aside the later appearance stories of the Gospels, it is a reasonable assumption that the list of appearances was supposed to be definitive. In some respects, what is not said is just as important as what is said. The tradition is altogether lacking in circumstantial details. No dates or locations are specified and there are no descriptions of the events. Peter and James alone are named. Although there are references to "the twelve" and to "all the apostles", nothing is said about them, and it is not even clear whether they are two different groups or the same group. The statement that there was an otherwise undocumented appearance witnessed by "more than five hundred brothers and sisters" contains no details other than the gloss, "most of whom are still alive, though some have died". There is no apparent awareness of the Judas story. If the Judas story had been known, the tradition would surely have had Jesus appearing to "the eleven" rather than to "the twelve".

Paul's statement that he was passing on a tradition that he himself had received tends to confirm the theory that the tradition was used in the instruction of converts. Early Aramaic and Greek versions of the tradition may have been circulating side by side in the bilingual Christian communities in Jerusalem and Syria, including in the important community in Damascus where Paul apparently received instruction after his own experience of encounter with the risen Christ. Although the date of Paul's experience cannot be determined with certainty, the biographical information in his letter to the Christians in Galatia suggests that it was between one and three years after the death of Jesus. In the first instance, Paul was only briefly in Damascus, but he subsequently returned for an extended stay of three years, probably from 34 to 37 CE. If the appearances tradition (or a part of that tradition) was passed on to Paul at the time of his initial instruction, the tradition itself must have had its origins very close indeed to the Easter events. The expansion of the basic faith formula by the appending of additional explanatory clauses, and the forging of the connection between the faith formula and the appearances tradition must also have taken place at a very early stage, probably in Jerusalem and almost certainly prior to Paul's first arrival in Damascus.

Resurrection "on the third day"

The tripartite faith formula associated with the appearances tradition also contains the earliest reference to the tradition that the resurrection took place "on the third day". This tradition seems to have had no particular significance for Paul, which suggests that it was attached to the traditional resurrection faith formula prior to his encounter with the risen Christ on the road to Damascus. The undoubtedly early tradition that the resurrection took place "on the third day" does not necessarily imply the existence of a related empty-tomb tradition. The empty-tomb tradition first appears some thirty-five years later in the Gospel of Mark. Even then, Mark's tradition says only that the tomb was visited "on the third day" and discovered to be empty, not that Jesus rose "on the third day". The omission of any reference to an empty tomb in Paul's writings is puzzling. If Paul had known of such a tradition, one might have expected him to have referred to it, either directly or indirectly, in his teaching about the resurrection of Jesus and the transformation of the human body after death. The lack of any such reference suggests that the empty-tomb tradition was unknown to Paul, and therefore probably unknown to the communities with which he was involved. On the other hand, he might have been taking it for granted that the resurrection of Jesus must necessarily have included the rising of Jesus' transformed body from the place in which it had been buried. If so, belief in an empty grave or tomb would have been a corollary. We conclude that the empty-tomb tradition was either unknown to Paul, or that he knew of it but regarded it as a matter of little or no consequence: something simply taken for granted. Paul's views concerning the nature of the resurrection body and its relationship to the physical remains of the deceased person are discussed later in this chapter.

Surprisingly, the earliest narrative evidence for the resurrection of Jesus having taken place "on the third day" is an extraordinary and historically worthless story appearing in the second century in the non-canonical pseudepigraphical Gospel of Peter. Jesus is depicted emerging from the tomb, accompanied by a gigantic wooden cross:

> [the guards] saw . . . three men [two angels and Jesus] come out of the sepulchre, and two of them sustaining the other, and a cross following after them. And of the two they saw that their heads reached unto heaven, but of him that was led by them that it overpassed the heavens. And they heard a voice out of the heavens saying: Hast thou preached to them that sleep? And an answer was heard from the cross, saying: Yea.
>
> *Gospel of Peter, fragment 1, IX:35—X:42*[74]

The lack of any connection between the early tradition of resurrection "on the third day" and the much later empty-tomb traditions of the Gospels suggests that the two traditions may have had independent origins. One possibility, first put forward by Strauss, is that the tradition of resurrection "on the third day" originated in early Christian reflection on the scriptures, rather than in any specific recollection of historical events. These verses from Hosea are often suggested as most likely to have given rise to the third day tradition:

> "Come, let us return to the LORD,
> . . . he will heal us;
> he has struck down, and he will bind us up.
> After two days he will revive us;
> on the third day he will raise us up,
> that we may live before him."
>
> *Hosea 6:1–2*

There is, in fact, no evidence that this text was ever used by the early Christians in connection with the resurrection of Jesus. An alternative suggestion is that the well-known story of Jonah and the Whale gave rise to the tradition. Jonah was three days and three nights in the belly of a "large fish" before he was spewed out on to the dry land:

> But the LORD provided a large fish to swallow
> up Jonah; and Jonah was in the belly of the fish
> for three days and three nights . . .
> "I went down to the land
> whose bars closed upon me for ever
> yet you brought up my life from the Pit [i.e. *Sheol*],
> O LORD my God."
>
> *Jonah 1:17; 2:6*

We have evidence that the significance of this text was recognized. Matthew attributes to Jesus a saying that directly relates the death and resurrection of Jesus to Jonah's sojourn in the belly of the monster:

> "For just as Jonah was for three days and three nights in the belly
> of the sea monster, so for three days and three nights the Son of
> Man will be in the heart of the earth."
>
> *Matthew 12:40*

An oddity of this saying is that, taken literally, the phrase "for three days and three nights" contradicts both the early 1 Corinthians 15 tradition that God raised Jesus "on the third day" and the later empty tomb traditions in the Gospels which say that Jesus was in the tomb for two rather than three nights. The "passion-prediction" sayings (Mark 8:31; Matthew 16:21; Luke 9:22) and the "temple-rebuilding" saying (Mark 14:58; cf. John 2:19, Matthew 26:61) also exhibit fluidity in the way that they utilize the "third-day" tradition. The Mark 8:31 saying represents Jesus as having predicted his suffering, rejection, death, and resurrection "after three days". Matthew 16:21 and Luke 9:22 correct Mark, saying that Jesus must be raised "on the third day". The Johannine "temple-rebuilding" saying represents Jesus as having declared that if "this temple" (that is, his body) were to be destroyed, he would raise it up "in three days". It is widely agreed that—in their present form—these sayings are creations of the early post-Easter community of Jesus' followers. They have been retrojected into the tradition upon which the Gospel writers were drawing. Nevertheless, they may reflect underlying authentic sayings of Jesus.

More generally, there are repeated references in the Hebrew scriptures to particularly significant events involving release, revelation, or revival having taken place on the third day.[75] One commentator identifies no fewer than thirty instances in the Hebrew scriptures in which "the third day" is the critical or decisive day. The abundance of these references suggests that the third day motif was conventionally used in connection with significant events. Alternatively or additionally, it may simply have been a convenient way of indicating a period of time longer than a day but shorter than a week. Also deserving mention in this connection is a Jewish tradition that the soul of a dead person remained in the vicinity of the body of the deceased for three days before finally descending into *Sheol*. This tradition is attested at a somewhat later date in *midrashim* Genesis Rabbah 100:7 and Leviticus Rabbah 18:1. There are also *midrashim* and *targumim*' albeit of a much later date but possibly reflecting earlier traditions, that speak of the general resurrection for judgement taking place on the third day or three days after the end of the world. (Midrashim are traditional expositions of the first four books of the Hebrew scriptures. Targumim are Aramaic translations or paraphrases of the Hebrew scriptures, originally spoken.)

Lack of reference to the women

Another surprising feature of the 1 Corinthians 15:5–8 resurrection-appearances tradition is the lack of any reference to appearances of the risen Christ to Mary Magdalene, or to any other woman or women. Appearances of the risen Christ to women feature prominently in the Gospels of Matthew and John, so the lack of reference to any such appearances in the earliest tradition is perplexing and has given rise to much speculation. One possibility is that references to appearances to women were omitted from the "official" list in 1 Corinthians 15 on the grounds that women were held to be incapable of giving valid testimony on matters of consequence. Whether this was in fact the case in first-century Judaism is doubtful.

A second possibility is that the tradition contains no references to appearances to women because women formed no part of the ongoing leadership of the earliest community of Jesus' post-Easter followers. Another possibility is that Mary Magdalene and the women were in competition with Peter and his followers for recognition as the earliest witnesses to the resurrection, and that Peter and his followers were the eventual winners. References to the role of Mary Magdalene and the other women might then have been retrospectively expunged from the earliest resurrection-appearances tradition. All these suggestions are speculative—no firm conclusions are possible. There are, however, some slight indications of tension between Mary Magdalene and Peter, even during Jesus' lifetime. The non-canonical, second-century pseudepigraphical Gospel of Thomas has a strange passage which reads:

> Simon Peter said to them: Let Mary go from among us, because women are not worthy of the Life. Jesus said: See, I shall lead her, so that I will make her male, that she too may become a living spirit, resembling you males. For every woman who makes herself male will enter the Kingdom of Heaven.
>
> *Gospel of Thomas, logion 114*[76]

It is difficult to assess the implications (if any) of this extraordinary saying, but it seems to presuppose conflict or competition between Mary and Peter. Although Peter's assertion that women are by nature inferior to men and unworthy of eternal life goes unchallenged, Jesus does say that Mary will be granted spiritual equality with the male disciples. For the purpose of establishing the earliest form of the appearances tradition, this text is valueless.

Drawing the threads together: the tradition in 1 Corinthians 15:5–8 is the earliest certain evidence we have concerning experiences of encounter with the risen Christ. This tradition is very early, and it—or parts of it—must have originated no more than a year or so after the Easter events themselves. Paul appears to consider his own experience of encounter with the risen Christ to be in all significant respects identical to the experiences of James and Peter and the other apostles and disciples. His testimony may be brief and lacking in detail, but the historical quality is outstanding. Some three years after his conversion, long before he wrote 1 Corinthians, Paul had visited Jerusalem, where he stayed with Peter and met James, the brother of Jesus. As one commentator says, we can safely assume that they had considerably more to talk about than the weather. At the very least, Paul must have been made aware of the circumstances surrounding the appearances to Peter and James. He must have been given details of the other appearances listed in 1 Corinthians 15 as well. That Paul would have quoted the traditional formula knowing it to be false is inconceivable. This is the earliest testimony concerning appearances of the risen Jesus, and it is the testimony of an eyewitness who had personally met and talked to other eyewitnesses. This is a conclusion of the utmost importance. Paul's more or less explicit assertion that the appearance of the risen Christ to him differed in no significant way from those to James, Peter, and the others must be respected. This means that if we can establish the nature of Paul's experience, we will have a baseline for evaluating the much later appearance stories of the Gospels.

Paul's revelation

In his letter to the Christians in Galatia, Paul declares that the gospel he is proclaiming is authoritative because it is of divine origin, not man-made. He also declares that his own personal authority or commission stems from a direct divine calling and a personal revelation of Jesus Christ. His commission, he says, was part and parcel of his revelatory experience:

> For I want you to know, brothers and sisters, that the gospel that was proclaimed by me is not of human origin; for I did not receive it from a human source, nor was I taught it, but I received it through a revelation of Jesus Christ ... God, who had set me apart before I was born and called me through his grace, was pleased to reveal his Son to/in me ...
>
> *Galatians 1:11–12, 15–16*

The lack of descriptive detail troubles some commentators. The deficiency is probably less significant than it seems. Paul's restraint in speaking about his experience is probably deliberate. Some years later, he had an ecstatic visionary experience about which he also speaks with the utmost discretion and restraint, saying only that he was caught up into the third heaven where he "heard things that no mortal is permitted to repeat" (2 Corinthians 12:1-4). That Paul felt it necessary to be reticent about such intensely personal experiences is understandable. In any case, when he is speaking of his initial revelatory experience he is focusing not on the experience in itself, but on its intelligible content in terms of the God-given understandings that comprised the "gospel" he was being called to proclaim.

On closer examination, Paul is anyway less reticent than at first appears. The Greek term used by Paul to describe his experience implies a sudden and dramatic revelation, almost always with a visual or an aural component, or both. Elsewhere in his writings there are passages in which he uses language and imagery which are thought by many scholars to reflect this initial visionary experience. When he speaks of Christ being raised in glory (1 Corinthians 15:43), of his being highly exalted (Philippians 2:9), and of his being at the right hand of God (Romans 8:34), Paul may only be transmitting received tradition. But when he contrasts the veiled and fading glory of the temporarily transformed Moses with the unveiled and enduring light of the glory of Christ, we seem to be moving into different territory:

> And all of us, with unveiled faces, seeing the glory of the Lord as though reflected in a mirror, are being transformed into the same image from one degree of glory to another ...
>
> *2 Corinthians 3:18*

> ... the god of this world has blinded the minds of unbelievers, to keep them from seeing the light of the gospel of the glory of Christ, who is the image of God ... For it is the God who said, "Let light shine out of darkness", who has shone in our hearts to give the light of the knowledge of the glory of God in the face of Jesus Christ.
>
> *2 Corinthians 4:4,6*

There are parallels here with Philippians 2:6–11 and other early christological hymns and hymnic fragments. There are also parallels with Jewish wisdom traditions. The reference to God having "shone in our hearts to give the light of the knowledge of the glory of God in the face of Jesus Christ" may well be a reference to Paul's own conversion and prophetic calling experience, which he understood to be a transforming personal encounter with the risen Jesus revealed to him as Messiah, Lord, and Son of God. This experience seems to have involved the visual perception of Jesus as a heavenly being suffused with the light of radiant divine glory. It also involved the communication of information and understandings comprising the gospel that Paul was being called to proclaim.

This understanding of Paul's experience is broadly compatible with the three much later accounts of his conversion in the Acts of the Apostles. In Acts, Paul's conversion or calling is depicted as a visionary experience involving blinding heavenly light and encounter with Jesus, who is either in heaven, or coming to Paul from heaven. We have to be cautious in drawing inferences from these accounts. The author of Acts, writing forty years or more after the events he is describing, has his own agenda. In particular, he wants to contradict Paul's claim to be a fully-fledged apostle. He also wishes to undermine Paul's implicit assertion that he experienced a resurrection appearance in all respects the same as those vouchsafed to Peter, James, and the other disciples. The author of Acts seeks to achieve this objective not by questioning Paul's experience, which he correctly represents as a revelatory vision involving light and perception, but by emphasizing and enhancing the physicality of the appearance stories in his own Gospel. Nevertheless, he endorses Paul's own testimony in all essentials. Paul experienced a revelatory encounter with Jesus, the cognitive content of which included a prophetic call that led to his conversion, not to a new religion (Paul remained a devout Jew) but rather to a complete change of direction.

Physical or spiritual resurrection?

The earliest strata of historical testimony bearing on appearances of the risen Christ make no reference to an empty-tomb tradition and speak only of the burial of Jesus. Paul's testimony—and by inference, the testimony of those listed in the earliest appearances tradition—is that the resurrection appearances were visionary experiences of encounter with the risen Christ, perceived as a heavenly being radiant with glory. This raises the question of what was believed at this time about the fate of Jesus' corpse. Does the very early traditional resurrection faith formula's assertion that Jesus was "raised from the dead" necessarily imply belief in the restoration to some form of life of his dead body? Or to put it another way, does the metaphor of "resurrection" absolutely exclude the idea of the spirit of Jesus ascending to heaven whilst leaving his physical body behind to suffer decay and dissolution in the normal way?

Second Temple afterlife beliefs were fluid and variously expressed. Belief in vindication by heavenly exaltation and by resurrection had first come into clear focus in the Maccabean period in connection with the rewarding of righteous martyrs and the vindication of righteous men who had suffered unjustly. At about the same time, the concepts of vindication, heavenly exaltation, and glorious transformation become associated with one another. In the first instance, resurrection is envisaged as the future resurrection of exceptionally righteous or exceptionally wicked people, either for reward or punishment. There is evidence that it was sometimes believed that exceptional individuals might already have bypassed *Sheol* and proceeded directly, with or without their physical bodies, to new life in heaven.

The Wisdom of Solomon and 1 Enoch both reflect a fusion of Greek and Hebrew thinking. The implicit assumption is that the soul can be parted from the body and can enter into the presence of God whilst still retaining identity and recognizability. To assert that there was a single Greek concept (the inherent immortality of the soul) opposed to a single Jewish orthodoxy (the resurrection of the physical body) is to do violence to the evidence. We have to be wary of the assertion that already existing Jewish afterlife beliefs would have determined absolutely the significance of the term "resurrection" as it was first applied to Jesus, or that they would have dictated exactly what Jesus' followers could—or could not—have believed about the fate of his body after his death. Given the observed fluidity in Second Temple afterlife beliefs, we have to allow for the possibility that there may have been a significant element of creative innovation in the application of already existing ideas to the specific instance of Jesus.

The starting point for understanding Paul's beliefs concerning the nature of resurrection and the resurrection body is an extended discussion in the first letter to the Corinthians. Much of what Paul says about the believer applies by extension to Jesus. Opposing some Christians in Corinth, who were apparently saying that there was no resurrection of the dead, Paul addresses directly the question of the connection between the body that is buried and the believer's future, gloriously transformed resurrection body. In so doing, he sets out his own anthropology or psychology.

A human being, says Paul, has three distinct components. There is the "flesh", there is the "psychic body", and potentially there is the "spiritual body". Each of the three is radically different from the others. It appears that Paul envisaged resurrection as the transformation, with continuity of identity, of the "psychic body" into a "spiritual body". The question is, did he understand the "flesh" and the "psychic body", although distinct, to be inseparable? If he did, he must have believed that the "flesh" would be included in the process of resurrection transformation. That is, there could be no residue (such as a corpse) "left behind" when the transformation had taken place. On the other hand, if he believed the "psychic body" to be separable from the "flesh", he could have believed that the "flesh" would be left behind on earth, to suffer decay and dissolution in the normal way. This latter interpretation seems to be confirmed when, towards the climax of his argument, Paul says:

> What I am saying, brothers and sisters, is this: flesh and blood cannot inherit the kingdom of God, nor does the perishable inherit the imperishable.
>
> *1 Corinthians 15:50*

The apparent implication is that when a believer is raised from the dead, his or her physical corpse will be discarded, abandoned, and left behind. If Paul believed that the "essential Jesus"—that is, his "psychic body"—had been separated from his "flesh" by death and transformed into a "spiritual body", the subsequent fate of Jesus' untransformed "flesh"—that is, his corpse—would have been a matter of little interest. This might explain the absence of any reference to an empty-tomb tradition in Paul's writings.

On the other hand, Paul may have considered the "flesh" and the "psychic body" to be distinguishable but nevertheless inseparable entities. In which case, he must have believed that resurrection of necessity involved the transformation of both the "flesh" and its parallel "psychic body" into a "spiritual body" capable of entering into heaven. In which case, Paul would have taken it for granted that the tomb of Jesus had been empty from the moment of resurrection onwards. The emptiness of the tomb would have been a natural corollary of resurrection belief, requiring no further explanation or comment. This, too, would explain the lack of any reference to an empty-tomb tradition in Paul's writings.

Towards the end of 1 Corinthians 15, Paul deploys a different metaphor, speaking of immortality as a garment or clothing:

> For the trumpet will sound, and the dead will be raised imperishable, and we will be changed. For this perishable body must put on imperishability, and this mortal body must put on immortality. When this perishable body puts on imperishability, and this mortal body puts on immortality, then the saying that is written will be fulfilled: "Death has been swallowed up in victory."
>
> *1 Corinthians 15:52–54*

Precisely what is involved in "putting on" imperishability or immortality is not specified. It could be that Paul is thinking of immortality being "put on" over something else that is already there, rather like one coat being put on over another. Alternatively, the idea may be exchange: Paul may be envisaging the old clothing (the perishable human body) being exchanged for the new clothing (the imperishable clothing of immortality).

In a slightly later letter to the Christians in Corinth, Paul again addresses the question of the relationship between the earthly body and the resurrection body. In this letter the idea of exchange is much more prominent. A person's body is a kind of tent. The death and resurrection of the believer, says Paul, involves putting off "this earthly tent" and putting on a new heavenly dwelling, "a house not made with hands":

> For we know that if the earthly tent we live in is destroyed, we have a building from God, a house not made with hands, eternal in the heavens. For in this tent we groan, longing to be clothed with our heavenly dwelling—if indeed, when we have taken it off we will not be found naked. For while we are still in this tent, we groan under our burden, because we wish not to be unclothed but to be further clothed, so that what is mortal may be swallowed up by life.... we know that while we are at home in the body we are away from the Lord...
>
> *2 Corinthians 5:1-6*

The idea of old garments being exchanged for new ones on entry into heaven features in many ascent apocalypses. It has its origins in Jerusalem temple ritual. On the Day of Atonement, before entering the innermost sanctuary, the Holy of Holies, the High Priest was divested of his ordinary clothing and put on special holy vestments (Leviticus 16:4). Likewise, in the ascent apocalypses, the visitor to heaven puts off his old clothing and is vested in glorious new raiment. In 2 Corinthians 5:1-5, Paul seems to be regarding what he calls "our earthly tent" as the shell within which a person has identity and being. The longed-for "heavenly dwelling" is the spiritual body or shell which will clothe the believer in heaven. The implication seems to be that when the believer dies, the former will be taken off and discarded or destroyed so that the latter may be put on. To be clothed in new raiment when we die is essential because to be left naked would be to perish.

Some commentators detect a possible development in Paul's thinking. He was becoming (it is suggested) increasingly fearful that he might die before the return of Jesus. He was therefore increasingly conscious of the need for believers to come to terms with continuing, contingent being here on earth. Hence the frank admission in 2 Corinthians 5 that waiting for death is burdensome. Ideally, we would all like mortality to be swallowed up by immortality here and now. Nevertheless, says Paul, we have no choice in the matter. We have to wait. Only when the dead are raised will they exchange their "earthly tent" for a "heavenly dwelling".

Whether there really is any such development in Paul's thinking is doubtful. The two letters to the Corinthians are only a year or so apart in date. In both letters, the essential understanding is that when the believer is raised from the dead, his or her physical body will be transformed, but continuity of identity will be preserved. In setting forward this understanding, Paul deploys a variety of metaphors, none of which is entirely consonant with the others. Significantly, when Paul wrote to the Philippian Christians some five years later, he was still using the metaphor of transformation in the same way that he did in 1 Corinthians 15:51–52:

> But our citizenship is in heaven, and it is from there that we are expecting a Saviour, the Lord Jesus Christ. He will transform the body of our humiliation so that it may be conformed to the body of his glory . . .
>
> *Philippians 3:20–21*

Before arriving at any conclusions, we need to consider two other matters that cast additional light on Paul's thinking. The first, which has already been mentioned, is the brief, anonymous account in 2 Corinthians of Paul's own personal experience of visionary heavenly ascent. Paul says:

> I know a person in Christ who fourteen years ago was caught up to the third heaven—whether in the body or out of the body, I do not know; God knows. And I know that such a person—whether in the body or out of the body I do not know; God knows—was caught up into paradise and heard things that are not to be told, that no mortal is permitted to repeat.
>
> *2 Corinthians 12:2–4*

The date Paul gives—"fourteen years ago"—rules out any possibility that this is a reference to his revelatory encounter with the risen Christ on the road to Damascus. We know nothing about the circumstances of this second visionary experience, but so far as Paul was concerned, it was evidently a real experience, something that actually happened. What is particularly interesting and relevant for present purposes is the outright ambivalence. Paul seems to have thought that heavenly ascent was possible with or without the physical body. How this is to be reconciled with his dictum that "flesh and blood cannot inherit the kingdom of God", and with the concept of entry into heaven involving a necessary change of clothing, is not clear. Paul may have been making a distinction between the rules that applied to temporary ascent during a person's lifetime and those that would apply to ascent into heaven after death. Nevertheless, he appears to believe that a physical body could temporarily enter heaven. And if temporarily, why not permanently?

The second matter is Paul's understanding of the eschatological significance of resurrection. Paul believed the resurrection of Jesus to be an eschatological act of God signalling the end of the old era and the inauguration of the new age. Writing to the Christians at Corinth, he says:

> But in fact Christ has been raised from the dead, the first fruits of those who have died. For since death came through a human being, the resurrection of the dead has also come through a human being; for as all die in Adam, so all will be made alive in Christ. But each in his own order: Christ the first fruits, then at his coming those who belong to Christ. Then comes the end, when he hands over the kingdom to God the Father . . .
>
> *1 Corinthians 15:20–24*

In Second Temple Judaism, it was believed in some circles that the end of the present age and the commencement of the new age and the rule of God would be accompanied by the resurrection of the righteous dead. Jesus, says Paul, has already been raised by God. He is the first fruits of the harvest of the dead, but believers are still waiting for their own resurrection. In effect, Christians are living in an interim period between the inauguration of the new age, which commenced with the resurrection of Jesus, and the full realization of the new age, which will involve the coming again of Jesus Christ, the keeping safe of living believers, the resurrection of dead believers, and the handing over of the new kingdom by Christ to God. For example:

> . . . you turned to God from idols, to serve a living and true God, and to wait for his Son from heaven, whom he raised from the dead—Jesus, who rescues us from the wrath that is coming.
>
> *1 Thessalonians 1:9–10*

> For the Lord himself . . . will descend from heaven, and the dead in Christ will rise first. Then we who are alive, who are left, will be caught up in the clouds together with them to meet the Lord in the air; and so we will be with the Lord for ever.
>
> *1 Thessalonians 4:16–17*

> Then comes the end, when he hands over the kingdom to God the Father, after he has destroyed every ruler and every authority and power. For he must reign until he has put all his enemies under his feet. The last enemy to be destroyed is death . . . When all things are subjected to him, then the Son himself will also be subjected to the one who put all things in subjection under him, so that God may be all in all.
>
> *1 Corinthians 15:24–26,28*

The understanding that the resurrection of Jesus is the eschatological act of God conditions all Paul's thinking. In Second Temple Judaism, resurrection for life in the new age was understood to involve the physical rising of the bodies of the righteous dead from their graves. This understanding of resurrection, some say, must govern any interpretation of the metaphors used by Paul in connection with the resurrection of Jesus and of believers. Nevertheless, the evidence is slight, and key texts such as Daniel 12:2–3 are capable of more than one interpretation. Even if it is true that "resurrection" without an empty grave would have been unthinkable, allowance must still be made for the possibility of innovation on the part of Jesus' earliest followers. In declaring that the forthcoming resurrection of the dead had already taken place in the specific instance of Jesus, a new dynamic was unleashed. Instead of existing Jewish understandings determining or constraining the thinking of Jesus' followers, experience of Jesus was redefining existing Second Temple categories and beliefs. The imprecision and fluidity of Paul's metaphors suggests that although the thinking of Jesus' earliest followers had moved on beyond existing categories, it was not yet entirely systematized.

We can sum up by saying that Paul probably took it for granted that the resurrection of Jesus included the raising of Jesus' dead body from the grave in which it had been buried, but he does not say this in so many words. His silence leaves open the possibility that he may have believed that Jesus' corpse had remained permanently in its grave, discarded like unwanted old clothing. The problem is that Paul's complicated threefold anthropology is ambiguous, and his views concerning the nature of the resurrection body cannot be established with certainty. He oscillates between the concepts of abandonment, exchange, and transformation using a variety of metaphors, the implications of which are not entirely consistent. A similar fluidity is evident in his cryptic reference to his own heavenly ascent experience. He seems to have believed that it was possible to enter heaven, at least temporarily, with or without one's ordinary human body. All we can say with certainty is that twenty years after Jesus' death, basic questions concerning the nature and circumstances of his resurrection were still the subject of continuing debate (cf. 1 Corinthians 15:12).

The relationship between exaltation and resurrection

In addition to the apparent lack of clarity in Paul's thinking, there is evidence that there may have been an initial disconnection between the ideas of exaltation and resurrection. The very early pre-Pauline faith formula makes no mention of Jesus' heavenly exaltation, while the probably pre-Pauline christological hymns and fragments focus on Jesus' extreme heavenly exaltation, making no explicit reference to his resurrection. This leads some commentators to suggest that resurrection faith and belief in Jesus' heavenly exaltation may have had independent origins, perhaps among different groups of Jesus' followers in different geographical and linguistic settings. If so, the two traditions could have developed briefly in parallel prior to becoming assimilated one to another. Another possibility is that resurrection faith emerged as a secondary expansion of initial exaltation belief. Once the merger of the two parallel or sequential traditions had taken place, resurrection faith—freighted as it is with dynamic eschatological implications—would have subsumed belief in Jesus' vindication by heavenly exaltation.

Either of these processes would explain why in the very earliest traditions we find references to Jesus' exaltation without any mention of his resurrection, references to his resurrection without any mention of exaltation, and references to resurrection juxtaposed with references to exaltation (e.g. Romans 8:34). It would explain the non-eschatological nature of the very earliest formulaic assertions of Jesus' resurrection, the lack of any reference to an empty tomb, and the absence of any suggestion that resurrection necessarily involved the bringing back to physical life of Jesus' dead body.

Conclusion

The earliest pre-Pauline evidence for the resurrection and the resurrection appearances of Jesus is embedded in the writings of Paul and others. There seems to have been a very brief and very early resurrection faith formula in the form "God raised Jesus [or Christ] from the dead" and/or "Jesus [or Christ] died and rose again". This formula came into being no more than a year or so after the death of Jesus at the latest. A number of probably pre-Pauline christological hymns and fragments have also been identified. They make no explicit reference to Jesus' resurrection, but emphasize instead his pre-existence and hyper-exalted status as a heavenly being. There is also early evidence that in worship, both Aramaic- and Greek-speaking Christians used the Aramaic term *marana tha* (meaning "Our Lord, come!") as an invocation addressed to Christ as exalted heavenly Lord.

The earliest evidence for appearances of the risen Jesus to his followers is the tradition quoted by Paul in 1 Corinthians 15:5–8. This may have been part of Paul's initial instruction, and if so, it is very early indeed. It asserts the resurrection but makes no mention of any eschatological implications. It lists appearances to Cephas [Peter], James, "the twelve", "all the apostles", and a large group of "more than five hundred brothers and sisters", but it contains no circumstantial details. Paul adds himself to the list of those to whom Christ appeared and implies that the experiences of Peter and the others listed in the 1 Corinthians 15 tradition were similar in all respects to his own.

The circumstances and content of Paul's experience of encounter with the risen Jesus Christ can to some extent be inferred from statements and allusions in his letter to the Galatians and elsewhere in his writings. They also receive a measure of corroboration from the author of the considerably later Acts of the Apostles. Paul experienced a revelatory encounter in which the risen Christ seems to have appeared to him as a heavenly being, radiant and shining with the reflected light of the glory of God. Through this encounter experience, the gospel was communicated to Paul, and he found himself challenged to commit to discipleship and to the proclamation of Christ among the Gentiles. We know that long before he wrote any of his letters, Paul had visited Jerusalem and met Peter and James. He would certainly have known if their experiences of encounter with the risen Christ had been significantly different from his own. His implicit testimony must therefore be accepted. The appearances of the risen Christ were all broadly similar. They all involved visionary perceptions of the risen Jesus Christ as an exalted, radiant, heavenly being.

What Paul says about the nature of the believer's resurrection body and, by extension, that of Jesus, is conditioned by his complex and not entirely consistent anthropology. He uses a variety of metaphors, all of which are capable of more than one interpretation. He makes no reference to any empty tomb tradition, possibly because he took the empty tomb for granted as a corollary of Jesus' resurrection.

The absence of any reference to heavenly exaltation in the very early resurrection faith formula, and the equally puzzling lack of any explicit reference to the resurrection of Jesus in the christological hymns and hymnic fragments, suggest that the concepts of exaltation and resurrection may have had separate origins within different communities of Jesus' followers. If so, the earliest form of resurrection belief could have been belief in Jesus' post-mortem vindication by heavenly exaltation.

The quality of the historical evidence for multiple visionary experiences having been interpreted as appearances of the risen, heavenly Jesus Christ, is outstanding, but at this stage the resurrection of Jesus as a historical event resolutely refuses to come into focus.

CHAPTER 8

Resurrection Belief: Twenty Years On

In the previous chapter, we examined the very earliest stratum of historical evidence bearing on the resurrection of Jesus. This evidence included the early formulaic assertions of the resurrection, the probably pre-Pauline christological hymns and fragments and the resurrection-appearances tradition of 1 Corinthians 15. In order to understand the nature and content of these resurrection appearances we examined Paul's testimony concerning his own visionary experience of encounter with the risen Jesus. In this chapter we focus on the second layer or stratum, this being the period between the first emergence of resurrection faith and the writing of the first Gospel in around 70 CE. In practice, this means we focus on Paul's authentic letters, written during the fifties CE.

These letters show that by the time Paul was writing to the various communities with which he was connected, many important additional understandings concerning the resurrection of Jesus had already been formulated. These included the understanding that the resurrection of Jesus signifies the inauguration of a new age, explicit belief in the coming again (or *parousia*) of Jesus, belief that associated with the resurrection there is outpouring of the Spirit of God, and the realization that, far from being a mistake, the death of Jesus is providential and confers benefits on believers.

Scriptural exegesis

The earliest resurrection testimony makes no specific reference to the Hebrew scriptures apart from the probably secondary assertion that the resurrection of Jesus on the third day was "in accordance with the scriptures". By the fifties things have changed considerably. Jesus' followers have evidently for some time been diligently searching the Hebrew scriptures in their Greek translation for passages or significant texts that might throw light on what had happened, either because the texts could be identified as prophecies literally fulfilled in the events of Jesus' death and resurrection, or because they supported emergent understandings of these events.

Numerous examples of significant connections are given in the following sections, but one text in particular—Psalm 110—requires special mention, because it was extraordinarily influential from a very early stage. This psalm itself is either quoted or alluded to no fewer than thirty-three times in the New Testament. The first verse, in particular, is quoted explicitly no fewer than eight times. If direct quotations and allusions are added together, Psalm 110:1 is referred to more frequently in the New Testament than any other text from the Septuagint. Verse 1 reads:

> The LORD [God] says to my lord,
> "Sit at my right hand
> until I make your enemies your footstool."
>
> *Psalm 110:1*

Common to all the early Christian interpretations and applications of this verse are the ideas of Jesus' exaltation and lordship. It was regarded as conferring on Jesus as "lord" the status and glory associated with being seated at the right hand of God himself (the place at the right hand being the place traditionally reserved for a king's son and heir). Session at God's right hand signals Jesus' supreme exaltation and, additionally, his heavenly lordship and messianic enthronement.

It is not suggested that reflection on Psalm 110:1 or any other biblical text actually generated belief in Jesus' heavenly exaltation. Exaltation belief seems to have come about as a result of theological reflection on the significance of Jesus' death interacting iteratively with visions of Jesus perceived as a gloriously transformed heavenly being. Nevertheless, the Christian messianic interpretation of Psalm 110:1 undoubtedly served as the point of entry into emergent christological thinking of a number of important ideas. In particular, it bound together the three key concepts of Jesus as lord, Messiah, and son of God so that they reinforced and intensified one another. To see how this works, Psalm 110:1 needs to be read in conjunction with Romans 1:3-4, Psalm 2, and Nathan's prophecy concerning a coming king who is called the son of God:

> ...I [God] will establish the throne of his [David's promised descendant's] kingdom for ever. I will be a father to him, and he shall be a son to me.
>
> *2 Samuel 7:13-14*

> He [God] said to me, "You are my son; today I have begotten you..."
>
> *Psalm 2:7*

> ...the gospel concerning his Son, who was descended from David according to the flesh and was declared to be Son of God with power according to the spirit of holiness by resurrection from the dead...
>
> *Romans 1:3-4*

One of the questions asked in connection with the Christian messianic understanding of Psalm 110:1 is whether it reflects a time when the idea of exaltation was more important than the idea of resurrection. Could a messianic interpretation of Psalm 110:1 have emerged in an Aramaic-speaking milieu, as a more or less immediate consequence of the belief that the dead Jesus had been vindicated by heavenly exaltation rather than by resurrection, or could it only have originated at a somewhat later stage among the Greek-speaking, LXX-reading, Jewish followers of Jesus? In this connection, reference is sometimes made to two texts in the letter to the Hebrews that use Psalm 110:1 to express belief in Jesus' supreme exaltation to God's right hand without any mention of his resurrection (Hebrews 10:12 and 12:2). Unfortunately, the letter to the Hebrews is far too late—possibly as late as the nineties—for it to be safely used as evidence for developments taking place in the thirties and forties. Nevertheless, it does seem probable that the Christian messianic interpretation of Psalm 110:1 took place at a very early stage. Linguistic considerations are not decisive. Scholars today are less inclined than formerly to assert that particular developments could only have taken place in a Greek-speaking milieu (i.e. later) rather than in an Aramaic-speaking milieu (i.e. earlier). As we have seen, the two linguistic communities in Jerusalem coexisted alongside one another more or less from the outset. Many members would have been bilingual, and thinking in the two communities probably developed more or less in parallel. If, as now seems probable, independent Jewish messianic interpretations of Psalm 110:1 were already available in Aramaic-speaking, first-century Judaism, the Christian interpretation of Psalm 110:1 could have been very early indeed. All that the Christian interpreters would have been doing was adopting and developing existing lines of Jewish messianic exegesis. This conclusion is compatible with the understanding that exaltation belief may have preceded resurrection belief or, at least, may have had independent origins.

It has been suggested that the messianic interpretation of Psalm 110:1 may even be derived from Jesus himself. Mark represents Jesus as having quoted the verse in a way that interprets the phrase "my lord" in Psalm 110:1 as a reference to the Messiah:

> While Jesus was teaching in the temple, he said, "How can the scribes say that the Messiah is the son of David? David himself, by the Holy Spirit, declared,
> 'The Lord said to my Lord,
> "Sit at my right hand,
> until I put your enemies under your feet."'"
> *Mark 12:35–36*

Few scholars would regard this as an authentic saying of Jesus. Nevertheless, the attribution of the saying to him is another indication that the Christian understanding of Psalm 110:1 as a reference to Jesus' supreme exaltation and heavenly enthronement was important and early. In addition to unifying key christological affirmations, including Jesus' lordship, messiahship, and his being seated at God's right hand, Psalm 110:1 emphasizes his supreme heavenly glory and paves the way for the slightly later understanding that his exaltation and vindication include supremacy over all powers whatsoever, whether on earth or in heaven. Indeed, it has been said that the imagery implicit in the Christian messianic interpretation of the first verse of Psalm 110 goes about as far as it is possible to go without compromising monotheism.

Of the three interlocking concepts, it was probably the understanding of Jesus' exalted lordship, reflected in the *marana tha* invocation in worship, that was initially the most influential (see pp. 178–180). It connected directly with the idea that the kingdom of God had been decisively inaugurated by Jesus' resurrection, and that it would soon be completely established. It also facilitated, as we have seen, the transfer of attributes and functions of Yhwh as Lord to the risen Jesus as exalted heavenly Lord. This was a development of the utmost importance. Attention has already been given to the probably pre-Pauline christological hymn Philippians 2:6–11, which uses Isaiah 45:23 as a bridge to transfer to Jesus the universal homage previously believed to be due only to God himself. In Isaiah 45:23, God declares that, "To me every knee shall bow, every tongue shall swear." The author of the Philippians hymn adapts this, declaring that God highly exalted Jesus so that "at the name of Jesus every knee should bend, in heaven and on earth and under the earth, and every tongue should confess that Jesus Christ is Lord." There are other instances of the same process in Paul's writings.[77] In one instance, Paul uses the title "Lord" to transform a statement about the name of God in the book of Joel into an equivalent statement about Jesus:

> Everyone who calls on the name of the Lord [God] shall be saved.
> *Joel 2:32*

> "Everyone who calls on the name of the Lord [Jesus] shall be saved."
> *Romans 10:13*

The author of the Philippians hymn does not specify the "name above every name" awarded to Jesus. The general assumption is that it must be "Lord". The exaltation ascribed to Jesus is, however, so startling that we have to consider another possibility. In Chapter 3, we noted a number of important traditions concerning an angel of exceptional status who is described as having "God's Name in him". This angel functions as God's representative, even at times speaking as if he were God himself. The underlying idea seems to be that in encountering this particular angel there is a form of encounter with God. This suggests that the "name above every name" awarded to the hyper-exalted Jesus in Philippians 2:9 may be the divine name, Yhwh. This may seem extraordinary, but so also are the other instances of the transfer to Jesus of the divinity associated with the lordship of God.

This admittedly speculative interpretation receives indirect support from the Similitudes of Enoch. The Similitudes contain a vivid description of the revelation of the hidden and hitherto unknown name of the heavenly being called the Son of Man. In a passage bearing striking similarities to the Philippians hymn, the unknown author says:

> And they [the angels] had great joy, and they blessed and glorified and exalted, because the name of that son of man had been revealed to them.
> And he sat on the throne of his glory, and the whole judgement was given to the Son of Man . . .
>
> *1 Enoch 69:26–27*[78]

As in Philippians, the "name" is not specified, but evidently something very special is implied. Earlier in the Similitudes, it is said that the Son of Man was given his secret "name" by God before the creation of the world. If the underlying concept is the same as that in the Divine Name angel traditions, the secret name revealed to the heavenly host could be Yhwh, the Name of God. This would explain the paean of angelic praise. The Jewish Similitudes of Enoch and the Christian hymn in Philippians 2:6–11 may be two different instances of a shared interpretive tradition involving a heavenly redeemer endowed with the Divine Name of God.

There is another example of the transfer of the Divine Name (or divine attributes) from God to Jesus in the Revelation to John. Some scholars suggest that the Revelation, which is generally supposed to date from around 95 CE, could in fact have been written just before the destruction of the Jerusalem temple in 70 CE. The author has a vision in which he sees Jesus as a radiantly glorious heavenly being. This awesome figure says to John:

> "Do not be afraid; I [Jesus] am the first and the last, and the living one. I was dead, and see, I am alive for ever and ever . . ."
>
> *Revelation 1:17–18*

Compare this with:

> "I [God] am the first and I am the last; besides me there is no god."
>
> *Isaiah 44:6*

Resurrection as the inauguration of the new age

Other concepts derived from the Hebrew scriptures also contributed to the ongoing development of the earliest understandings associated with the resurrection of Jesus. One of the most important of these was the concept of resurrection as a sign of the dawning of a hoped-for new age. As we have seen, in the pluriform Judaism of the Second Temple period there was no settled orthodoxy. Afterlife beliefs, in particular, were fluid and loosely defined. Nevertheless, there appears to have been a widespread, variously expressed expectation of a blessed age to come. Before long, it was believed, the people of God would be decisively delivered from their enemies, and then they would undergo renewal and restoration tantamount to a new creation. For example:

> [Thus says the Lord GOD:]
> For I am about to create new heavens
> and a new earth;
> the former things shall not be remembered

> or come to mind.
> Be glad and rejoice for ever
> in what I am creating ...
>
> Isaiah 65:17; cf. Isaiah 66:22

The concept of the coming new age reflects various earlier promises of restoration articulated by—among others—the authors of Isaiah, Jeremiah, and Ezekiel. As to how this hoped-for state of affairs would come about, opinions were divided. Some texts seem to envisage military action under the leadership of a messianic figure, either human or quasi-divine. Others appear to believe that God's kingly rule over his people will be established by direct divine action. The theme of God ruling as king, either through an intermediary or directly, is an important component of the expectation. For example, the Jewish text, the Testament of Moses (probably pre-70 CE), announces a forthcoming act of decisive divine intervention which will lead to the establishment of the kingdom or rule of God:

> "Then his kingdom will appear throughout
> his whole creation ...
> For the Heavenly One will arise from his kingly throne.
> Yea, he will go forth from his holy habitation
> with indignation and wrath on behalf of his sons ...
> For God Most High shall surge forth,
> the Eternal One alone.
> In full view will he come to work vengeance on the nations ...
> Then will you be happy, O Israel! ...
> And God will raise you to the heights.
> Yea, he will fix you firmly in the heaven of the stars,
> in the place of their habitations.
> And you will behold from on high.
> Yea, you will see your enemies on the earth.
> And recognizing them, you will rejoice.
> And you will give thanks.
> Yea, you will confess your creator.
>
> Testament of Moses 10:1,3,7–10[79]

Divine action and human initiative are not mutually exclusive; they may be seen as two sides of the same coin. War in heaven may proceed in parallel with war on earth; military victory on earth may reflect both divine agency and human effort. The angels of God may even, at times, fight alongside humans on earth.

It was in the wider context of hoped-for national restoration, and the narrower and more specific context of the persecution associated with the Maccabean rebellion, that the idea of resurrection first emerged. Belief in the resurrection of the dead vindicated divine providence in the face of evident human evil and injustice. The martyrs and the righteous dead would be raised from the dead to be rewarded by participation in the coming new kingdom of God, the blessed new age to come. Limited pain now would deliver unlimited gain hereafter. The Maccabean martyrs who suffered such dreadful fates would be raised to "everlasting renewal of life" and "ever-flowing life" (2 Maccabees 7:9,36). The author of the Wisdom of Solomon speaks of the souls of the righteous being created for incorruption; they are formed in the image of God's own eternity (Wisdom of Solomon 2:23). Daniel speaks of "everlasting life" and of the righteous "shining like the stars for ever and ever". His vision of resurrection serves the interest of justice very directly. Resurrection is not for everyone. For the very righteous it will facilitate reward, and for the very wicked it will facilitate punishment:

> Many of those who sleep in the dust of the earth shall awake, some to everlasting life, and some to shame and everlasting contempt.
> *Daniel 12:2*

First-century CE Jewish eschatological expectations concerning the coming new age are variously expressed and not always consistent. In 4 Ezra, at the coming of the Messiah all the assembled hostile nations will be judged and destroyed. The messianic kingdom lasts for four hundred years, ending in seven days of primeval silence. Then the world reawakens for the resurrection of the dead and the last judgement. (4 Ezra 7:30–44). The scheme used in 4 Ezra makes no mention of resurrection for participation in the messianic kingdom, but it specifies that the ten lost tribes of Israel will return. The writer of 2 Baruch foresees a time of tribulation culminating in the glorious revelation of the Messiah, who will triumph over his enemies. This triumph will inaugurate a new age of messianic rule for the living righteous. Then comes the final day of judgement when the books will be opened. The righteous dead will rise to live in Paradise or on a transformed earth. They will no longer be corruptible, but will be like the angels and equal to the stars. The souls of the wicked, however, will waste away in torment (2 Baruch 30:1–5; 40:3; 50:2; 72:1—73:2). In the Similitudes of Enoch there are various schemes. There is general resurrection for judgement (51:1–5), and there is resurrection of the righteous (61:5). In both instances the righteous, resurrected dead are rewarded with ongoing life on a transformed earth from which sin and sinners have been eliminated:

> In those days, mountains shall dance like rams; and the hills shall leap like kids satiated with milk. And the faces of all the angels in heaven shall glow with joy, because on that day the Elect One [the Messiah] has arisen. And the earth shall rejoice; and the righteous ones shall dwell upon her and the elect ones shall walk upon her.
>
> *1 Enoch 51:4–5*[80]

Elsewhere in the Similitudes, the righteous dead have already risen from *Sheol* and are in heaven, transformed and wearing garments of glory (39:4–5; 62:15). These conflicting traditions do not, apparently, trouble the author.

Similar motifs appear in early Christian writings, particularly in the book of Revelation. Towards the end of Revelation, the author has a vision in which he sees heaven opened. Angelic armies emerge, led by the Word of God, who is a mighty being seated on a white horse. The kings of the earth and their armies are defeated, many being slain by a sword that emerges from the mouth of the Word of God, who is Christ. Satan is bound and consigned to a sealed pit. There is an initial resurrection of the faithful dead martyrs, who enjoy a blessed new life with Christ on earth for a thousand years. After that, Satan is released from bondage. In the ensuing, climactic war, the wicked nations of the earth are finally annihilated and Satan is cast for ever into a lake of fire. Then comes the general resurrection of the dead, good and bad alike, for the last judgement (Revelation 20:1–15).

It is against this rather confusing background of eschatological and apocalyptic traditions, often Daniel-based, that we have to assess Paul's thinking concerning the resurrection of Jesus and the age to come. For Paul, the resurrection of Jesus signals the inauguration of the coming new age. He declares:

> . . . Christ has been raised from the dead, the first fruits of those who have died.
> 1 Corinthians 15:20

Significantly, Paul forges a strong link between the ideas of resurrection and creation. In Romans 4:17, he speaks of God as the one "who gives life to the dead and calls into existence the things that do not exist". In Romans 5:12–19, He contrasts Christ with Adam. Death, says Paul, entered the world through Adam, but Christ's act of righteousness leads to justification and life for all (believers). In 1 Corinthians 15:20–24 (see above), Paul further develops this theme, arguing that just as death entered the world through a human being (Adam), so now life in the form of resurrection from the dead enters the world through a human being (Christ). We who were dead will be made alive in Christ, who is the first fruits of the harvest of the dead.

The "first fruits" were the initial and choicest portions of the harvest produce, traditionally offered at the annual festival of *Shavuot* in the Jerusalem temple (Exodus 23:16–19; Deuteronomy 26). The reference to the risen Christ as the "first fruits of those who have died" implies the belief that there will be a resurrection of dead believers when Jesus comes again and the new era is fully implemented. For Paul, the resurrection of Jesus is an act of God which has significant parallels with God's act of initial creation. It signals the inauguration of a completely new dispensation, thereby also conferring retrospective significance on Jesus' death. Nevertheless, common sense and everyday reality oblige Paul to make a distinction between God's already accomplished act of raising Jesus from the dead and his eagerly anticipated final act of deliverance for all believers. For the time being, believers have to wait:

> ... [we] wait for his Son from heaven, whom he raised from the dead—Jesus, who delivers us from the wrath that is coming.
>
> *1 Thessalonians 1:10*

The scheme is reasonably clear. First there is the resurrection of Jesus, who represents the "first fruits" of the coming new age. Then, after the period of waiting, there will be the full implementation of the new age and the full realization of its benefits. These include the return of Jesus, the resurrection of believers, the crushing of all hostile powers, and the final handing over of the kingdom to God (1 Corinthians 15:24). But for now, the kingdom of God in all its fullness remains a future hope. It is something to which the believer has been called, but into which he or she has not yet entered (1 Thessalonians 2:12). Yet although believers must wait, they do not wait passively. They are already connected or united with the death of Jesus by baptism. In due course they will be similarly united with Jesus by resurrection from the dead:

> Therefore we have been buried with him by baptism into death ... For if we have been united with him in a death like his, we will certainly be united with him in a resurrection like his.
>
> *Romans 6:4–5*

Resurrection and *parousia*

From a very early stage, perhaps from the very beginning, a corollary of the belief that God had raised Jesus from the dead was the expectation that Jesus would return again, to complete God's already initiated work of salvation and judgement by establishing the kingdom of God in power. Christians are presently waiting for this coming of God's Son from heaven (1 Thessalonians 1:10). When the day comes, God's trumpet will sound, the Lord Jesus will descend from heaven, and those Christians who have already died will be raised from the dead and reunited with those who are still living (1 Thessalonians 4:16–17). For the moment we are exiles, but "our citizenship is in heaven", and we must stand firm and be patient while we wait for the expected Saviour, the Lord Jesus Christ (Philippians

3:20). But everything must take place in due order. Christ, the first fruits, has already been raised from the dead. Then, when Christ returns, dead believers also will be raised (1 Corinthians 15:23).

The Greek term frequently used in connection with the return of Jesus (*parousia*) means "arrival" or "being present". Belief in Jesus' *parousia* was already well established by the fifties, when Paul was writing. It seems to have emerged at a very early stage indeed. Despite the "health warnings" we have already attached to Aramaic/Greek linguistic arguments, *parousia* belief probably did originate in an Aramaic rather than Greek-speaking environment. It is hard to think of any other reason why the Aramaic invocation *marana tha* ("O Lord, come!") should have been used in worship even in faraway Greek-speaking churches. *Parousia* belief is central to early Christian thinking, and we shall argue below that it was—almost from the very outset—an integral component of the earliest exaltation and resurrection faith.

Parousia belief almost certainly reflects the very early identification of the risen and exalted Jesus with the heavenly figure described in Daniel 7:13-14 as "one like a son of man". In Daniel's vision, this exalted figure comes to God with the clouds of heaven and is awarded everlasting dominion, glory, and kingship over all the peoples, nations, and languages. Exactly when and how the identification of Jesus with this figure came about is not known. Nevertheless, it was a critically important development. In addition to supporting the idea of Jesus being vindicated after his death by coming to God in heaven, Daniel 7 facilitated the connection of belief in Jesus' coming to God (his vindication by resurrection and exaltation) with belief in his future revelation (*parousia*), or his appearing in power to make believers safe, to overcome all enemies, and to exercise universal dominion. It is not necessarily that belief in the Son of Man's "coming to God" morphed into belief in his "coming to earth". The task awarded to the figure who comes to God in Daniel 7:13-14 necessarily involves his subsequent coming to earth in order to exercise the delegated divine powers which have been awarded to him. Whatever the precise mechanism, by one route or another the identification of the risen and exalted heavenly Jesus with the Danielic figure led to the formation of sayings about the future coming of Jesus, the Son of Man, which were absorbed into the pre-Gospel Jesus tradition and which later surface in the Gospels themselves. The identification of the heavenly Jesus with the figure in Daniel 7 also intensified other emergent christological understandings, including Jesus' heavenly lordship and, probably, belief in his pre-existence.

If the identification of Jesus with the Danielic figure was as significant as it appears to have been, we have to explain the puzzling lack of any explicit reference to the Son of Man, or to Jesus as the Son of Man, in the writings of Paul. There are several issues here. There are, in fact, very few references to any of Jesus' sayings or activities in Paul's writings. It may be that Paul had only limited access to information about Jesus and therefore had little or no knowledge of this particular aspect of the developing Jesus tradition. Paul's failure to refer to Jesus as the Son of Man may anyway be more apparent than real. There are *parousia* passages (1 Thessalonians 1:10; 4:16–17; 1 Corinthians 4:5; 15:23–25) in which Paul deploys ideas and imagery closely similar to those in the Gospel sayings about the coming of the Son of Man in power. Additionally, in Romans 5:15 the term "one man" may be a substitute for what would otherwise have been a reference to the Son of Man. There is also a possible allusion or echo of the Son of Man tradition in Paul's use of Psalm 8:4–6 in 1 Corinthians 15:27. Nearer to the mark may be the fact that Paul's theology, especially his Adam–Christ typology, is intricate and precisely focused. He could well have regarded the rather loosely articulated and ambiguous Son of Man sayings as potentially confusing to his Gentile readers, and therefore best set aside.

The simplest and most straightforward explanation for Paul's lack of explicit reference to Jesus as Son of Man is that by the time he was writing, the term was already redundant. Once the risen and exalted Jesus had been identified with the Son of Man in Daniel 7:13–14, Jesus himself became the primary focus of interest. Cryptic allusions were no longer necessary, especially in a Gentile context. Jesus himself was now identified as the one expected to come from heaven to exercise delegated divine powers, to make safe the righteous, and to establish on God's behalf an everlasting, universal kingdom embracing all nations upon earth. In other words, once Jesus had been identified with the Son of Man, references to the future actions of the Son of Man would have naturally mutated into references to the future coming and actions of the heavenly Jesus.

In the tradition underlying the Gospels, sayings about the coming Son of Man are preserved (not necessarily unchanged) until they finally surface in the Gospel texts. In the meantime, in Paul's writings, the coming one has already been explicitly identified as Jesus himself. Thus we have the Marcan saying:

> Then they will see "the Son of Man coming on the clouds" [Matthew adds "of heaven"] with power and great glory. [Luke stops at this point] And he will send out the angels [Matthew adds "with a loud trumpet call"], and they will gather his elect from the four winds, from the ends of the earth to the ends of heaven.
>
> Mark 13:26-27; cf. Matthew 24:30-31, Luke 21:27

Compare this with Paul's well-known rapture passage in 1 Thessalonians, where closely similar imagery and sentiments were already being applied explicitly to Jesus in the early fifties:

> For the Lord [Jesus] himself, with a cry of command, with the archangel's call and with the sound of God's trumpet, will descend from heaven, and the dead in Christ will rise first. Then we who are alive, who are left, will be caught up in the clouds together with them to meet the Lord in the air; and so we will be with the Lord for ever.
>
> 1 Thessalonians 4:16-17

Neither saying gives any certain details concerning the ongoing state of those who will be "gathered in", "raised", or "caught up", beyond the assertion that they will be "with the Lord for ever". In both cases, the primary concern is to reassure faithful believers that at the time of the *parousia* or appearance of Jesus from heaven, they will be protected and kept safe. In Paul's writings it is not always clear whether it is anticipated that the new, transformed life of believers will be in heaven or on earth. The "flesh and blood" saying in 1 Corinthians 15:50-52 seems to envisage a general transformation of believers and a non-physical, heavenly kingdom. On the other hand, the assertion that Jesus will destroy every rule and authority and power (1 Corinthians 15:24–25) seems to imply that the kingdom which will eventually be handed over to God is a kingdom on earth. Perhaps Paul supposed that once Christ had exercised his overwhelming power and judgement, the distinction between life on earth and life in heaven would be irrelevant, or even non-existent.

Finally, there is the book of Revelation, which could be earlier than is generally supposed. Revelation contains a description of a vision in which the risen and gloriously transformed Jesus Christ, who is described as "one like a son of man", commands the author to write to seven named churches, delivering a message to each church in turn. Some churches are praised, some are rebuked, and others are promised conditional rewards. The church in Philadelphia is praised for its patient endurance, with a promise of reward:

> ... I will keep you from the hour of trial that is coming on the whole world to test the inhabitants of the earth. I am coming soon; hold fast to what you have, so that no one may seize your crown. If you conquer, I will make you a pillar in the temple of my God; you will never go out of it. I will write on you the name of my God, and the name of the city of my God, the new Jerusalem that comes down from my God out of heaven, and my own new name.
> *Revelation 3:10–12*

Here, as in Paul's letters and in the Gospels, the primary motif associated with the *parousia* is reassurance. There is to be a time of trial, and believers must hold fast. Jesus Christ is coming soon from heaven. The "new Jerusalem" coming down from God in heaven is a symbol for the eschatological kingdom of God (cf. Revelation 21:2–4), which is evidently here on earth. For those who stay firm and true, there is the promise of honourable participation in the coming new order. The promise that Jesus will "write on you the name of my God" echoes the christological hymn in Philippians 2:6–11, where the exalted heavenly Jesus is awarded "the name that is above every name". It also brings to mind the climactic scene in 1 Enoch 69:26–27 where the revelation of the secret name of the Son of Man generates a paean of angelic praise. All three passages may be independent reflections of a Jewish angelomorphic tradition in which the highest conceivable honour and status is investiture with the Divine Name.

Resurrection and the Spirit of God

Another unfolding implication of resurrection faith influenced by concepts and texts drawn from the Hebrew scriptures is the belief that there was a special outpouring of the Spirit of God associated with the resurrection of Jesus. The Hebrew word for spirit (*ruach*) means "breath", "wind", or even "gale". The term denotes the outgoing torrent of divine energy manifested in the act of creation and subsequently motivating and empowering individuals to undertake special commissions or to communicate divine revelation by prophecy or otherwise. The Genesis account of the creation says that "in the beginning":

> ... the earth was a formless void and darkness covered the face of the deep, while a wind [*ruach*] from God swept over the face of the waters. Then God said, "Let there be light"; and there was light.
>
> *Genesis 1:1–3*

The creating and re-creating aspect of the Spirit of God is dramatically captured in Ezekiel's vision of the valley of the dry bones (chapter 37). The restoration of the metaphorically dead people of God begins with the reassembling of their dry bones, which are then brought back to life by the infusion of divine *ruach*. Ezekiel is commanded to prophesy and say to the bones:

> "O dry bones, hear the word of the LORD. Thus says the Lord God to these bones: I will cause breath [*ruach*] to enter you, and you shall live. I will lay sinews on you, and will cause flesh to come upon you, and cover you with skin, and put breath [*ruach*] in you, and you shall live; and you shall know that I am the LORD."
>
> *Ezekiel 37:4–6; cf. Genesis 2:7*

The Spirit of God is sometimes spoken of as something that will be "poured out". The anticipated outpouring of the Spirit may be associated with the promise of national restoration (Ezekiel 36:27–28), with the general blessing of God's people (Isaiah 44:3), or with a specific eschatological act of divine intervention taking the form of an anticipated "Day of the Lord" on which God's power and glory will be decisively manifested. On the Day of the Lord, God's enemies will be defeated, a new social order will be established, and a new era of abundant blessing and joy will be inaugurated. The pouring out of the Spirit on the fast-approaching, eschatological Day of the Lord is depicted in an oracle of unknown date in the book of Joel:

> Let all the inhabitants of the land tremble,
> for the day of the LORD is coming, it is near . . .
> Then afterwards
> I will pour out my spirit [*ruach*] on all flesh.
>
> *Joel 2:1,28*

Luke quotes Joel 2:28–32 in his account of the pouring out of the Holy Spirit on the day of Pentecost (Acts 2:17–21).

The earliest reference that we have to the gift of the Spirit of God or the Holy Spirit to the followers of Jesus makes no direct connection with the resurrection of Jesus. Writing probably in 50 or 51 CE, Paul reminds the Thessalonian Christians that they were called to live in a manner that is pleasing to God and that they possess the ongoing gift of God's Holy Spirit:

> For God did not call us to impurity but in holiness. Therefore whoever rejects this rejects not human authority but God, who also gives his Holy Spirit to you.
>
> *1 Thessalonians 4:7–8*

A few years later, however, Paul does make an explicit connection between the gift of the Spirit of God and the resurrection of Jesus. Writing to Christians in Rome, he says that God, who raised Jesus from the dead, will also give resurrection life to believers through the agency of his indwelling Spirit:

> If the Spirit of him who raised Jesus from the dead dwells in you, he who raised Christ from the dead will give life to your mortal bodies also through his Spirit that dwells in you.
>
> *Romans 8:11*

Although much later in date, there is a particularly interesting example of the connection between the heavenly exaltation of Jesus and the outpouring of the Holy Spirit in an anonymous, non-Pauline letter to the Christians in Ephesus. Writing perhaps in the eighties, the author begs his readers to be forbearing with one another and to maintain "the unity of the Spirit in the bond of peace". He continues:

> But each of us was given grace according to the measure of Christ's gift. Therefore it is said,
>> "When he ascended on high he made captivity itself a captive; he gave gifts to his people."
>
> *Ephesians 4:7-8*

The quotation is from Psalm 68. The author of Ephesians is apparently interpreting it as a reference to the heavenly exaltation of Jesus. This psalm, which itself probably comprises a variety of very ancient traditions, celebrates the awesome power of God and the victories won over the enemies of his people. Describing what may be some form of cultic re-enactment of such a victory, the psalmist says:

> You ascended the high mount,
> leading captives in your train
> and receiving gifts from people . . .
>
> *Psalm 68:18*

The victorious one, who ascends the high mount, leading captives and receiving gifts, is either God or the king. In the Christian exegesis of the psalm in Ephesians, the recipient of the gifts becomes the donor of the gifts. When the risen Jesus Christ ascends on high, he does not receive gifts. On the contrary, he gives gifts. According to the author of Ephesians, these gifts are the various functions or ministries necessary for building up the community of believers. In 1 Corinthians 12 there is a somewhat similar list of gifts described as being given "through the Spirit" for the common good. In both cases, the underlying concept seems to be that the risen and ascended Jesus gives the gift or gifts of the Holy Spirit to his followers.

The author of Ephesians is not necessarily playing fast and loose in his exegesis of Psalm 68. There is a fourth- or fifth-century Jewish Aramaic Targum to Psalms, probably reflecting much earlier interpretations, that makes exactly the same reversal. According to the Targum, the one who ascends on high is Moses. Moses ascends (Mount Sinai) and then gives gifts (the words of the law) to the people. That both Jews and Christians should have so similarly reinterpreted Psalm 68 suggests a shared early Jewish interpretive tradition in which someone ascends on high to receive gifts from God, which are then transmitted onwards and downwards to the people.

The idea of the Holy Spirit being the gift of the risen and exalted heavenly Jesus to his followers also appears in the Acts of the Apostles. In an extended narrative account of events in Jerusalem on the day of Pentecost, the author says that Jesus received from his Father the promise of the Spirit of God. Having received the gift, Jesus then poured it out on his followers. The author of Acts describes how Peter declares to the astonished onlookers:

> "This Jesus God raised up, and of that all of us are witnesses. Being therefore exalted at the right hand of God, and having received from the Father the promise of the Holy Spirit, he [Jesus] has poured out this that you both see and hear."
>
> *Acts 2:32–33*

Jesus was, in effect, the conduit through which God's Spirit was delivered. The Gospels of Luke and John also associate the pouring out of God's Spirit with the resurrection of Jesus, albeit in very different ways. In Luke's Gospel, the risen Jesus commands his disciples to remain in Jerusalem pending the gift of the Spirit, which will "clothe them with power from on high":

> "Thus it is written," [says Jesus] "that the Messiah is to suffer and to rise from the dead on the third day, and that repentance and forgiveness of sins is to be proclaimed in his name to all nations, beginning from Jerusalem. You are witnesses of these things. And see, I am sending upon you what my Father promised; so stay here in the city until you have been clothed with power from on high."
>
> *Luke 24:46–49*

John has no account of any Pentecost event because he prefers to represent the Holy Spirit as the personal gift of the risen Jesus, a gift quietly bestowed on the inner circle of his faithful disciples. The gift is bestowed on the evening of the day on which the tomb was discovered to be empty:

> Jesus said to them again, "Peace be with you. As the Father has sent me, so I send you." When he had said this, he breathed on them and said to them, "Receive the Holy Spirit. If you forgive the sins of any, they are forgiven them; if you retain the sins of any, they are retained."
>
> *John 20:21–23; cf. Genesis 2:7*

Despite the intimacy of the occasion, John appears to be implying that Jesus' action parallels the act of God in the first creation of man. For John, Jesus' gift of the Holy Spirit marks the beginning of a new act of creation. While Luke and John disagree on the timing and on the circumstances, they are nevertheless agreed that the Holy Spirit is given by or through Jesus to his faithful followers, and that this gift is made possible by Jesus' resurrection and exaltation. Also, that it is associated with the forgiveness of sins and with ongoing mission.

Resurrection and atonement

Belief in Jesus' heavenly exaltation spoke primarily about the past and present status of Jesus, whilst belief in his resurrection had forward-looking or eschatological implications from the outset. Resurrection faith also addressed the immediate psychological needs of Jesus' followers. By confirming the rightness of his teaching and actions, it enabled his followers to understand that his ministry, death, and heavenly exaltation were all part of God's overarching, saving purpose. What these convictions did not, however, explain was why God had allowed Jesus to die in the first place. Even though Jesus himself may have made no explicit claim to the title of Messiah, he was probably believed to be an anointed or messianic figure, and it was this that brought about his death. At that time the idea of a suffering messiah was unprecedented. It appears nowhere else in Judaism until well into the second century CE. The question that had to be addressed by Jesus' followers was, what divine purpose could possibly have been served by the death and resurrection of Jesus that could not have been served equally well by his continuing to live until the hoped-for kingdom of God came in power? Also, how could Jesus be the Messiah (by definition a victorious figure) if he died by crucifixion? The Law of Moses is explicit. Anyone executed "on a tree" must be accursed by God:

> When someone ... is executed, and you hang him on a tree, his corpse must not remain all night upon the tree; you shall bury him that same day, for anyone hung on a tree is under God's curse.
> *Deuteronomy 21:22-23; cf. Galatians 3:13*

Theories of the atonement address these questions. They emerge alongside exaltation and resurrection faith as an attempt by Jesus' followers to understand how his death could have had positive value, and how and why it was "in accordance with the scriptures" and "for our sins" (1 Corinthians 15:3). Resurrection faith and theories of the atonement both interpret the death of Jesus, but whereas resurrection looks forwards to the coming new age, theories of atonement—at least in the first instance—look backwards, seeking to discover meaning in what has already happened.

Atonement belief, like belief in the resurrection and heavenly exaltation of Jesus, had its roots in the life and teaching of Jesus during his lifetime. Jesus was widely regarded as a prophetic figure. To his own followers, he was a prophet and more than a prophet. He was God's final eschatological envoy to his people (1 Thessalonians 2:15–16; Luke 11:49–51; cf. Matthew 23:34–36). The belief that Jesus was God's final envoy was consonant with his urgent teaching concerning the coming kingdom of God. His absolute commitment to God's cause also propelled him into the category of exceptionally righteous men. Likewise, his death at the hands of wicked men whilst engaged in God's work elevated him to the ranks of the martyrs. The initial understanding of his disciples was probably that Jesus had died as an unjustly persecuted righteous man or as a martyr persecuted for his religious faith—or both. These very early understandings lie at the heart of belief in Jesus' resurrection and vindication by exaltation.

The belief that Jesus died as an unjustly persecuted righteous man or martyr, and the further understanding that his death was "for us", probably reflect the conviction in some Jewish circles contemporary with Jesus that the death of martyrs was beneficial for the people as a whole. In the story of the seven brothers in 2 Maccabees, the last brother to be killed by Antiochus says:

> "I, like my brothers, give up body and life for the laws of our ancestors . . . and through me and my brothers to bring to an end the wrath of the Almighty that has justly fallen on our whole nation."
>
> *2 Maccabees 7:37–38*

In the later 4 Maccabees, the priestly martyr Eleazar prays as he dies:

> "Be merciful to your people, and let our punishment suffice for them. Make my blood their [i.e. the people's] purification, and take my life in exchange for theirs."
>
> *4 Maccabees 6:28–29*

The belief that there was benefit for others in the death of martyrs probably lies behind the earliest perceptions of necessity and advantage in the death of Jesus. His death was not a tragedy, as his followers must initially have supposed. It was not even a setback needing to be overcome. There was purpose and positive value in what had happened to Jesus; indeed, the death of Jesus was part of the divine intention. Hence the formation and retrojection into the tradition at an early stage of sayings that represent Jesus emphasizing the necessity of the suffering and death of the Son of Man. It was something that had been intended and had to happen:

> Then he began to teach them that the Son of Man must undergo great suffering, and be rejected by the elders, the chief priests, and the scribes, and be killed, and after three days rise again. He said all this quite openly.
>
> *Mark 8:31–32*

Although possibly not part of the very earliest faith formula, the understanding that Christ died "for us" forms part of the pre-Pauline resurrection and appearances tradition in 1 Corinthians:

> For I handed on to you as of first importance what I in turn had received: that Christ died for our sins . . .
>
> *1 Corinthians 15:3*

It has already been suggested that the 1 Corinthians 15 tradition could have been part of the initial instruction given to Paul in Damascus immediately following his visionary encounter with the risen Jesus. If Paul received the tradition that Christ died "for us" at the same time, it could have originated within two or three years of Jesus' death, if not earlier.

A further indication that the understanding that Christ's death was "for us" may be very early is the phrase, "This is my body [broken] for you" in Paul's account of the last supper of Jesus with his followers. Paul declares that he received the tradition directly from the Lord:

> For I [Paul] received from the Lord what I also handed on to you, that the Lord Jesus on the night when he was betrayed took a loaf of bread, and when he had given thanks, he broke it and said, "This is my body that is for you. Do this in remembrance of me." In the same way he took the cup also, after supper, saying, "This cup is the new covenant in my blood. Do this, as often as you drink it, in remembrance of me."
>
> *1 Corinthians 11:23–25*

The words attributed to Jesus and the description of the event may not be historically accurate, but the phrase, "I received from the Lord what I also passed on to you" is significant. Paul may mean only that he was passing on a received liturgical tradition, but it seems more likely that he believed he was communicating knowledge of the actual actions and sayings of Jesus. His statement that he received the tradition "from the Lord" seems to imply that the tradition was authenticated by his own defining encounter with the risen Jesus Christ. This also suggests that the understanding of Jesus' death being "for us" is very early indeed. It could even have its origins in an authentic saying of Jesus himself.

The so-called "words of institution" reappear, somewhat later, in the Gospels. Mark's version, which is probably based on an earlier tradition, differs slightly from that given by Paul:

> ... he [Jesus] took a loaf of bread, and after blessing it he broke it, gave it to them, and said, "Take; this is my body." Then he took a cup, and after giving thanks he gave it to them, and all of them drank from it. He said to them, "This is my blood of the [new] covenant, which is poured out for many."
>
> *Mark 14:22–24*

Despite these differences, the Pauline and the Marcan versions of the words of institution both clearly imply that the death of Jesus and the shedding of his blood constituted a cultic sacrifice. In the case of the Pauline tradition, the focus is on the new covenant. The obvious allusion is to the new covenant promised by God in Jeremiah 31:31. In the case of the Marcan tradition, the implication is that the death of Jesus is akin to—or even a renewal of—the covenant sacrifice performed by Moses and the people of Israel at the time of the giving of the Law:

> Moses took the blood and dashed it on the people, and said, "See the blood of the covenant that the LORD has made with you . . ."
>
> *Exodus 24:8*

There may be a further echo of the pre-Pauline eucharistic tradition, also expressed in sacrificial imagery, in 1 Corinthians. Paul rebukes boastfulness and likens its social effect within the community of believers to that of yeast contaminating what should be unleavened bread. He says:

> For our paschal lamb, Christ, has been sacrificed. Therefore, let us celebrate the festival, not with the old yeast, the yeast of malice and evil, but with the unleavened bread of sincerity and truth.
>
> *1 Corinthians 5:7-8*

Alongside the basic statement that Christ "died for us", the New Testament documents contain a number of other, more complex statements of purpose that reflect the sacrificial cult of the Jerusalem temple. They all revolve around the idea of the death of Jesus being the final, atoning sacrifice serving God's eschatological purpose. For example, in a passage widely held to be part of an earlier pre-Pauline, Jewish-Christian liturgical tradition, Paul speaks of Christ Jesus:

> . . . whom God put forward as a sacrifice of atonement by his blood, effective through faith. He did this to show his righteousness, because in his divine forbearance he had passed over the sins previously committed . . .
>
> *Romans 3:25*

Different aspects of the same idea are developed further in later New Testament writings.[81]

The interpretation of the death of Jesus as an atoning sacrifice probably originated within the parallel Aramaic-speaking and Greek-speaking communities of Jesus' Jewish followers in Jerusalem. We know that both communities remained closely associated with the temple and its cult for some years after the death of Jesus. In this context the understanding that Jesus died as an atoning sacrifice would have much more resonance than the basic assertion that he died "for our sins".

It was perhaps in the same milieu that the concept of the "surrender" or "handing over" of Jesus originated. "Surrender" is always implicit in the idea of an atoning sacrifice as something offered to God. Sometimes it is explicit. It may be God who surrenders Jesus, or it may be Jesus who surrenders himself. Examples of the belief that it was God who surrendered Jesus include:

> He[God] who did not withhold his own Son, but gave him up for all of us . . .
>
> *Romans 8:32; cf. Genesis 22:12*

> [God] who raised Jesus our Lord from the dead, who was handed over to death for our trespasses and was raised for our justification.
>
> *Romans 4:24–25*

The second of these statements is particularly important because it connects atonement with resurrection and justification. The somewhat formulaic structure of the text suggests that it is reflecting pre-Pauline tradition, and perhaps also the well-known passage in which Isaiah speaks of the self-offering of an anonymous servant of God who bears the sins of the people and pours himself out in death:

> Surely he has borne our infirmities . . .
> All we like sheep have gone astray . . .
> and the Lord has laid on him
> the iniquity of us all.
> . . . The righteous one, my servant, shall make many righteous,
> and he shall bear their iniquities.
> Therefore I will allot him a portion with the great,
> and he shall divide the spoil with the strong;
> because he poured out himself to death,
> and was numbered with the transgressors . . .
>
> *Isaiah 53:4,6,11–12*

Isaiah connects the idea of the self-giving of God's righteous servant with the idea of vindication by exaltation. In the past, too much may have been asserted on the basis of Isaiah 52—53 taken in isolation. In addition to Isaiah 52—53, a number of other passages (for example, Psalms 22, 31, 34, 41, 69, and 109, and Zechariah 9:11) may have contributed to the understanding that Christ's death was "for us" and "in accordance with the scriptures". Nevertheless, there are ten possible verbal echoes and thirty-two possible allusions to Isaiah 52:13—53:12 in the New Testament, so we can still say with reasonable confidence that this particular passage exerted a significant influence on the proclamation of Jesus' earliest post-Easter followers. For example, the influence of Isaiah 52:13—53:12 can perhaps be seen in Mark 10:45, one of several passages in which it is said that Jesus voluntarily surrendered himself to death:

> "For the Son of Man came not to be served but to serve, and to give his life as a ransom for many."
>
> *Mark 10:45*

> And the life I now live in the flesh I live by faith in the Son of God, who loved me and gave himself for me.
>
> *Galatians 2:20*

> Therefore be imitators of God, as beloved children, and live in love, as Christ loved us and gave himself up for us, a fragrant offering and sacrifice to God.
>
> *Ephesians 5:1–2*

We also need to consider the possibility that the perception of significance in the suffering and death of Jesus may go back behind the scriptural exegesis of the post-Easter Aramaic-speaking and Greek-speaking communities to Jesus himself during his lifetime. Whether Jesus anticipated personal suffering and death in the detailed way suggested by the three major passion predictions in Mark (8:31; 9:31 and 10:33–34), we do not know. But if Jesus regarded himself as God's final prophetic envoy to his people Israel, and if he was implicitly defining himself as God's righteous servant and the point of presence of the coming new Israel and kingdom of God, he must have anticipated opposition. Over and above this, he may also have anticipated personal suffering, particularly towards the end of his life when he was making his final journey up to Jerusalem. That Jesus spoke of the possibility of his suffering and that he also affirmed his complete confidence in eventual vindication are reasonable assumptions. After his death, general statements giving expression to this understanding were probably "sharpened up" in the traditioning process, eventually becoming the suspiciously over-precise passion predictions we find in the Gospels. Although now overlaid with secondary details derived from the eucharistic practices of the post-Easter community, the early Pauline and Marcan traditions of the Last Supper probably contain a core of genuine historical remembrance. Towards the end of his life, Jesus may even have anticipated martyrdom, regarding it as a possibly necessary part of the eschatological event through which God's saving purpose for his people was being brought about. This understanding, recollected by his followers, would explain the post-Easter emergence of the belief that Jesus gave himself—or God gave Jesus—"for us".

Conclusion

By the fifties, when Paul was writing his letters, basic belief in Jesus' resurrection and heavenly exaltation had expanded to incorporate a number of important additional understandings, many of which were latent in the initial post-Easter beliefs concerning Jesus' exaltation and resurrection, or even further back, in the life and ministry of Jesus himself.

One of the most marked features associated with these unfolding understandings is the use they make of the Hebrew scriptures in their Greek translation. Although basic belief in Jesus' resurrection and exaltation appears to have been arrived at independently of the scriptures, by the 50s, Jesus' followers had evidently for some time past been searching the scriptures for passages and texts that might throw light on what had happened, either because they could be identified as prophecies literally fulfilled in the events of Jesus' death and resurrection, or because they supported emergent understandings and interpretations of events.

Consequently, at a very early stage resurrection belief came to signify much more than the simple transfer of Jesus from life on earth to life in heaven. It was believed that the resurrection of Jesus signalled nothing less than the dawn of the promised new age of salvation for God's people, the coming kingdom or rule of God. At a very early stage the risen and exalted Jesus was identified as the heavenly being spoken of in the book of Daniel—the being who would come to God to be awarded everlasting dominion, glory, and kingship over all peoples and nations. If the risen and highly exalted Jesus had been awarded these awesome delegated divine powers, they must surely be exercised. Jesus would therefore shortly be revealed, in awesome power and majesty (the *parousia*). He would descend from heaven, keeping believers safe, while the powers of this world were being overthrown and God's work of salvation was being brought to completion.

In Jewish expectation, one of the hallmarks of the coming new age was the hoped-for outpouring of the creative and re-creating Spirit of God. Jesus' followers believed that this had happened at the time of the resurrection and/or was happening now. In pouring out his Holy Spirit through Jesus, God was engaging in what was, in effect, a new act of creation. Resurrection faith also enabled Jesus' followers to perceive purpose and necessity in the completed life and death of Jesus. They came to understand that the death of Jesus had not been a mistake requiring rectification, nor was it an accident of history. On the contrary, Jesus had deliberately surrendered himself (or God had surrendered him) in a sacrificial act of atonement. His death, as much as his life, was a necessary part of God's overarching purpose. It was "for us".

In the previous chapter, we reviewed the earliest evidence for the emergence of resurrection and exaltation faith. In this chapter, we have observed further key understandings unfolding out of the initial cognition. Now, at last, we come to the four Gospels. Compared to the documents and traditions we have been considering, the testimony of the Gospels is late, secondary and—in many respects—riddled with contradictions. Nevertheless, this does not mean that the Gospels are without value as historical sources. What it does mean is that the testimony of the Gospels concerning the resurrection of Jesus, like all other historical testimony, must be systematically assessed and interpreted, taking due account of the perspectives and intentions of the individual authors. This is the objective of the next chapter.

CHAPTER 9

Resurrection Belief: Later Narratives and Stories

Each of the four canonical Gospels contains an extended narrative account of the death and burial of Jesus, followed by a description of a visit on the first day of the week by women—or a woman—to the place where the body of Jesus had been buried. Three of the four Gospels also contain accounts of appearances of the risen Jesus to individuals or groups. The exception is the Gospel of Mark, which contains no account of any appearances of the risen Jesus.

Mark is the earliest of the four Gospels. It was written at some time between the years 66 and 75 CE. The three other Gospels were written somewhat later, probably towards the end of the first century. At one time, all four Gospels were believed to be historical accounts of the life of Jesus, written either by eyewitnesses, or by writers with access to reliable, first-hand testimony, but it is now agreed that none of the Gospel authors witnessed the events they describe. Moreover, many of the traditions in the Gospels have undergone a process of development prior to their incorporation into the final, written texts. This means that the Gospels cannot be read either as straightforward history, or as biography in the modern sense. As a literary genre, they are regarded as falling somewhere within the broad spectrum of Graeco-Roman biography, but with significant differences. Although each Gospel reflects the particular circumstances and individual concerns of its own author, all the authors share the conviction that the "Jesus-event"—that is, the life, death, and resurrection of Jesus of Nazareth—constitutes God's saving action.

The purpose of the Gospels is much debated. The simplest explanation is that, by the last third of the first century CE, the age of eyewitnesses and of clear remembrance of Jesus and his teaching was beginning to draw to a close. It was therefore essential for basic information about Jesus to be preserved in writing. The authors were not just writing to tell their readers what happened in the past, nor were they intending to present Jesus as merely a moral exemplar. Each author, in his own way, was seeking to direct his readers' attention to what the author believed to be the present significance of the events that he was describing. This means that, in addition to communicating information about Jesus, the Gospel authors are revealing something about themselves and about their own beliefs. They do this by their selection of material, by the way in which they amend material having a common origin, and especially through their individual theological and christological emphases. The testimony of the Gospels merits particularly careful evaluation because it has both a historical and a theological dimension.

The empty tomb narratives in the Gospels

According to all four Gospels, the body of Jesus was handed over by Pilate to Joseph of Arimathea, who buried it in a rock tomb sealed by a large stone. Unless this tradition is a Marcan composition, it must have been circulating prior to 65–70 CE. The only earlier evidence we have concerning the fate of Jesus' body after his death is the much earlier pre-Pauline tradition in 1 Corinthians 15:4, which simply says that "he [Jesus] was buried and [that he] was raised on the third day". Paul's puzzling failure to make any reference to the empty tomb tradition has already been discussed. The Pauline and pre-Pauline testimony makes no reference to an empty tomb or to a visit by the women. Neither does it say anything about an abortive search for the dead body of Jesus.

There is one other reference to the burial of Jesus that is not in the Gospels. This also lacks any reference to Joseph of Arimathea and makes no mention of the empty tomb tradition or the role of the women. It takes the form of a brief, compressed statement set in the context of a sermon represented by the author as having been preached by Paul in Antioch:

> ...they [the residents of Jerusalem and their leaders] took him [Jesus] down from the tree and laid him in a tomb.
>
> *Acts 13:29*

This so-called "rival burial tradition" can be disposed of quickly. Given that the authors of Luke and this section of Acts are generally accepted to be the same person, the very brief summary statement about the burial in Acts must have been regarded by its author as being compatible with the fuller Joseph of Arimathea burial tradition he had already incorporated into his own Gospel. Even if this were not so, the evidence is insufficient to indicate the existence of two competing traditions. The most that we can perhaps say about Acts 13:29 is that it tends to confirm that the burial tradition may have been fluid for some years following Jesus' death.

The empty-tomb tradition first appears in Mark 16:1–8. It includes the burial of the body of Jesus by Joseph of Arimathea in a rock tomb, the subsequent visit by the women early on the morning of the day following the Passover, and their discovery that the tomb was empty. The empty-tomb tradition is central to the resurrection narratives in all four Gospels, but it is only very loosely connected with the appearance stories. The problem with the empty tomb narratives in the Gospels is that, although at first sight they may appear to be broadly in agreement, closer examination reveals major inconsistencies which resist attempts at harmonization. A comprehensive discussion of these problems is beyond the scope of this book, but the principal issues are highlighted in the following paragraphs.

First, there is a basic framework carried over from the Gospel of Mark into Matthew and Luke. In the Gospel of John, the framework is somewhat different. Nevertheless, all four Gospels agree on the day (the first day of the week; that is, the day after the Sabbath), the time (early morning), and that in the first instance only women (or one woman) went to the tomb. The origins of the "third-day" tradition and its possible or probable disconnection from the empty tomb tradition were discussed in Chapter 7. Luke and Matthew can be observed trying in different ways to connect the two traditions by introducing references to "the third day" into empty-tomb narratives (Luke 24:21, cf. 24:1; and Matthew 27:64, cf. 28:1). On the question of the names of the women who visited the tomb, there is disagreement. All four Gospels name Mary Magdalene, but they vary as to the others. John says that Mary Magdalene went to the tomb alone, but then he implies that other women were present by making Mary say to the disciples, "We [sic] do not know where they have laid him." There are minor inconsistencies in the reasons given for the women's visit to the tomb. According to Mark, they intended to anoint the body of Jesus with spices. Luke follows Mark, adding a few extra details. Matthew says only that the women went to see the grave. John says that Mary Magdalene went to the grave alone, but not why she went.

More significant divergences begin to emerge when the women arrive at the tomb. In Mark, the door-stone of the tomb has already been rolled away before the women arrive. Inside the tomb, the women see a young man in a white robe. They are amazed. The young man, apparently an angelic being, proclaims the resurrection:

> "Do not be alarmed; you are looking for Jesus of Nazareth, who was crucified. He has been raised; he is not here. Look, there is the place they laid him. But go, tell his disciples and Peter that he is going ahead of you to Galilee; there you will see him, just as he told you." So they went out and fled from the tomb, for terror and amazement had seized them; and they said nothing to anyone, for they were afraid.
>
> Mark 16:6–8

According to Matthew, the tomb was still closed when the women arrived. They saw an angel of the Lord descending from heaven. The angel's appearance was like lightning, and he was clothed in raiment that was as white as snow. The angel rolled away the door-stone while the women looked on. Matthew interweaves with this narrative a story about the chief priests' setting a guard on the tomb. He describes the soldiers' terror and amazement when the angel descended from heaven and rolled back the stone. The story of the guards is clearly secondary apologetic. Matthew is seeking either to pre-empt or to reply to an allegation that Jesus' disciples must have stolen his body in order, falsely, to proclaim his resurrection. The body could not have been stolen, says Matthew, because the tomb was guarded.

Luke's account also differs from that of Mark. In Luke, the door-stone has already been rolled away, but there is no young man or angel waiting inside the tomb. Instead, two angels in dazzling clothes suddenly appear and stand beside the women. In John, as in Mark and Luke, the stone has already been rolled away before anyone arrives. The first visitor to the tomb is Mary Magdalene. She does not enter but runs to fetch Peter and "the disciple whom Jesus loved". The two men enter the tomb and discover that the body of Jesus has gone. Finally, when they have gone back to their homes, Mary Magdalene herself peers into the empty tomb. She sees two angels seated (not standing) in the place where the body of Jesus had been deposited.

From the moment of the angelic announcement of the resurrection onwards, the four narratives begin to diverge in a more serious way. Mark says that the angel told the women that the risen Jesus was going ahead of them into Galilee and that they would see him there; the women then fled in terror and amazement, saying nothing to anyone (Mark 16:7–8). At this point, Matthew follows Mark. Mark's statement about the women's fear and their subsequent silence creates difficulties for Matthew and Luke and—if he knew Mark's Gospel—for John as well. Matthew's problem is that he wants to introduce a story about an appearance of Jesus to the women returning from the tomb. He therefore omits the statement that the women said nothing to anyone and asserts the exact opposite; that is, that Mary Magdalene and the other Mary ran to tell the disciples. Matthew also modifies the women's emotional reaction. Whereas Mark had said that they were trembling and amazed, Matthew says that although they were fearful, they were also filled with joy (Matthew 28:8). Luke and John make no reference to the women remaining silent; indeed, they also assert the opposite. Luke says that the women "told all this to the eleven and to all the rest" (Luke 24:9). John simply says that "she [Mary Magdalene] went to Simon Peter and the other disciple, the one whom Jesus loved" (John 20:2).

Luke has another problem, because he intends to represent all the resurrection appearances of Jesus as having taken place in or around Jerusalem, despite the fact that Mark's angel had predicted that the disciples would see Jesus in Galilee (Mark 16:7, cf. Mark 14:28). Luke solves his problem by omitting Mark 14:28 and altering the angelic message. He makes the two angels say to the women:

> "He is not here, but has risen. Remember how he told you, while he was still in Galilee, that the Son of Man must be handed over to sinners, and be crucified, and on the third day rise again."
>
> *Luke 24:5–6; cf. 9:22*

This is a deliberate alteration. It involves not just the shading or embellishment of the Marcan text but the complete replacement of one saying of Jesus by another (Luke 9:22). In Mark and in Matthew, the angelic message is that the disciples may expect to see Jesus in Galilee in the future. In Luke, on the other hand, the disciples are reminded of something that Jesus said in Galilee in the past. In representing all the appearances as having taken place in Jerusalem, Luke directly and deliberately contradicts Mark.

The historicity of the empty-tomb tradition

Given the discrepancies and contradictions in the empty-tomb tradition as presented in the Gospels, given the freedom with which Matthew and Luke modify Mark, and given the fact that the empty-tomb tradition receives no mention in Paul's writings, we have to ask whether the burial and empty-tomb traditions are historical or whether they are secondary constructions emerging into the light of day at some later stage, possibly after Paul was writing in the fifties but before the writing of the first Gospel.

Paul's lack of reference to the empty-tomb tradition has already been discussed in connection with the undoubtedly very early but probably exegesis-based tradition that resurrection took place "on the third day", and his beliefs concerning the relationship between the believer's transformed "spiritual" resurrection body and the "flesh". Various possible explanations were suggested. The simplest is that the empty-tomb tradition was unknown to Paul because the tradition is not historical and had not yet been formulated. This would explain his silence and also the lack of any reference to women in the very early 1 Corinthians 15 resurrection-appearances tradition. It is also compatible with the apparent fluidity in Paul's thinking concerning the relationship between the body that is buried and the transformed resurrection body.

The problem can be simplified by setting aside the question of the apparent ambiguities in Paul's thinking concerning the nature of the resurrection body. These ambiguities, or apparent ambiguities, reflect Paul's unusual threefold anthropology and his choice of metaphors, especially the variably and sometimes inconsistently applied metaphor of transformation. The circle can quite reasonably be squared by assuming that Paul believed that when the dead were raised—both in general and specifically in the case of Jesus—the "flesh" and the "psychic body" would be together transformed into a new "spiritual body". In other words, it is only *untransformed* flesh and blood that cannot inherit the kingdom of God.

The problem can be further simplified by observing that there is an important historical fixed point. As already noted, some three years after his conversion Paul stayed with Peter in Jerusalem for two weeks. While he was in Jerusalem with Peter, Paul also met James, the brother of Jesus (Galatians 1:18–19). It is inconceivable that Peter and James did not tell Paul about the death of Jesus and what happened afterwards. If the empty-tomb tradition is more or less historical in the form that appears in the Gospels, Paul would have known and would almost certainly have referred to it, even if only indirectly, when writing about the resurrection. On the other hand, if the empty-tomb tradition is late and the core of historicity is very slight or even non-existent, there would have been nothing for Paul to refer to. He would have been silent because he and Peter and James were unaware of any tradition. They knew nothing because there was nothing to know.

Paul's lack of reference to the empty-tomb tradition of the Gospels should not be taken to mean that he—or Peter and James—supposed Jesus' corpse still to be somewhere in Jerusalem, buried or disposed of by some other natural means. There is no evidence that Jesus' followers ever believed the resurrection of Jesus not to have included his physical body. As we saw in the previous chapter, basic belief in Jesus' resurrection quickly expanded to include the further understanding that he was "the first fruits of the harvest of the dead", and that his resurrection signified the inauguration of the hoped-for new age. In Second Temple Judaism the use of the term "resurrection" may or may not always and necessarily have implied belief in the restoration of the corpse to some form of physical being, but in this instance the question is irrelevant. When Paul's ambiguities are satisfactorily explained, the evidence is that the earliest followers of Jesus took it for granted that the act of resurrection included Jesus' body. For all practical purposes, the emptiness of the tomb—or rather, the inability ever to find or recover the body of Jesus—and the affirmation of his resurrection march together.

These considerations tend to support the thesis that there may only be a minimal core of historicity in the empty-tomb tradition. As to what constitutes that minimal core, we can only speculate. Jesus died by crucifixion. His corpse could have been cast into a communal pit, the normal way of disposing of the bodies of executed criminals. That some of his followers, including women, later sought to retrieve his body, either for reverential reasons or to complete the burial process with proper ceremony, is a reasonable assumption. An abortive search for the corpse of Jesus could be the nucleus or core of historicity around which the empty-tomb tradition(s) subsequently crystallized.

Finally, we need to consider the suggestion that it was the discovery of the empty tomb that triggered the first visions of the risen Jesus Christ, and thereby indirectly gave rise to belief in his resurrection. If anything, the evidence points in the opposite direction. A failure to locate a corpse which had been buried some days previously is unlikely in itself to have given rise to belief in resurrection, especially resurrection signifying the dawning of a new age. Other, more prosaic explanations would have suggested themselves. If Jesus was buried in an expensive tomb, the obvious explanation for the absence of his body would be theft; the tombs of the rich were always prime targets for robbers. If Jesus' body was cast into a communal pit, scavenging animals would probably have made short work of it.

More importantly, there is no evidence prior to the Gospels that the empty-tomb tradition in any way contributed to the emergence of belief in the resurrection of Jesus. And nowhere in the Gospels is the discovery of the empty tomb represented as having generated belief in Jesus' resurrection. Only Matthew, deliberately contradicting Mark, represents the women at the empty tomb reacting with something approaching faith. Even then, their response is occasioned by the angel's announcement of the resurrection, not by the emptiness of the tomb. In the earliest tradition, the resurrection is nowhere deduced from the empty tomb. If anything, it is the empty tomb that is asserted on the basis of experience of encounter with the risen Christ.

The appearance stories of the Gospels

The Gospels contain nine stories of appearances of the risen Jesus to his followers. These stories are divided between the Gospels of Matthew, Luke, and John, the shorter (original) ending of Mark's Gospel having no appearance stories. Matthew has two, one set in Jerusalem and the other in Galilee. John has three stories of appearances in Jerusalem and one of an appearance in Galilee. Luke contains three appearance stories, all set in or near to Jerusalem. There is only one direct narrative account of an appearance to an individual (Mary Magdalene), although there is a brief, hearsay report of an individual appearance to Simon (Luke 24:34). All the other appearances are to smaller or larger groups of followers.

Even on the basis of a cursory examination, it is apparent that these stories are strikingly at variance with the appearances of the risen Jesus referred to in the pre-Pauline tradition. They are quite unlike Paul's account of his own encounter with the risen Jesus Christ. Also, the appearance stories in the Gospels frequently contradict one another, and not only on matters of detail. Individual Gospels, and sometimes even individual stories, lack internal consistency and coherence. A comprehensive discussion of these inconsistencies is beyond the scope of this book. What follows is an overview highlighting the key issues, followed by an assessment of the significance of the stories for charting the emergence of resurrection faith.

First of all, there is a general problem concerning identity of the witnesses to the resurrection. In all four Gospels, it is women who discover the empty tomb. In Matthew and John, the first appearances of the risen Jesus are to women. Yet, as we have seen, in the earlier Pauline and pre-Pauline tradition there is no mention of any involvement of women in connection with either the burial or the resurrection of Jesus. Second, there are specific problems arising in connection with named witnesses. None of the Gospels has a narrative account of an individual appearance of Jesus to Peter, despite the fact that an appearance to Peter takes pride of place in the pre-Pauline tradition. All we have is the hearsay reference in Luke 24:34 to a report of an appearance to Simon (Peter).

The Gospels are also completely silent on the matter of an appearance of Jesus to his brother James. Given that James was destined later to become the leader of the Jerusalem church, this omission is particularly surprising. One suggestion is that James has been deliberately "airbrushed" out of the story, perhaps because Mark and his community were contesting the authority of the Jerusalem mother-church. Mark's Gospel is elsewhere notably negative towards the family of Jesus. In addition to the lack of any account of an appearance to Peter, and the absence of any reference to James, the Gospels also fail to mention the admittedly difficult-to-envisage appearance of Jesus to five hundred disciples at the same time. Another difference, apparently minor but nevertheless significant, is that the Gospels of Matthew and Luke both speak of Jesus appearing to "the eleven". The much earlier pre-Pauline tradition, on the other hand, speaks of appearances to "the twelve" and to "all the apostles". John speaks only of appearances to "the disciples". This suggests that the story of Judas's betrayal of Jesus may not have been part of the earliest tradition.

Another striking difference between the Gospels and the earliest pre-Pauline tradition is that Matthew, Luke, and John all have narrative descriptions of appearances of Jesus in the form of stories, whereas the earliest tradition simply asserts the resurrection and then lists the appearances to individuals and groups. The nearest we have to a narrative prior to the Gospels is the vestigial information given by Paul in his letter to the Galatians and in his second letter to the Corinthians.

Although certainly not part of the early tradition, there are two other narrative descriptions of appearances of the risen Christ that should be mentioned. One is the description, in the first chapter of Revelation, of a visionary "seeing" of the risen and gloriously transformed heavenly Jesus Christ. The other is a narrative description of the resurrection in the fragmentary, second-century, non-canonical Gospel of Peter. Despite its fanciful description of a gigantic Jesus emerging from the tomb, supported by angels and followed by a talking cross, the Gospel of Peter may possibly contain much earlier traditions. For example, it has been suggested that an early form of the Gospel of Peter could have influenced the author of Matthew. (It has to be said that this suggestion has not gained general acceptance.) Given its extraordinary embellishments and its many departures from the canonical texts, no further account will be taken of the Gospel of Peter.

Despite repeated attempts over many years, it has not proved possible to harmonize the empty tomb narratives and the appearance stories of the Gospels with the much earlier 1 Corinthians 15 pre-Pauline appearances tradition. We therefore focus on what the Gospel stories have in common. Some preliminary simplification will assist: we exclude from consideration Luke's passing reference to a reported appearance of Jesus to Simon Peter. Although this may be an indirect indication that Luke was aware of the 1 Corinthians 15 tradition, it is definitely not a narrative. We also set aside Matthew's very brief reference to an appearance of Jesus to the women returning from the tomb. Although this story may be connected in some distant way with the Mary Magdalene tradition in John, the words attributed to Jesus duplicate those attributed to the angel three verses earlier. When these are removed, the story has virtually no narrative content. It was probably composed by Matthew to replace Mark 16:8 (the silence of the women) and to make a bridge between Matthew's version of the empty tomb story and his own subsequent Galilee mountain appearance story. John's two "Doubting Thomas" stories are to be treated as two components of one entity. The narratives requiring analysis are therefore: one story of an appearance to an individual (Mary Magdalene in John 20); two stories of appearances to small groups (the Luke 24 "Emmaus road" story and the John 21 "Galilean lakeside" story); three stories of appearances to a larger group, comprising the inner core of Jesus' followers designated either "the eleven" (in Matthew and Luke) or "the disciples" (in John).

Examination shows there to be a number of motifs common to all five group-appearance stories. First, the risen Jesus is not presented as a glorious heavenly being. He is nothing like the figure depicted in the pre-Pauline christological hymns and fragments. Nor is he anything like the radiantly glorious being encountered by Paul and (by implication) those listed in the 1 Corinthians 15 resurrection-appearances tradition. On the contrary, the appearance stories of the Gospels represent Jesus as having appeared in human form. In these stories, he walks and talks with his followers. In two instances it is implied that he might be touched. It is Luke, not John or Mark, who most nearly understands the resurrection of Jesus in a physical or quasi-physical way when he describes the risen Jesus eating a piece of broiled fish (Luke 24:42–43; cf. Acts 10:41).

Second, in every story Jesus comes unbidden. His presence is not solicited or prayed for. Suddenly and unexpectedly, he is with his disciples; then, just as suddenly, he is gone.

Third, in each story recognition is an issue. All the stories say that some of Jesus' closest followers doubted or disbelieved that they were seeing him, or that he had been raised from the dead. In his account of an appearance of Jesus to "the eleven", Matthew says that some believed that they were seeing Jesus, but others doubted. Luke depicts Jesus suddenly appearing and standing among "the eleven" and their companions in Jerusalem. Their initial reaction is to think they are seeing a ghost. When Jesus rebukes them for their doubts they are terrified, joyful, and yet also disbelieving. In the story of the appearance of Jesus on the road to Emmaus, Jesus is not recognized until he breaks bread with his former disciples. In the John 20 group-appearance story, Jesus comes in the evening and stands among his disciples. Thomas is absent, and when told what has happened, he declares that he will not believe unless he sees the mark of the nails on Jesus' hands and places his own hand in Jesus' wounded side.

Fourth, despite his human form, in none of the stories is Jesus represented as a dead body resuscitated or restored to normal human life and functioning. Confusion sometimes arises because the Gospels do contain two stories of just such resuscitations. One is the story of the raising of the undoubtedly dead Lazarus (John 11:17–44). The other is the story of the restoration or raising of Jairus's possibly dead daughter (Mark 5:35–43 and parallels). The implication in both these stories is that Lazarus and Jairus's daughter have been restored to human normality, and that in the fullness of time they will have to die natural deaths all over again.

The idea of Jesus being raised from the dead as a normally functioning physical human being—that is, rising "in the flesh"—is foreign to early Christian thinking. It does not appear until the mid-second century, first in Justin Martyr and then, slightly later, in Irenaeus. Of the three Gospel writers with appearance stories, it is Luke who most nearly understands the resurrection of Jesus in a physical or quasi-physical way. But even Luke stops well short of suggesting that the risen Jesus Christ is simply the corpse of Jesus brought back to normal human life. Luke indicates that he believes the risen Jesus to have been changed or transformed, albeit in some unspecified way, by placing emphasis on the way in which the risen Jesus could suddenly vanish (Luke 24:31) and, equally suddenly, reappear (Luke 24:36).

Finally, in each of the stories Jesus gives significant guidance or instructions to his disciples. This takes various forms: in Matthew, Jesus commissions "the eleven" to go and make disciples of all nations; in Luke, Jesus teaches his disciples that everything that has happened, and everything that is going to happen, is in fulfilment of the scriptures. The disciples are now to be God's agents proclaiming repentance and forgiveness of sins to all nations. In the John 20 (Jerusalem) tradition, Jesus delivers his own divine commission to his disciples, saying, "As the Father has sent me, so I send you" (verse 21). In respect of their communication of significant content, the appearance stories are quite unlike bereavement apparitions. Bereavement apparitions are well-attested psychological phenomena. Typically, they involve unexpected transient apparitions or sightings of a deceased person, usually a "significant other". Bereavement apparitions rarely communicate any significant cognitive content.

The motifs that appear in the shorter group-appearance stories also appear in the three more extended narratives; that is, the John 21 freestanding Galilean lakeside story, the Luke 24 Emmaus road story, and the John 20 Mary Magdalene Jerusalem story.

In the freestanding John 21 narrative, the disciples are fishing unsuccessfully from a boat on the "Sea of Tiberias". They see Jesus on the shore but fail to recognize him. He gives them instructions, and when they obey these instructions they catch many fish. Then Peter recognizes Jesus. They come to land and discover that Jesus has prepared a meal. He takes bread and gives it to them, and likewise fish. Jesus then interrogates Peter, commissioning him for leadership and defining his (prospective) lifelong discipleship in terms of personal affection and devotion.

The second extended narrative is the Luke 24 story of the walk to Emmaus, a village near Jerusalem. Two disciples, one named and the other anonymous, are walking along the road. The risen Jesus joins them incognito and asks them why they are so dejected. They express surprise—has he not heard of the death of Jesus, the prophet in whom they and many others had placed so much hope? Without revealing his identity, Jesus then interprets to them "the things about himself in all the scriptures". Arriving at their destination, they invite him to enter and eat with them. Jesus takes bread, breaks it, and gives it to them. They recognize him, but immediately he vanishes from their sight. The key features are that Jesus appears unbidden and in human form. He is not recognized; he gives significant instruction; then he is recognized. Finally he disappears again.

Similar motifs appear in the John 20 Mary Magdalene individual appearance story. Like Luke's story of the walk to Emmaus, this narrative possibly originated as a freestanding unit of tradition. A rather clumsy introduction connects the Mary Magdalene story to the preceding story of the visit to the empty tomb. Peter and "the disciple whom Jesus loved" have visited and inspected the empty tomb, and then gone home. Mary has remained outside the tomb weeping. She looks in and sees two angels, but apparently does not recognize them as such. She tells them that the body of her Lord has been taken away, but she knows not where. She then turns and sees a man whom she supposes to be the gardener. She asks him where the body of Jesus is. Only when the supposed gardener speaks to her does she recognize him as Jesus. He says to her:

> "Do not hold on to me, because I have not yet ascended to the Father. But go to my brothers and say to them, 'I am ascending to my Father and your Father, to my God and your God.'"
>
> *John 20:17*

The story ends abruptly. Mary goes back to the disciples, announces that she has seen the Lord, and tells them what Jesus has said to her. The significance of Jesus' prohibition is much debated by commentators. Interpretations divide according to whether it is supposed that Mary had already taken hold of Jesus, or whether she had not yet actually made physical contact. It would be unwise to try to draw specific conclusions about the author's understanding of the nature of the corporeality of the risen Jesus from this story. As elsewhere in the Gospel of John, a specific encounter with Jesus is being used as a vehicle for communicating theological insights and understandings of general application. Nevertheless, in this freestanding Mary Magdalene story we find the same motifs that appear in the other appearance stories—an appearance in human form, an unsolicited and unexpected encounter, a recognition, and a specific command or commission.

John's Mary Magdalene story raises complicated redactional and historical issues. In the Marcan tradition, which is adopted with amendments by Matthew and Luke, Mary Magdalene is the one person who is always mentioned in the accounts of visits to the tomb. This suggests that the story of Mary Magdalene's visit to the tomb may have a historical basis. The Mary Magdalene story in John, and perhaps also Matthew's brief account of an appearance of Jesus to "Mary Magdalene and the other Mary" (Matthew 28:1–10), may both be reflections of an earlier, free-floating Mary Magdalene tradition which subsequently became merged with an originally separate tradition of a visit by a group of women to the tomb. Nevertheless, in its present form, the story of Jesus' appearance to Mary Magdalene has a distinctively Johannine character, and its substance reflects characteristically Johannine interests.

In three of the appearance stories we find the additional motif of Jesus being "worshipped" as if he were in some sense divine. Matthew says that when the women encountered Jesus on their way back from the empty tomb, "they took hold of his feet and worshipped him" (28:9). In Matthew's account of the appearance of Jesus to "the eleven" on a mountain in Galilee, it is said that "they worshipped him" (28:17). The same phrase is used by Matthew when writing about Jesus during his lifetime. When Jesus walks on water the amazed disciples declare him to be the Son of God; then, says Matthew, "they worshipped him" (14:33). In all three instances, Matthew is probably using the term "worship" to signify extreme reverence rather than the kind of worship due to the deity, but in John's "Doubting Thomas" story (John 20:24–29) something rather more serious seems to be implied. Thomas is invited to touch Jesus in order to verify his identity and reality; Thomas replies, "My Lord and my God!" This may be an intentional harking back to the beginning of the Gospel where (according to the best manuscripts) Jesus Christ, although definitely not God (*ho theos*) absolutely, is nevertheless "God the only Son". He is the one who has made God known (John 1:18; cf. John 1:1).

We may say that, despite their variety, the appearance stories of the Gospels exhibit a significant number of unifying motifs. In particular, there is the unsolicited coming of Jesus, there is his appearance incognito in human form, there is an encounter involving recognition, and there is the delivery of an instruction or a commission. There may also be reverence, as if Jesus were in some sense divine or a representative of God. Surprisingly, in this last respect we find that the testimony of the Gospel writers, Matthew and John, matches that of Pliny, the pagan Roman governor of Bithynia (now north-east Turkey). Pliny wrote to the emperor Trajan in about 112 CE seeking advice on how to handle the problem of Christians. He told Trajan that he had discovered by investigation, including torture, that Christians were meeting early before daylight on a certain day "to sing a hymn to Christ as if to a god" (*carmenque Christo quasi deo dicere*). This does not necessarily mean that the Bithynian Christians were equating Christ with God, but it does indicate that they revered the risen Christ in the way that one might revere a god.

The significance of the appearance stories

The appearance stories of the Gospels seem to be a specific family or genre of stories having many similarities with the angelomorphic transformation stories of the Hebrew scriptures. The assumption underlying the angelomorphic transformation stories is that angels may take on human form and visit earth incognito. They may also represent and speak on behalf of God; sometimes they may even speak as if they were God. For example, in the story of Moses and the burning bush, the angel of the Lord appears to Moses and speaks as though he were God himself (Exodus 3:1–6). In the extended story of Abraham and Sarah, three messenger angels present themselves in human form to Abraham by the oak trees at Mamre (Genesis 18:1–15). Throughout the ensuing story, their identities fluctuate. They appear to be men, but they are angels in human form. They are three, but they are also one. They speak as if they are men, and as if they are angels. One of them speaks as if he were Yhwh himself. This fluctuation of identity is carried over into the immediately following story of the debate between Abraham and Yhwh concerning the destruction of Sodom and Gomorrah.

The same phenomenon can be observed in the book of Judges. An angel appears in human form and speaks to the dejected Gideon. Gideon complains to the angel that Yhwh has abandoned the people of Israel, thus allowing their enemies to triumph over them. Suddenly, the angel begins to speak not just for, but as Yhwh:

> Then the Lord turned and said to him, "Go in this might of yours and deliver Israel from the hand of Midian; I hereby commission you."
>
> *Judges 6:14*

Still supposing the angel to be a human being, Gideon offers him a present of food, and asks him to wait while it is prepared. When the food is ready, the angel stretches out his staff and touches the food. Fire springs up, the food is consumed by the fire, and the angel vanishes. Gideon is terrified. He believes that he will die because, he says, he has seen the angel of Yhwh face to face, and no man can see God and live. Nor do angels need food, as Gideon should have known. The implication is that to see the angel of Yhwh is in some sense to see Yhwh himself. This fluidity of reference cannot be dismissed as textual corruption or misinterpretation. It is integral to the story itself.

There is a similar fluidity of reference in the story of Manoah and his wife, the parents of Samson. An unknown "man of God" comes to them to announce that Manoah's barren wife will conceive. The man of God is the angel of Yhwh, who has temporarily assumed human form. He declines the offer of food (because angels don't eat) but instead proposes a sacrifice. While the sacrifice is being prepared, they ask the man of

God for his name. He replies that his name is too wonderful for them to know (cf. the "angel who has God's Name in him", the "Name above every name" awarded to Jesus in Philippians 2, and the secret "Name" of the Son of Man in 1 Enoch 69). The sacrifice is duly offered, and the angel disappears in the flame of sacrificial fire. Manoah and his wife now realize that the man of God was more than an angel. In encountering God's angelic representative, they had in some way been encountering God himself:

> And Manoah said to his wife, "We shall surely die, for we have seen God."
>
> *Judges 13:22*

In the Hebrew scriptures, in the Apocrypha, and in the Pseudepigrapha there are other instances of stories involving the motif of encounter with a stranger who is subsequently revealed to be the angel of YHWH. For example, in the probably second-century BCE book of Tobit, Tobias the son of Tobit undertakes a journey lasting many months. He takes with him his dog and a young man, who is employed to be his companion and guide. Tobit is unaware that this young man, who is even offered a bonus payment at one point, is in fact the archangel Raphael in human form. When, at long last, Raphael's true identity is disclosed, Tobias and his father are terrified. They fall face down before Raphael, who commands them to get up, to acknowledge God who sent him, and never to forget to bless God each and every day. There is an interesting sidelight to the story. Because Raphael has been eating and drinking, something that angels do not do, the author has a problem. He solves it neatly by making Raphael say, "Although you were watching me, I did not really eat or drink. What you saw was a vision" (Tobit 12:19).

In the possibly late first-century or early second-century CE text known as the Testament of Abraham, there is another story of encounter with an angel. The story has some similarities with Luke's Emmaus story. The archangel Michael, incognito in human form, meets the aged Abraham walking along a road. Abraham invites the unknown traveller to come with him to his home, so that the traveller may eat and then rest. As they make their way into the city, Abraham begins to suspect that his visitor is a "man of God" rather than an ordinary mortal. By the time that Abraham is washing his guest's feet at the entrance to his house, he is certain that he is entertaining an angel. This unknown traveller, it transpires, is none other than the archangel Michael, commander in chief of the heavenly host. Michael has come incognito as a messenger and helper to prepare Abraham for his impending death and heavenly ascension.[82]

The appearance stories of the Gospels never suggest that the risen Jesus is an angel, although the letter to the Hebrews denies this possibility so fiercely that one suspects there may have been those who thought he was. In the Gospels, the risen Jesus is clearly himself, but he also has an angel-like ability to appear and disappear without warning. Taken as a whole, the Gospel appearance stories have many obvious similarities and points of connection with the angelomorphic angel traditions cited above. For example, the appearance stories of the Gospels, like the angelomorphic transformation stories, seem always to involve the delivery of a significant message or command. Similarly, the motif of disclosure taking place in the context of a meal appears, variously applied, in the appearance stories and in the angelomorphic angel traditions. No devout, first-century Jew reading the story of the walk to Emmaus could possibly fail to be aware of its implications. In the Galilean lakeside appearance story, the disciples' fearful understanding that they are with Jesus only becomes explicit in the context of a meal involving fire, bread, and fish. And, as noted above, Jesus is worshipped—or accorded the kind of reverence due to a deity—in both of Matthew's appearance stories and in John's "Doubting Thomas" story. Thomas's confession of faith ("My Lord, and my God!") would immediately prompt recollection of the stories of Gideon and Manoah, both of whom realize that in seeing the angel of YHWH they have seen God. In functional terms, the Jesus encountered in the appearance stories of the Gospels has two aspects. He is Jesus, but he is also a heavenly being capable, when necessary, of appearing in human form.

The traditions in the Hebrew scriptures in which encounter with the divine is mediated by angelomorphic entities seem to have provided a ready-made model which Christians were able to use to articulate in story form their conviction that, in encountering the risen Jesus, one was encountering God. When this is understood, the stories, which at first sight seem to be to be little more than naive and fanciful tales, can be seen to be a family of theologically significant narratives, each one redacted as necessary to meet the particular requirements and circumstances of the individual author. They probably circulated in oral form prior to being committed to writing sometime after Paul's last genuine letter. Where they came from, and how they came into being, we do not know. Appearances of Jesus to "the twelve" and to "all the apostles" are attested in the pre-Pauline 1 Corinthians 15:5 tradition. It can reasonably be assumed that the same event or events lie behind the group-appearance stories in Matthew, Luke, and John 20. Luke's brief reference to a report that there had been an appearance to Peter may be a direct reflection of the Peter tradition in 1 Corinthians 15:5. The memory of an appearance to Peter may also lie (a long way back) behind the story of Simon Peter's commissioning in John 21.

Although it receives no mention in the 1 Corinthians 15 appearances tradition, there may also be an authentic experience underlying the Mary Magdalene encounter story in John 20. Paul's silence on the matter is not conclusive. Paul or his tradition may have deliberately expunged from the record references to resurrection appearances involving women, either because there was rivalry between Mary Magdalene and Peter for pre-eminence as primary witness to the resurrection, or possibly because only males counted as witnesses in Jewish law. As for the other appearance stories, we know nothing of their origins and have no way of assessing their historicity.

The appearance stories and the empty-tomb traditions probably have separate origins, and they seem to have been becoming connected to one another only at the time of the earliest Gospel (see Mark 16:8). In the first instance, the appearance stories seem to have been intended not as proofs of the resurrection, but rather to protect the connection between the risen and exalted heavenly Jesus Christ of the Church and the historical Jesus of Nazareth. They do this by making it clear that the risen and exalted one is none other than the earthly Jesus. This intention accords with the wider purpose of the Gospel writers, which is to support the faith and practice of the early Christian communities by anchoring them in the history of Jesus and emphasizing the duty of Jesus' followers to carry forward his work into the future.

Conclusion

The empty-tomb traditions cannot be regarded as historical in their present form. Despite repeated attempts over several centuries, it has never proved possible to harmonize them without introducing speculative assumptions or doing violence to one or another of the strands of tradition. To paraphrase the New Testament scholar Christopher Evans (1909–2012), the problem facing the would-be harmonizer is that he or she is trying to combine, not scattered fragments from an originally single matrix, but rather a variety of freestanding, partly disconnected expressions of resurrection faith.[83] The gaps in the tradition cannot be made good either by critical reconstruction or by inspired guesswork, because they are not gaps in a single whole, but rather gaps between separate wholes. Other than where the later Gospels are taking Mark 16:1–8 as their starting point, the empty-tomb traditions and the appearance stories of the Gospels seem to be independent, free-standing expressions of Easter faith.

On the specific question of the historicity or otherwise of the story of the burial of Jesus by Joseph of Arimathea and discovery of the empty tomb by the women on the day following the Sabbath, Paul's silence is probably less significant than it appears. The apparent ambiguity of Paul's views on the nature of the resurrection body can now be seen to be something of a red herring; it reflects his complex threefold anthropology and his choice of not always consistently applied metaphors, especially the metaphor of transformation. The ambiguity dissolves when we assume that Paul understood resurrection to involve the transformation of both the "flesh" and the "psychic body" into one "spiritual body". Although not conclusive, the evidence tends to suggest that Paul always understood the resurrection of Jesus to have included his body. If the historical core of the empty-tomb tradition is as slight as we are suggesting, Paul probably saw no need to spell matters out. The emptiness of the tomb—if there was a tomb—would have been something taken for granted as a corollary of belief in Jesus' resurrection.

The first part of this enquiry into the origins of resurrection faith—that is, the historical part—is now almost complete. The remaining task is to build on what has already been established and to demonstrate that there is at least one credible historical pathway, with variants, whereby belief in the resurrection of Jesus could have evolved without any miraculous divine intervention involving an overturning of the natural order. This is the aim of the next chapter. If this can be achieved, we shall have "cleared the decks" and will be in a position to move on, in the final chapter, to the much more important question of whether Christians today can understand and affirm the resurrection of Jesus in a way that is compatible with modern scientific and critical-historical methods and assumptions and that, also, allows for the possibility that in the emergence of resurrection faith there is a revelation of the divine.

CHAPTER 10

The Resurrection as History: What Actually Happened

This concluding historical chapter suggests that the belief that God had raised Jesus from the dead, together with the associated understandings that unfolded out of this primary conviction, emerged without any miraculous divine intervention involving an overturning of the natural course of historical events. It argues that resurrection faith, although wholly innovatory and undoubtedly reflecting the visionary experiences and theological reflections of Jesus' followers after his death, has to be understood in the wider context of eschatological Second Temple Judaism as well as in the narrower context of the remembered teaching and person of Jesus.

Events

The immediate starting point for the emergence of resurrection faith was the situation of Jesus' disciples in the hours and days immediately following his apparently unexpected death. Like Jesus himself during his lifetime, his disciples had been fervently committed to belief in the imminently coming kingdom or rule of God, the hoped-for new age of justice, peace, and plenty for God's righteous people. They may also have believed that they, with Jesus, would have a central place in this coming kingdom (Mark 10:29–30; Matthew 19:28). In pursuit of their convictions they had forsaken everything. They had abandoned their occupations, their homes, and their families. They had endured privation and physical hardship. Trusting Jesus and suppressing any doubts, they had invested their hopes and expectations in the anticipated coming kingdom of God.

Jesus' ministry and message had been brief and divisive. He and his followers experienced opposition almost from the outset. They may well have been anticipating further opposition, trouble, or even suffering when they made their fateful, final ascent to Jerusalem as pilgrims for the Passover festival. Nevertheless, there is no undisputed evidence that the disciples expected Jesus to be killed, or that it was ever thought possible that the eagerly awaited kingdom of God might not come about. Then, suddenly and without warning, Jesus had been arrested, tried, sentenced, and executed, all within twenty-four hours. The date of his death is generally agreed to be 14 or 15 Nisan, either 30 or 33 CE. (The doubt arises because the chronology of the passion story in John's Gospel differs slightly from that in the three synoptic Gospels, but all four place the death of Jesus on a Friday before the Sabbath close to Passover.) That Jesus died in Jerusalem at around the time of the Passover festival may be taken as historical fact. Even if all the traditions in the Gospels are set aside, we have the much earlier, perhaps pre-Pauline statement, that "our paschal [Passover] lamb, Christ, has been sacrificed" (1 Corinthians 5:7b).

When Jesus was killed, the hopes and expectations of his followers must surely have lain in ruins. They would have been confused, distressed, and frightened, and they were also in mortal danger, or so they would have reasonably supposed. Whenever there was the remotest possibility of insurrection, the Roman military reaction was swift and brutal. They took no prisoners, other than for torture and exemplary execution. Pontius Pilate, the Roman prefect of Judaea, who apparently ordered Jesus' death, was exceptionally ruthless, even for a Roman governor. According to Josephus, Pilate's extreme brutality in Samaria, just a few years after the death of Jesus, led to his being called back to Rome and summarily dismissed from his post. In the case of actual or potential revolutionary activity, it was normal practice for both leaders and followers to be hunted down and slaughtered, as in the case of religious insurrections led by Theudas and "the Egyptian" (see pp. 133–134). In the first hours and days following Jesus' arrest and execution, the priority of his followers would have been to escape and survive. Some of them probably went into hiding in Jerusalem. Others may have made their way back to Galilee, as quickly and unobtrusively as possible.

That they were able to survive is interesting and possibly significant. There can be no doubt that the Romans could have hunted them down and arrested them, so how it came about that Jesus alone was killed and that his followers were spared is a puzzle. It suggests that Jesus may have been regarded as a relatively harmless eccentric (like his namesake Jesus ben Ananias, who—in 66 CE—went around Jerusalem proclaiming the city's impending destruction) rather than as a serious potential insurgent. Another speculative possibility is that Jesus brokered his own surrender to the authorities, perhaps through a middleman, in return for a promise that his followers would be spared. This could be the historical nucleus of the Judas story of the Gospels. It would help to explain how it first came to be said that the death of Jesus was "for us" and that Jesus had "given" his life to save his followers (1 Corinthians 15:3).

According to the tradition in the Gospels, Jesus died quickly. The fate of his body is much debated. Three possibilities were outlined in the previous chapter. It may have happened much as the Gospels report. That is, the body may have been hastily buried on the eve of the Sabbath in a rock tomb belonging to Joseph of Arimathea. In that case, the tradition of the visit of the women to the empty tomb on the first day after the Sabbath is probably historical. Alternatively, the empty-tomb tradition as we now have it in the Gospels may be a secondary creation, but with an inner core of historicity. If the dead body of Jesus was cast into a common grave in accordance with normal practice, or disposed of in some other unknown way, the historical core could be that on the day after the Sabbath, some of the followers of Jesus searched for his body and discovered it to be missing from the place where they expected it to be. And that it was never seen again. In which case, the story of the burial in Joseph of Arimathea's rock tomb, the visit of the named women, and other circumstantial details must be secondary embellishments of this (hypothetical) primary tradition. The third possibility is that the burial and empty-tomb traditions are entirely secondary creations lacking any historicity whatsoever. The body of Jesus was never "lost" at all. It was just disposed of in some natural way that we cannot now determine. This possibility has to be considered, because the empty-tomb tradition does not make its first appearance until some forty years after the death of Jesus (although there may have been an earlier version of Mark's account, lacking what is now Mark 16:7), and because there is no evidence prior to the Gospels that an empty-tomb tradition contributed in any way to the emergence of belief in the exaltation and resurrection of Jesus. Nor is there any reason why it should have done. Resurrection is an unlikely explanation for the emptiness of a tomb or an inability to find a corpse. As suggested in the previous chapter, there are other, more mundane explanations.

On the basis of the historical data, we cannot determine with certainty exactly what did or did not happen. The third possibility seems improbable, given that the earliest community of Jesus' followers could scarcely have proclaimed the resurrection of Jesus if the location of his corpse had been known and was potentially available for inspection by anyone prepared to take the trouble. Unless we want to argue the case for "spiritual resurrection", we have to accept that the proclamation of Jesus' resurrection presupposes at least a core empty-tomb tradition. Although the evidence suggests that the latter did not give rise to the former, the earliest proclamation of the resurrection and the earliest belief in an empty tomb or grave must nevertheless have marched together. The probability is, therefore, that behind the earliest empty-tomb tradition there is a core of historicity, and that the core historical events possibly included a search by women for the body of Jesus, and their discovery that the body had gone from the place where it had been buried.

In the first instance, the discovery that the body of Jesus was missing probably stood slightly to one side of the mainstream of events. Shortly after the death of Jesus, probably within hours or days, Jesus' followers must have begun to engage in a process of urgent reappraisal and reflection on the significance of his death. What did it mean? Had their shared convictions concerning the imminently coming kingdom of God been a delusion? Was the kingdom of God still going to come, as Jesus had said? If so, when and how? And why had God allowed Jesus to be killed? What divine purpose or intention could possibly have been served by his death? If they had been expecting that Jesus would prove to be a Davidic messiah-king, that was a hope that could no longer be entertained. But were there perhaps other ways of understanding messiahship that might have warranted the ascription of messianic status to Jesus? And most especially, given that Jesus' followers—like the Pharisees—believed in life after death, what had happened to Jesus himself? Where was Jesus now?

This process of questioning and reflection probably began in a haphazard and unstructured way. However, as Jesus' followers gained confidence and began to regroup, some rudimentary form of organization must have come into being, and provisional leaders must have emerged. On the question of their location during the days and weeks immediately after the death of Jesus, we have no historical data other than the much later and conflicting traditions in the Gospels. Some or all of them may have returned to Galilee, where they had families and other commitments. Others may have remained in Jerusalem and never gone back to Galilee at all.

Interwoven with this initial process of questioning and reflection were, we suggest, individual and group experiences understood by those concerned to be visionary encounters with the now exalted and transformed heavenly Jesus Christ. The earliest tradition does not specify where and when these events took place. As to those involved, we have the traditional list in 1 Corinthians 15:5–8. This can be regarded as reliable, but not necessarily comprehensive. As it stands, the list implies that Peter was the first to experience a vision of the risen Christ. No date is given, but it was probably very shortly after the death of Jesus, possibly on what has become known as Easter Sunday (cf. Luke 24:12,34). If so, Peter must have remained in Jerusalem. The structure of the traditional list suggests that at some time prior to the writing of 1 Corinthians, the Peter tradition may have become merged with a rival tradition that had given primacy to James, the brother of Jesus. If we accept the theory that the role of the women was for some reason deliberately erased from the earliest tradition, Mary Magdalene rather than Peter could have been the first disciple to see the risen Christ.

The series of visionary experiences probably extended over a period of time, possibly weeks rather than days, or perhaps even longer. The appearance of the risen Christ to Paul (cf. 1 Corinthians 15:8) probably took place between one and three years after the death of Jesus. Reports of the earliest of these visionary experiences must have circulated quickly among Jesus' followers, whether in Jerusalem or Galilee. They would have created a climate of extreme excitement and expectation. One can envisage a process of iterative interaction between visions and reflective interpretation of visions. The German New Testament scholar Gerd Lüdemann (1946–) suggests that the first vision was "infectious" and that the visions collectively constituted "an explosive dynamic, a whirlpool that would have drawn the scattered followers and family of Jesus back into Jerusalem".

As to the precise content of these visions of the risen and exalted Jesus, we have two semi-narrative accounts. The first, Paul's reference to his own experience, is suggestive only. The second is the very much later depiction of the exalted Son of Man in the first chapter of the book of Revelation. In both instances, visual or ocular seeing appears to be implied, but there is an underlying element of uncertainty. In Galatians 1:12–16, Paul says that he received the gospel "through a revelation (*apocalypsis*) of Jesus Christ" and that God was "pleased to reveal his Son to me" (or possibly, "in me"). In Revelation 1:10, the author says that he was "in the Spirit" when he saw the heavenly Jesus. None of these statements necessarily implies ocular seeing. The Greek term used by Paul to describe the appearances listed in the tradition of 1 Corinthians 15:5–8 is similarly ambiguous. The verb in question can function metaphorically in Greek, just as it does in English. It may denote either physical or mental seeing.

This gives rise to the possibility that the visionary "appearances" or "seeings" of the risen Jesus may in the first instance have involved mental insight rather than ocular seeing. The New Testament scholar Willi Marxsen (1919–1993) has suggested that some of the disciples initially arrived at a rational, reflective understanding concerning Jesus' post-mortem exaltation in heaven.[84] This understanding was first spoken of as something that they had "seen" in a metaphorical sense. At a slightly later stage this experience came to be regarded and spoken of as a sudden moment of insight, or a sudden moment of vision and illumination.

Marxsen admits that his suggestion is speculative, and it is difficult to see how it can be reconciled either with the plain sense of the appearance tradition in 1 Corinthians 15:5–8 or with what some commentators believe to be Paul's descriptions of his own initial revelatory experience in 2 Corinthians 3:18 and 4:6. Where Marxsen is surely correct, however, is in his theological assertion that the truth of the resurrection consists not in a historically accessible, miraculous restoration to life of Jesus' corpse, but rather in an action of God located in the life, death, and resurrection of Jesus. Nevertheless, Marxsen's "insight" theory cautions against forcing into the straitjacket of a single, rigid interpretation what may originally have been a variety of slightly different ways of giving expression to the conviction that God had raised Jesus from the dead and was now making him known within the community of his followers.

Christians who subscribe to a modern scientific world view may find it surprising and slightly compromising that visions and visionary experiences appear to have played such a prominent part in the emergence of resurrection faith. But the historical evidence that they did is overwhelming. This ought not to be surprising. Understandings and imperatives claimed to have been received in dreams and visions were common in the ancient world, and they have a long history in both Judaism and Christianity. The theologian Andrew Chester argues that early Christianity reflects a strong and powerful visionary tradition going back to Jesus himself, and that Jesus' own specific visionary experiences—and his wider, overarching vision of the world and human society being transformed by God—helped to facilitate the post-Easter visionary experiences of his followers.[85]

Even so, some readers may still find it hard to take seriously understandings arrived at as a result of a process involving visionary experiences. They suspect that phenomena such as visions, dreams, and hallucinations are the product of irrational, disordered, or even pathological mental processes. That this is sometimes the case is undeniable. Bereavement apparitions, which were alluded to briefly in the previous chapter, are a well-known psychological phenomenon. Celsus, an anti-Christian philosopher and polemicist writing in the late second century CE, dismissed the resurrection appearances of Jesus as hallucinations due to "some mistaken notion, an experience which has happened to thousands". Modern epidemiological studies suggest that some 16% of all bereaved persons experience one or more hallucinatory sightings of their deceased partner or friend, but these apparitions are fleeting phenomena lasting no more than a few seconds. They lack any cognitive content other than recognition and they deliver no specific understanding or message. In this respect, they stand in sharp contrast with Paul's account of his own revelatory experience and with the appearance stories of the Gospels, all of which are heavily freighted with significant content.

Nor are insights and understandings arrived at through processes such as visions, auditions, dreams, or hallucinations necessarily disconnected from rational thought. In the case of matters of current concern to an individual, the mental processes underlying his or her dreams and visions may even contribute positively to the formulation of rational conclusions. For example, a number of important scientific discoveries are said to have had their origins in dreams. To give just two out of several well-known instances: Friedrich August Kekulé (1829–1896) claimed that his discovery of the ring structure of the benzene molecule originated in a dream in which he saw a snake biting its own tail. Albert Einstein (1879–1955) said that the idea of relativity came to him in a dream in which he was in his pyjamas on a sledge accelerating downhill through the snow. As the sledge went faster and faster, the colours and relative positions of the stars began to change. So far as we know, there never was a snake in Kekulé's bedroom, and Einstein never went tobogganing in his pyjamas. Nevertheless, both their understandings have proved to be true.

Even apparently wild and chaotic dreams may prove, on analysis, to have unexpectedly rational content. Andrew Chester has examined the internal logic of visionary experiences, including the Jewish and Christian visions of human angelomorphic transformation described in Chapter 3 above. He argues in favour of a nuanced and discerning perspective for interpreting the strongly imminent eschatological expectation of Jesus and his earliest followers, suggesting that even apocalyptic visions having bizarre and lurid content need to be taken seriously. Once the incidental details are stripped away, these visions can sometimes be seen to be visions of the world not as it is—plagued by never-ending oppression, injustice, and exploitation of the poor—but of the world as it could and should be in a God-given future. The truth of an understanding does not necessarily depend on the way in which it was arrived at.

Understandings

It must have been very shortly after the death of Jesus that the first tentative understandings concerning his present whereabouts would have begun to circulate among his followers. The basic understanding, that Jesus had bypassed *Sheol* and was now highly exalted in heaven, was probably a significant part of the content of the earliest visions, but it may have been arrived at by straightforward reflection even before the first vision. There are numerous examples of significant figures who were apparently believed to have bypassed *Sheol* and entered directly into heaven. These include Enoch, Noah, Abraham, Isaac, Jacob, Moses, Elijah, David, Zephaniah, and Ezra. Some of these were believed to have bypassed death altogether, having been taken up to heaven whilst still in their mortal bodies. Others had apparently left their mortal bodies behind on earth. The story of the Transfiguration of Jesus (see Chapter 6) seems to reflect both possibilities. At the Transfiguration, both Elijah and Moses appear as radiant, heavenly beings. Elijah had been taken up to heaven in his earthly body; the body of Moses, on the other hand, was buried, although no one knows where.

Even if these examples were not available, there are two powerful separate but related reasons why it would almost certainly have been supposed that Jesus had gone directly to heaven. Firstly, Jesus was an unjustly persecuted righteous man. In the Judaism of the period, particularly in the wisdom literature, there was a tradition concerning the vindication of an unjustly persecuted righteous man (see Chapter 2). Jesus was just such a man. He had been derided, reproached, and held in contempt by wicked men. Since he was dead, he could not be vindicated in his lifetime here on earth. Like the anonymous figures in Wisdom 5:4–5, Jesus must therefore have been vindicated by exaltation in the presence of God in heaven. In due course, friends and enemies alike would come to see and understand that this righteous man, Jesus, was in fact numbered among the children of God, that God had saved him, and that Jesus had been right in all that he said and did. Furthermore, since Jesus was now alive with God in heaven, he must have been transformed into a glorious and radiant being, just like the other inhabitants of heaven (see Chapter 3). That Jesus was believed to have suffered as an exceptionally righteous or even sinless man receives strong confirmation a little later as doctrines of atonement begin to emerge.

Secondly, it was evident that Jesus had also died as a martyr. Since the time of the Maccabean rebellion, if not before, it had been believed that some righteous martyrs might—in due course—enjoy eventual resurrection to new life on a radically changed earth. This belief is explicit in the book of Daniel, where resurrection for reward or punishment is set in the near future. In the slightly later second book of Maccabees it is suggested that the dead martyrs enter into some form of blessed afterlife immediately after death. This blessing was almost certainly thought to involve transformation into glorious, angel-like beings shining "like the brightness of the sky . . . like the stars for ever and ever" (Daniel 12:3).

Earliest belief in the resurrection of Jesus may have emerged independently but in parallel with belief in his heavenly exaltation, possibly in different communities of his earliest followers. Or it may have unfolded as an inference drawn from belief in his heavenly exaltation. Attention has already been drawn to the apparently pre-Pauline christological hymns, which depict the extreme exaltation of Jesus without making any mention of his resurrection, and the very early, formulaic assertions of the resurrection which make no clear mention of Jesus' heavenly exaltation. This early disconnection between the two concepts may be pointing towards independent origins. On the other hand, the very early Aramaic worship imperative invocation *marana tha* is compatible with both exaltation (because Jesus is being acclaimed or invoked as heavenly Lord) and resurrection (because the "coming" of Jesus which is being prayed for is part of the package of ideas associated with the concept of resurrection—see 1 Thessalonians 4:14–16; cf. John 14:3). By the time of Paul, or even earlier if Romans 1:4 is pre-Pauline, Jesus' resurrection and his heavenly exaltation are explicitly connected.

No definite conclusion is possible. Belief in Jesus' vindication by heavenly exaltation and belief in his resurrection may have been united from the outset, or they could have had independent origins, possibly in different locations and among different groups of Jesus' followers. Whichever was the case, the two concepts became combined at a very early stage indeed. Also, once belief in Jesus' resurrection had become explicit and fused with belief in his heavenly exaltation, resurrection faith quickly assumed the greater importance. Belief in Jesus' heavenly exaltation served to explain where he was (exalted in heaven) and how he was (vindicated by his exaltation). It confirmed that Jesus had died as a righteous man and a martyr, and it retrospectively validated his mission and ministry. On the other hand, exaltation on its own had little or nothing to say about the coming kingdom of God, which had been such a central feature of Jesus' teaching. Nor did it explain why God had allowed Jesus to die. Resurrection faith, however, addressed the immediate practical and psychological needs of Jesus' followers by offering a powerful new perspective on the future. It could be interpreted as the eschatological act of God confirming not just the rightness of Jesus' past teaching and actions, but also their continuing validity and future relevance. Resurrection faith enabled Jesus' followers to understand that his earthly ministry, his death, and his heavenly exaltation were all part of God's overarching, ongoing saving purpose and intention.

Implications

Resurrection faith addressed the question of the future first and foremost by signalling the inauguration of God's hoped-for, coming new age. Resurrection meant that the new age had already begun and that the risen Jesus was the "first fruits" of those who had died (1 Corinthians 15:20). The implication of the metaphor is that what had been begun with the resurrection of Jesus must shortly be completed. The purpose of God, as articulated and enacted by Jesus, must be—and would be—fully achieved.

Resurrection faith also meant that a cluster of already related christological cognitions took on new and much sharper significance. The concepts of Jesus' messiahship, his lordship, and the understanding of divine sonship implicit in his *Abba*-relationship all had their origins in his authoritative teaching and absolute commitment to what he perceived to be the will and intention of his heavenly Father. In different ways, all three concepts were confirmed and intensified by resurrection faith. At a very early stage, Jesus' lordship, sonship, and messiahship gained strong additional support from a probably already existing Jewish messianic exegesis of key texts such as Psalm 110:1 ("The LORD said to my Lord, sit at my right hand . . .") and Psalm 2:7 ("You are my son; today I have begotten you"). The messianic interpretation of these texts served to validate the conviction that Jesus, as Messiah, Lord, and Son of God (by virtue of his messiahship), must be seated at God's right hand, the place of highest honour reserved for the king's own son (see Acts 2:34-36; 13:33-35). A whole cluster of christological ideas can be observed crystallizing and becoming locked together.

Another unfolding implication of resurrection faith was the belief that an outpouring of the Spirit of God must have been associated with the resurrection of Jesus. In the Hebrew scriptures, one of the hallmarks of the anticipated messianic age and kingdom of God is the universal outpouring of the creative and re-creating *ruach* or Spirit of God (Joel 2:28). By virtue of this outpouring of the Spirit of God on the followers of Jesus, an experience later schematized in rather different ways by Luke and John, the resurrection of Jesus was confirmed as the inauguration of the hoped-for new age. A new act of divine empowerment had taken place; an act of new creation was being manifested within the community of believers (Acts 2:1-21; John 20:22; cf. 2 Corinthians 5:5,17).

A further major development was the emergence of *parousia* belief; that is, the expectation that Jesus would be revealed by God from heaven, and that he would soon become present in power to complete God's already initiated work of salvation and judgement, keeping his followers safe and establishing the kingdom of God (cf. 1 Corinthians 15:23-25).

The emergence of *parousia* belief was closely associated with the very early identification of the risen Jesus as the "Son of Man" (cf. Mark 13:26-27; 14:62), the "Son of Man" being the heavenly figure described as "one like a son of man" who comes to God with the clouds of heaven and is awarded everlasting kingship and dominion over all the peoples and nations and languages on earth (Daniel 7:13-14). This identification is one of the few fixed points in the debate over the "coming" Son of Man sayings. As to how the identification came about, three possibilities have been considered. The first is that Jesus spoke in cryptic terms about the future coming of the Son of Man to God, intending thereby veiled reference to himself. He was using ideas drawn from Daniel 7:13-14 as an indirect way of giving expression to his confidence that he would eventually be vindicated after suffering. After his death, whatever it was that Jesus had said about his coming to God for vindication mutated into sayings about Jesus coming to earth to exercise universal dominion and to establish the kingdom of God. The second possibility is that during his lifetime Jesus spoke in cryptic terms about the future coming of the Son of Man from heaven, intending thereby reference to a figure other than himself. If so, after his death these sayings became changed into sayings of Jesus about Jesus himself as the coming one. The third possibility is that all the sayings in the Gospels about the coming of the Son of Man from heaven are post-Easter creations of Jesus' followers, retrojected into the Jesus tradition after his death. They reflect the emergence of *parousia* belief and the primitive community's own exegesis of Daniel 7:13–14.

So far as the emergence of resurrection faith is concerned, it does not matter greatly which of the three options we favour. However it came about, *parousia* belief was very early. The three pathways differ in their implications for Jesus' self-understanding, but in all three cases the outcome is that Jesus' messiahship and lordship are confirmed and underpinned by the understanding that he is the Son of Man, the figure in Daniel 7:13–14. First, he comes initially to God to be awarded everlasting dominion and kingship over all peoples and nations, and then (by implication) he comes to exercise these delegated divine functions on earth. So it is that Paul, although he makes no explicit reference to Jesus as the Son of Man, can say that the returning Jesus will reign until he has destroyed every ruler and every authority and power and put all enemies under his feet: "Then comes the end, when he hands over the kingdom to God the Father . . ." (1 Corinthians 15:24–25).

The conviction that Jesus' resurrection marked the inauguration of the age to come and that he would soon be returning to complete his messianic work led to a reappraisal of the significance of his death. Jesus' death could no longer be regarded as an accident subsequently rectified by his resurrection and exaltation. On the contrary, his death and resurrection could now be seen to be part of God's overarching, saving purpose. His death was necessary, it was good, and it was "in accordance with the scriptures". The emergence of the belief that Jesus died "for us" was pivotal. It expanded the idea that the death of a martyr was beneficial for God's people collectively, and it facilitated the interpretation of Jesus' death as an atoning sacrifice. Jesus could now be seen to have been a righteous, even sinless man who had voluntarily surrendered himself to suffering and death. These understandings added urgency to the search for scriptural texts and passages able to throw light on what had happened, what was happening, and what was expected to happen thereafter.

The Gospels suggest that many of these understandings originated on what became known as Easter Sunday. This is possible, especially in the case of the "heavenly exaltation" understanding, but an extended iterative process extending over a period of weeks or even longer—with understandings prompting visions, and visions then promoting further understandings—seems more likely. This is not detrimental to Christian faith. The Easter story as we have it in the Gospels may legitimately be regarded as a liturgically and doctrinally justified contraction of events whose truth is independent of its chronology.

Conclusion

Some readers, whilst willing to concede that there are problems with the Gospel records, will still want to maintain that there was a miraculous act of God involving the raising of the dead physical body of Jesus to new life, albeit transformed in some way that we cannot comprehend. The possibility of such a miraculous act of God cannot rationally be denied, but we have shown that there is nothing in the historical data behind the Gospels necessitating any such belief. Resurrection faith can be observed emerging naturally as a theological interpretation of the history of Israel, the totality of Jesus' completed life and death, and God's intended future for the world. The emergence of resurrection faith may have taken place over an extended period of time, although we need not rule out the possibility that some of the visionary experiences actually took place on what later became known as the first Easter Sunday. There is no need to presuppose any miraculous act of God overturning the natural order.

On the specific question of the historicity of the empty-tomb tradition as it appears in the Gospels, we have seen that the historical evidence is not strong enough to overcome a natural agnosticism. That there was an abortive search for his body after Jesus' death is a reasonable assumption. What seems certain is that after Jesus' death, his dead body was never seen again. It is also evident that emergent resurrection faith at some point became connected to an already existing and developing empty-tomb tradition, or with an earlier core tradition concerning an abortive search for the body of Jesus. Historically speaking, this intersection of traditions has shaped most Christian understandings of resurrection faith. It clarified and reinforced the conviction of Jesus' disciples that the exalted and glorious heavenly Jesus Christ, whom they were now revering "as if he were a god", was one and the same being as the historical Jesus of Nazareth. It might perhaps have played a part in the transformation of initial exaltation belief into subsequent full-blown resurrection-exaltation belief.

The conclusion must be that, although a miraculous divine intervention overthrowing the natural order cannot logically be excluded, a miraculous resurrection of Jesus is not something that can be proved by historical means. Nor is there anything in the historical testimony that cannot satisfactorily be explained using the methods of critical-historical science. Historically speaking, resurrection faith has to be regarded as a theological interpretation of historical events. This conclusion is about as far as we can go in terms of purely historical enquiry.

Nevertheless, to stop at this point would be to fail abysmally to do justice to the content and meaning of resurrection faith, both for Jesus' first followers and for ourselves. Rejecting the idea of divine action involving an overturning of the natural order does not mean rejecting the possibility of there being other modes of divine action that are both real and revelatory. With this possibility in mind, the final chapter takes the form of an Epilogue focusing on theological rather than historical issues. Historically speaking, the emergence of resurrection faith was set in the context of a powerful theological narrative about God's purpose for his people Israel, and the future which God intended to bring into being. The followers of Jesus believed that the climax of God's covenant with his people was manifested in God's eschatological self-revelation in the life and death of Jesus, the prophet-Messiah from Nazareth. Their resurrection faith was an intelligible, credible, and creative response to their experience of divine self-disclosure in the life and death of Jesus and its immediate aftermath. Those who, down the ages, have accepted the first generation's witness to Jesus crucified and risen have also been making, often in very different contexts, their own personal responses to what they perceive to be the decisive revelation of the mystery of God in Jesus, with all that this implies about living in God's world as God's people, and hoping and working for God's future in a transformed earthly reality. It is the nature and logic of this contemporary faith-response that we examine in the Epilogue. History tells us where we have come from. The questions are, how do we relate ourselves to our history, and where do we go from here?

CHAPTER 11

The Resurrection as Interpretation and Revelation

The assertion that God raised Jesus from the dead stands at the heart of the Christian faith. It is repeated in the Christian scriptures, creeds, and traditions. The declared intention of this book was to consider, in the light of the historical evidence, what a modern Christian might say in reply to the question, "Do you really believe that God raised Jesus from the dead on the first Easter Sunday?" Or to explain how modern Christians, committed to a post-Enlightenment scientific world view and discovering that there are natural historical pathways that satisfactorily account for the emergence of resurrection faith, may continue honestly to affirm belief in the resurrection of Jesus from the dead. If we accept a modern world view and reject the idea of a miraculous divine intervention overturning the natural order, are we not writing the idea of *any* divine action in history out of the script altogether? Or, to put it more positively, if we maintain that there is more to be said about life and spiritual experience than either scientists can measure or historians can assess, how does this influence our understanding of the resurrection of Jesus Christ?

In this final chapter we review a number of the ways some modern Christian thinkers have addressed these questions. Then we go on to consider the more specific question of whether—and if so how—meaning can rationally be attached to historical events. Developing this theme, we shall suggest that divine revelation may be delivered through the perception of intrinsic God-given significance in historical events and processes. In the case of the life and death of Jesus, we suggest that his resurrection, although not a historical event or an event involving an overturning of the natural order, nevertheless is a real event involving a revelatory act of divine self-disclosure. Finally, we suggest that, far from being a radical innovation, this is probably how the resurrection was experienced and understood by the first followers of Jesus.

Reactions to critical-historical scholarship

Christians who seek to explain the gap—whether 36 hours or several weeks—between the death of Jesus and the emergence of resurrection faith fall into three different groups. The first group comprises traditional Christians who reject the conclusion that the only historically accessible phenomena are the death of Jesus and the subsequent emergence of resurrection faith. Such Christians emphasize what they believe to be the historicity of the empty-tomb tradition, and they defend belief in a historical resurrection event that involves an overturning of the natural order. At the other end of the spectrum are the reductionists, who believe that modern critical historical enquiry has, in principle, satisfactorily explained everything that needs to be explained. They rest content with the conclusion that resurrection faith is nothing more than a rather complicated interpretive myth or metaphor. Third, there are those occupying the middle ground; that is, those who accept the validity of the historians' conclusion that resurrection faith is a theological interpretation of the completed life and death of Jesus, but nevertheless believe that there is more to be said about the resurrection of Jesus than the historians allow or the scientists can measure. There is, they say, a historical dimension, there is a theological dimension, and there is an experiential or existential dimension. In one way or another, scholars and thinkers in this third category argue for the reality of a divine act of resurrection. Jesus was raised from death to continuing but different—or new—life in God (cf. 2 Corinthians 5:17). The resurrection was and is real, but it is non-physical and inaccessible to historical investigation. The resurrection is an act of divine self-revelation located in the completed life and death of Jesus, understood to be Messiah, Lord, and Son of God. The resurrection is validated for the believer in his or her own faith-response to an existential challenge located in the historical events and the historical responses to these events. Or, to put it another way, there is a faith-response involving the perception of intrinsic significance in the history of Israel, the completed life and death of Jesus, and God's ongoing purpose for his people.

From its proponents' point of view, the conservative traditionalist or supernaturalist position has the merit of being incapable of falsification by historical methods. While conceding that there are some problems with the historical testimony in the Gospels, scholars like Nicholas Thomas Wright, Gary Robert Habermas, and William Lane Craig continue to argue that the "historical facts" point directly towards a resurrection event having taken place in history.[86] The tomb was empty on the third day, and it was empty because God had raised Jesus from the dead. This involved the transformation of the body of the risen Jesus in a way that is beyond our understanding. The critical historians' argument that events without historical antecedents (causes) and historical sequents (effects) cannot be called historical events is dismissed as mere quibbling. The point, the conservatives say, is that the resurrection of Jesus was a real event, taking place inside history and having major historical consequences. The conservatives also—and in this they are right—stress the significant novelty of Christian belief in the resurrection of Jesus as compared with other resurrection expectations in Second Temple Judaism. The innovatory nature of Christian resurrection faith, the empty tomb, the resurrection appearances, and everything that stemmed from these events point clearly, they say, to resurrection as a physical event. No other explanation, they say, fits the facts.

When it is objected that there is no analogy in human experience for a miraculous divine intervention overturning the natural historical process, and that any such overturning of the natural historical process is fundamentally inconsistent with our understanding of God's nature and intentions, the supernaturalists reply that an omnipotent creator-God must always be free to modify, adjust, or intervene in his creation as he wills. This may be true, but God's ability to do something does not mean that he has done it or will do it. It is impossible to prove that supernaturalists are wrong but, by the same token, they can never prove that they are right. There is also the practical problem that many people today reject a priori the idea of specific, local, miraculous, divine intervention in the natural process. They are therefore unwilling to engage with what they regard as Christian nonsense.

Reductionists assert that resurrection faith emerged as a result of an interaction between theological reflection on the completed life of Jesus and subjective visionary experiences of the risen Jesus Christ. This conclusion is not new. It was clearly articulated in 1835 in Strauss's *Life of Jesus*. A more modern exponent of this position is Willi Marxsen, who explicitly rejected belief in any form of resurrection event. Like Strauss, he accepted and stressed the historical importance of the disciples' visions of the risen Jesus for the formation of resurrection faith, but he declined to argue that these visions had any objective validity. Instead, Marxsen placed primary importance on the disciples' experiences of "coming to faith" after the death of Jesus, experiences which they externalized as "seeing" the risen Jesus. The disciples' "coming to faith" had prospective as well as retrospective implications. Retrospectively it generated the affirmation that Jesus had risen. Prospectively it generated the belief that Jesus' followers were called by God to carry forward the cause of Jesus— that is, the mission and ministry of Jesus—into the future. For Marxsen, the assertion that Jesus is risen is an interpretation, whereas the coming to faith of Jesus' followers is the historical datum. There is a miracle of resurrection, but the miracle is the experience of coming to faith. For Marxsen, the statement that Jesus has risen has no independent reality that can be separated from the experience of coming to faith. The reality of the resurrection is locked into the reality of the believer experiencing and finding faith. Ongoing discipleship consists in authentic living, complete openness to others, and believing that God can do anything. Jesus, says Marxsen, makes us free for limitless faith in this world and gives us utter confidence in God for the future.[87]

Different theological understandings of the resurrection of Jesus as a real but non-historical event have been advanced by many influential twentieth-century theologians, notably by Karl Barth (who insists on an empty tomb) and—very differently—by Rudolf Bultmann (who denies the empty tomb). The basic premise is that action starts with God and that we must distance ourselves from the relativity associated with historical enquiry. The resurrection of Jesus is essentially a revelatory and saving act of God. As such, it is a real but transcendent "eschatological event";

that is, an event having the capacity to bring us into present involvement with the life of the coming new age. The resurrection has to be spoken and thought of as something that takes place in time, only because we can speak of it in no other way. When spoken of as a real but non-historical event taking place within time, the resurrection signals the reality of Jesus leaving the realm of human history. It also signifies the relating of the whole of Jesus' historical life to God, which is why history cannot be dispensed with. However, the content of resurrection faith is not a time-bound act of mental assent to a proposition concerning historical facts, or even commitment to a theological understanding. The essential content of resurrection faith is the believer's response of obedience and trust to the self-revelatory act of God, a response in which the believer becomes conscious of his or her salvation. This underlying revelatory act of God is the real miracle—or better, the mystery—of the resurrection of Jesus.

Edward Schillebeeckx (1914–2009) was also convinced that the resurrection is a revelatory act of God, and that the raised Christ is real although non-physical. Schillebeeckx identifies a strong soteriological element in the historical Easter experience of encounter with the risen Christ, but he regards the empty-tomb tradition and the appearance stories of the Gospels as potentially more of a hindrance than a help. He does not, however, regard the Easter event and the Easter experience of Jesus' followers as being fundamentally inaccessible to historical judgement. According to Schillebeeckx, historical enquiry shows that there is a connection between Jesus' resurrection and the associated experiences of divine grace and conversion which his followers described as appearances of the risen Christ. That said, Schillebeeckx appears to downgrade the significance of the 1 Corinthians 15:5–8 appearances tradition when he suggests that in the very first instance, belief in the imminent return of Jesus (the *parousia*) may have been proclaimed without reliance on a resurrection-appearances tradition. Jesus, he has suggested, could have been held to be "the one who is to come" before he was believed to be "the one who is risen".

Like Schillebeeckx, Barth and Bultmann are agreed that there was a real though non-physical, revelatory resurrection event, and that this event has implications for salvation. Where they disagree is on the question of the relationship between the faith that is "come to" by the followers of Jesus after the first Easter and the earliest kerygma or proclamation through which faith is generated. Barth regards the resurrection as a non-physical fact, or an event of the objective order, which can be proclaimed as such. Bultmann, on the other hand, senses that Barth is in danger of placing an overlay of faith on top of understandings concerning the past that are not warranted by the historical evidence. Whilst accepting that the resurrection is a real but non-physical revelatory event, "the eschatological event par excellence", Bultmann rejects any attempt to present the resurrection as an objective event of the past. He insists that whenever we try to talk about the resurrection of Jesus in objective terms, we lapse into the realm of mythology. We can only legitimately speak of God out of the experience of God's Word acting on us in the present.

What initially appeared to be a minor difference between Barth and Bultmann soon became a much more fundamental disagreement. To some extent, the problem reflects the different ways in which Barth and Bultmann understand religious language (see below). It also reflects Bultmann's conviction that the essence of faith is the believer's present response to a divine call, not belief in anything objectively imagined or described. Although there has been some doubt on the matter (particularly in view of his gnomic assertions that "Jesus is risen in the kerygma" and that "To believe in the Christ present in the kerygma is the meaning of the Easter faith"), it seems that Bultmann did continue to affirm the truth and reality of the raised Jesus Christ as a real but non-physical object of encounter. On the basis of a private conversation, Hans Küng (1928–) reports that Bultmann's position is that "Jesus does not live because he is proclaimed; he is proclaimed because he lives."[88] Despite their significant differences, these major proponents of the resurrection as a "real but non-physical event" are therefore agreed that the resurrection is a revelatory act of God, that the risen Jesus Christ is real, and that at the heart of the earliest resurrection faith there was an experience of encounter with the living Jesus Christ.

Backtracking slightly, the problem of relating faith to history is not new. In 1892, Martin Kähler (1835–1912), in his essay *The So-called Historical Jesus and the Historic, Biblical Christ*, emphasized that "facts that first have to be established by [historical] science cannot *as such* become experiences of faith".[89] Although writing many years before Bultmann,

Kähler thought that faith and the historically established picture of Jesus repelled one another like oil and water, and that "the historical Jesus of modern authors conceals from us the living Christ." Kähler believed that faith is evoked in us by experience of encounter with Christ, who is our "supra-historical" saviour. Attempts to base faith on the resurrection as historical fact could be compared with Newtonian physics. In Newtonian physics it is assumed that the observer is detached, standing outside and apart from that which is being observed. By contrast, in Einstein's theory of relativity, it is understood that the observer can never be separated from that which is being observed, being always an integral part of the total system.

Before we can commit to understanding resurrection faith as a faith-response to a real (but non-physical) revelatory experience of encounter with the risen Christ, we need to address a number of related issues and anticipate some possible objections. Firstly, talking about God is never straightforward. God is not a person as we are, nor is God an object, or even a force that can be described. Talking about God is therefore very different from talking about everyday matters. We have to consider carefully the origins, nature, and ownership of theological language in order to show that it is capable of legitimately pointing to human experience of God. Secondly, we have to consider how meaning may be located and perceived in historical events. Thirdly, we have to expand this understanding to include the possibility that divine revelation may be delivered through human response to challenges latent in historical events.

Theological language

Our historical enquiry has led to the conclusion that resurrection faith emerged as a theological interpretation of the totality of the history of Israel, the life and death of Jesus, and what flowed from it. For the followers of Jesus, the resurrection of Jesus was not primarily a historical event requiring proofs, but first and foremost an understanding concerning a changed state of affairs. This changed state of affairs, which was apprehended in a saving experience involving their own conversion and coming to faith, had to be put into words. Putting this experience into words involved talk about God and talk about personal religious experience. That is, it involved the use of theological language. The affirmation that God had raised Jesus from the dead was Jesus' followers' way of giving expression to their understanding concerning this changed state of affairs, and their experience of arriving at this understanding. The statement that God raised Jesus from the dead is God-talk; that is, theological language.

Theological language requires explanation. It involves using words and concepts in unfamiliar ways, but nevertheless has its own inner logic and necessity. Theological language cannot define God, nor can it prove anything about God, but it can be used to speak about God in relation to the world, and about human experience of God. Theological language is used by believers to relate themselves to their experience of reality and of being or existing in relationship with reality. It is also used to advance the claim that God reveals God, or Godself, in and through the historical process.

When we use theological language, we have to anticipate and be ready to answer the objector who says that theological language, unlike the precise language of science, is nothing but a ragbag of different modes of discourse devoid of any essential unifying principle or inherent logic. We reply that theological language is indeed complex and multivalent. It has various elements and modes, including myth, symbol, metaphor, analogy, paradox, allegory, story, narrative, and interpreted history. All these may be flexibly deployed, alone or in combination, in such a way as to reinforce, intensify, limit, and correct one another. All may be observed in the Hebrew scriptures and in the New Testament, whose religious and theological language has its own inner logic and coherence.

Consider, for example, the role of myth in God-talk. Non-believers may be surprised to learn that many modern Christians take a positive rather than a negative view of myth, although they would probably want to draw a distinction between myth in itself and specific articulations of faith in mythical terms. Myth does not present an objective view of the world as it is, but it can serve to express our understanding of ourselves in relation to reality. Further, myth may be a particularly appropriate or even necessary vehicle for communicating divine revelation. Bultmann regarded all objectified descriptions of the resurrection of Jesus as mythological, although he was careful to say that this did not mean that the resurrection of Jesus was a mythical event "pure and simple". He was clear that revelation did not arise out of myth; on the contrary, myth is appropriated as one way of articulating the experience of revelation.

The theologian and philosopher John Macquarrie (1919–2007) argued that myth and symbol together constitute the matrix out of which all other theological language has emerged.[90] They unify all other theological language, and they have both an ontological and an existential dimension. The language of myth is dramatic, immediate, and evocative. It is freighted with overtones and connotations, embedded in community, but free of particularity. Myth has the important additional capacity to confront us with present possibilities. The mythical drama of the New Testament, says Macquarrie, bursts into history: it takes place not in the remote future but in the midst of the real history of Jesus of Nazareth and his first followers. The converse, of course, is also true; that is, in the earliest Christian texts we observe history becoming transmuted into Christian myth. Symbol functions in a similar way. A symbol has the capacity to draw human awareness towards something other than itself. Myth and symbol both have an irreducible existential core which finds its best expression in metaphor and analogy. Metaphor involves the transfer of meaning, but the underlying presumption is that there is something about one thing or person that is suggestive of something about another thing or person. Analogy, to be meaningful, also presupposes an intrinsic likeness or affinity between the analogue and that which it stands for. Paradox, on the other hand, operates in reverse. It serves to protect the "otherness" of God by keeping us alert to the inherent limitations and provisionality of theological language.

This multiplicity of modes of discourse involved in theological language should immediately alert us to the dangers and difficulties involved in interpreting the beliefs of one culture from the viewpoint of an alien culture. In stripping away what appear to be the "wrappings" of an ancient, alien belief—that is, the myths, allegories, metaphors, analogies, and symbols by means of which the alien belief is articulated—there is a real risk of losing essential content. This is not because the wrappings themselves constitute the reality which they appear to be enclosing, but because collectively they function to define the reality. The danger of demythologizing ancient, alien texts and traditions is that the process of "unwrapping" meaning may lead not to clearer understanding, but to a loss in definition of the reality to which the texts and traditions are referring.

This means that, wherever possible, theological texts should be assessed "from within". Theological language is the property of a particular linguistic and faith community. It serves to reflect the needs and interests of the community and it enables its members to identify with shared experiences and inherited traditions. Beliefs and traditions may lose much of their meaning when separated from the community and culture to which they belong. Unless comparisons of traditions take place from within the communities whose property they are, there will always be a danger that assessments will be defective. Modern interpreters do not necessarily have to be believers, but they do have to understand the logic and rules that govern the use of the theological language in the ancient texts and traditions they are assessing. Modern interpreters also have to be aware of the changing nature of theological language over time, and of the possibly different ways in which it may be functioning within particular sub-groups of the same faith community. The philosopher Alasdair MacIntyre (1929–) argues that only a critic who has fully entered into the thinking of a tradition can understand how rationality is understood and established within that tradition.[91] Much of the language actually in use in a community is intimately tied to the particular community's set of beliefs. This means that the accurate translation of ideas and concepts from one language to another requires translators to learn the second language as though it were their own first language.

There is also the question of the relationship between a linguistic or faith community and its wider environment. Faith communities seldom exist in isolation—they are usually set in the context of a constantly changing social and intellectual environment, or in juxtaposition with alien faith communities, or both. A rapidly changing external environment or collision of cultures may expose a faith community to sudden shock and epistemological challenge. A defensive retreat into isolationism is one possibility. Alternatively, ancient certitudes and traditions may be gradually eroded under the pressure of new knowledge and thinking. Particular elements of the tradition may be reformulated or reformed, or may fade away into relative insignificance. Alternatively, previously inconspicuous or marginal elements of the tradition may assume enhanced significance and prominence. In any assessment of the rationality of a religious tradition, one has to ask whether the tradition in question is demonstrating an ability to respond creatively to changing circumstances and epistemological challenge whilst preserving essential links with its past, including, where necessary, modes of linguistic expression. Or, to put it simply, we have to ask whether the tradition has fossilized, or whether it can respond positively when challenged, despite the fact that it may now be set in the context of a world view very different from that within which it originated. A tradition that is manifesting an ability to adapt creatively to changing circumstances, whilst still remaining faithful to its own past, cannot arbitrarily be dismissed as irrational, even though its beliefs and traditions may be expressed in unfamiliar theological language.

To summarize, religious language is primarily but not exclusively the property of a faith community. It is richly textured, complex, and multivalent. In this respect, it has something in common with poetry. Religious language serves to give expression to convictions concerning human experience of both physical and non-physical realities that, like Godself, may not be reduced to the status of mere objects or "matter in motion". The multiple components and genres of religious literature have—in varying degrees—both an ontological and an existential capacity. That is, they can be used to speak about reality, and about our experience of relationship with reality. Myth is particularly important: in its religious context, myth draws the one who knows into active engagement with that which is known. A particular myth may be of ancient origin and may be expressed in theological language, but there is no reason why it should not apply to present circumstances and possibilities. Like poetry, religious language has the capacity to express truths about the human condition which might otherwise be inexpressible. The Christian proclamation of the resurrection finds expression in theological language, and it includes a mythical component insofar as it joins together physical reality (the historical Jesus) with non-physical realities (God, the act of

God in raising Jesus, and the exalted, heavenly Jesus Christ), and it has the capacity to draw the hearer into active engagement with what he or she is hearing. The terms and concepts involved may seem strange to modern men and women but, subject to the proviso that it must be interpreted "from within", there is no necessary irrationality in the affirmation that "God raised Jesus from the dead."

Events and meaning

Accepting Bultmann's argument that any attempt to relate God to specific historical events inevitably generates myth, and accepting also that myth—with its ability to draw together physical and non-physical realities—is almost always a component of theological language, we have to ask whether historical events—that is, physical events taking place in space–time—can ever have meaning. Can historical events ever be freighted with the kind of intrinsic meaning that can reach out and draw the interpreter or observer into active present engagement with their significance? If not, attempts to discern an essential connection between the human Jesus and the post-resurrection, non-physical but real risen Jesus are futile. We therefore have to ask whether there can ever be, in any historical event, something of objective significance waiting for us to "lock on" to it, waiting for us to perceive it and understand it. Or are we, as interpreters of history, always imposing or projecting our own understandings on to what are actually random, meaningless happenings?

A useful starting point is to note that the assumption that historical events can have meaning underlies many of our day-to-day decisions and much of our orientation towards reality. Consider just three examples:

1. The *first example* is that of traffic lights controlling a highway intersection. Suppose that the lights I am approaching change from green to red. By the time I register this change it is a historical event, albeit a historical event in the very recent past. That this event has meaning is obvious. It tells me that I must stop my car, or there may be an accident. Equally, it is obvious that the meaning is not inherent in the redness as opposed to the

greenness of the lights. The meaning is projected on to the redness and the greenness of the lights by social and legal convention. This does not mean that the meaning is not real—it would be foolish and could be fatal to ignore it—but it is not intrinsic meaning. One could envisage another culture in which red meant "go" and green meant "stop".

2. The *second example* is more complex. Weather forecasting in the United Kingdom is based on meteorological data. Data concerning air pressure, winds, and cloud formations are collected by satellite cameras and other remote sensors far out in the Atlantic Ocean. These data are then transmitted to land-based meteorologists, by which time they have become historic data. Suppose that meteorologists interpret this data to forecast an approaching storm. Clearly, they are interpreting and projecting significance on to the data. But equally, one could argue that in this case the significance is also intrinsic to the data. The data, which are historical events in the form of measurements, have meaning that is not just externally imposed on them. Even if no human analysts were involved, they would still be signifying the same approaching storm.

3. The *third example* is especially important. Physicists assume that coherence and intrinsic rationality are part of the universal fabric of reality. This is an act of faith involving a projection of significance. No one can prove that there is not some faraway, inaccessible corner of the universe where the laws of physics are quite other than those applying in our own locality. The assumption that universal coherence and rationality are intrinsic properties of the fabric of reality is incapable of demonstration, either by reasoning or by experiment. We shall never know whether it is true, and if it *is* true, it is true regardless of our awareness or unawareness.

As all three examples show, we undoubtedly can and do project meaning on to historical events and natural processes. But sometimes, in addition to the act of projecting significance, we additionally suspect that we may be "locking on" to intrinsic meaning or significance already latent in the events and processes we are interpreting. An analogy might be a capsule "docking" with an orbiting space station. The claim that particular events are significant involves an act of faith—or rather, a response of faith—which is arrived at in the context of being drawn into active engagement with the events themselves. In this respect historical events function like myth; that is, they tell a story about the past that has the capacity to point to truth beyond themselves and confront us with present possibilities.

Understanding that historical events may have intrinsic significance in addition to the significance we project on to them opens the way to a possible understanding of divine revelation. Divine revelation may be thought of as something delivered, not through miracles involving an overturning of the natural order, but through the perception of God-given meaning located in historical events. In this connection, the theologian Helmut Richard Niebuhr (1894–1962) makes a helpful distinction between what he calls "inner" and "external" history.[92] For Niebuhr, external history is an impersonal process, detached from the non-participating observer or historian. It comprises matter in motion, a meaningless succession of events. External history involves the chronicling of these events and processes. Inner history, on the other hand, is personal; it comprises history as lived and experienced from within. Whereas external history-writing can be descriptive only, internal history involves experiencing. Both external and internal history are valid approaches to reality, but neither may be reduced to the other.

Niebuhr's distinction between external and inner history must not be pressed too far, but understanding how he and others think they can locate meaning in history suggests a possible way of combining the idea of divine revelation with commitment to a modern scientific world view. For Niebuhr, divine revelation and human perception of meaning are two different sides of the same coin. To perceive God-given intrinsic meaning in historical events is to receive revelation. Building on this understanding, Niebuhr argues that revelation involves an act of God (placing significance in events) intended to elicit the individual's perception of meaning and significance. This means that at the heart of the revelatory experience there is not just intellectual appreciation, there is an "encounter experience". That is, there are two living selves engaging in what Martin Buber (1878–1965) called an "I–Thou" relationship. In this experience of encounter there is a self-disclosure of God himself.

Revelation involves more than the perception of intrinsic significance in specific historical events. The core experience is an existential challenge to engage in a relationship of commitment to the One who is being disclosed through significant events.

The revelatory experience is therefore intensely personal, but seldom takes place in isolation. Revelation is usually located in the context of a faith community, or in some form of association with the traditions, scriptures, and cult of a faith community. Directly or indirectly, the faith community provides both the setting and the initial stimulus for the revelatory experience. By affording access to the whole range of interpretive possibilities embodied in the community's religious language and concepts, the faith community facilitates the subsequent articulation of revelatory experience. It also provides checks, balances, controls, and boundaries that determine the ongoing significance of the revelatory experience. Finally, the faith community is the context within which new perceptions of significance may be enhanced and intensified, by connection with the community's existing traditions.

How is the objective validity of a claimed revelation of God in historical events—for example, the life and death of Jesus and the emergence of belief in his resurrection—to be established? The answer is that such claims cannot be objectively validated because they involve acts of judgement and faith commitment on the part of the individual or individuals making the claim. Nevertheless, although claims cannot be objectively verified, they may and must be interrogated and tested for reasonableness, coherence and internal consistency. Depending on the nature of the claim, other considerations and criteria may also apply. For example, if a claim originates in the context of a faith community, or if it is articulated in terms of the religious language and concepts of a faith community, the standards applied in assessing the claim must commend themselves as the best and most appropriate standards available within the framework of that community's thinking. One might also wish to ask whether the claim stands alone, or whether it in some measure epitomizes, intensifies, integrates, or unifies other related perceptions of the faith community in question. If the claim is entirely dissimilar to all previous understandings, we may not necessarily reject it out of hand, but we will probably be cautious in forming any judgement.

Resurrection as revelation

In purely historical terms, resurrection faith emerged as a theological interpretation or understanding imposed on the events of Jesus' life and death by his followers. From their standpoint, matters were quite otherwise. They were on the inside of the process, participating in what Niebuhr calls "inner history". So far as they were concerned, they were not imposing understandings or projecting interpretations on to historical events. On the contrary, Jesus' followers discovered themselves to be on the inside of an unfolding revelatory act of God. They were being engaged by Godself through historical events that challenged them to perceive and to respond to what they were perceiving. Or rather, to *whom* they were perceiving, because, in some instances, the act of perception and response was associated with experiences which they could only adequately describe as direct encounters with Godself mediated through visionary "seeings" of the gloriously transformed, heavenly Jesus Christ.

The New Testament confirms that the earliest resurrection faith took the form of belief in an overarching revelatory act of God. The traditional resurrection faith formula rarely says that "Jesus rose from the dead", probably because it would have misleadingly implied that Jesus had risen from death to life in God, like a bubble naturally rising to the surface of a liquid. The earliest proclamation usually took the form of the statement that "God has raised Jesus from the dead". In the probably pre-Pauline christological hymn in Philippians 2:5-11, the centrality of the divine act is again explicit: it is God who has acted by highly exalting Jesus and giving him "the name that is above every name". In Galatians 1:15-16, Paul makes it clear that in his own experience of encounter with the risen Christ, he believed himself to be the recipient of a specific revelatory act of God. "God," says Paul, "was pleased to reveal his Son to me" (or "in me"). Elsewhere Paul emphasizes that in the matter of revelation, Jesus and God are not to be separated. Jesus is the living image of God; it is God who displays the light of his own glory in the face of Jesus Christ (2 Corinthians 4:4-6). The somewhat later appearance stories of the Gospels also imply that in encountering the risen Christ, there is encounter with the divine. In John 14:9; Jesus himself says, "Whoever has seen me has seen the Father."

In terms of external history, the resurrection of Jesus is a summary statement of faith unifying and encapsulating a complex package of perceptions and understandings concerning the totality of Israel's history, Jesus' life and death, and what was believed to be God's intended future. In respect of beliefs concerning the risen Jesus' person and function—that is, Christology—we observe numerous motifs and understandings already existing in Second Temple Judaism being drawn together and applied to the figure of the risen and exalted Jesus Christ. These include belief in the divine vindication of the unjustly persecuted righteous man; the idea of resurrection as a reward for dead martyrs; the possibility of bypassing *Sheol* and being taken directly to heaven; the concept of martyrdom conferring benefits on others; the belief that humans entering heaven will undergo transformation and become glorious angel-like beings; the concept of heavenly messiahship; and the idea of resurrection for participation in a new age or kingdom of God. Also integrated into resurrection faith at a very early stage indeed is the identification of Jesus with the heavenly being who comes to God to be awarded "dominion and glory and kingship, that all peoples, nations, and languages should serve him" (Daniel 7:13-14).

Further understandings quickly followed. These included the conviction that followers of Jesus were the beneficiaries of an outpouring of the Spirit of God; the understanding that they were now called and commissioned to continue Jesus' ministry; the conviction that Jesus would return to gather up and make safe his faithful followers and exercise his universal dominion; and the expectation that the mortal bodies of Jesus' followers would, in due course, undergo a transformation like that of Jesus (1 Corinthians 15:50-54). Paul even extends the hope of transformation to include the whole of creation (Romans 8:18-24). Not just believers, but the whole grinding natural process that first makes us and then breaks us is to be transformed. It will be "set free from its bondage to decay". That is, it will be liberated from contingency. Belief in the resurrection and transformation of Jesus is universalized and brought into association with belief in God as creator. The transformation of all things will be the culmination of God's already inaugurated act of new creation.

For the followers of Jesus, these understandings required no proof. So far as they were concerned, the historical events of Israel's history and Jesus' life were reaching forward out of the distant and more recent past into the present, freighted with challenging intrinsic significance, response to which took the form of perception experienced as encounter with the divine. The outcome of this experience was "salvation"—that is, the state of "being made safe"—and commitment to continuing the work of Jesus into the future. In terms of "inner history", the resurrection of Jesus was therefore not an event believed (or not believed) to have happened. Resurrection faith was something received through an act of perception and response to the challenge latent in the perception. It involved experience that could only be described as encounter with the divine. As Edward Schillebeeckx insists, the conviction that Jesus has risen is an assurance of faith that comes from God alone.

That said, belief in the resurrection of Jesus emerged in the context of an ancient faith community whose world view was very different from those of modern men and women. In giving expression to their faith, the followers of Jesus inevitably used theological language and concepts some of which are unfamiliar today. Nevertheless, their claims may still be assessed for reasonableness, providing that the assessment takes place as if from the standpoint of the language and traditions of the ancient community of faith. In this context, it can be seen that both the primary tests of coherence and consistency and the secondary tests of unifying, intensifying, and extending power are met. It can be seen that Jesus was located in the mainstream of already existing Jewish hopes for a coming new age. It can be seen that, in terms of external history, resurrection faith drew together and unified a constellation of already existing interpretive traditions and motifs, generating a coherent and consistent but nevertheless wholly innovatory understanding of Israel's history, of Jesus' life and death, and of God's future for his people. In terms of "inner history", resurrection faith is the response of the followers of Jesus to their experiences of a challenging personal encounter with the One who was reaching out to them, in and through the history of Israel and of Jesus.

Conclusion

The declared intention of this book was to address the question, "Can a modern Christian, fully committed to a post-Enlightenment scientific world view, honestly return a clear 'Yes' to the question, 'Do you really believe that God raised Jesus from the dead?'"

The question is deceptive in its simplicity, and any answer has to be qualified. As we have seen, there is a sufficient gap in the historical evidence to allow room for traditional belief in a miraculous resurrection event. That said, carefully focused critical-historical enquiry refutes the traditionalists' argument that "No other explanation fits the facts." Indeed, the earliest and best testimony does not even point in this direction. There is at least one possible historical pathway, with variations, by means of which belief in the resurrection of Jesus could have emerged naturally without the need for any miraculous overturning of the natural order.

Christians who reject a priori the idea of a miraculous overturning of nature find themselves in an invidious position. The problem is how to give expression to our faith without slipping over the cliff edge into reductionism and unbelief. Paradoxically, critical-historical enquiry assists in two distinct ways. First, it assists by showing that the earliest understanding of the resurrection never involved the resuscitation—that is, the restoration to normal, physical human life—of Jesus' corpse. Although it was certainly believed from the outset that after his death, Jesus was raised, transformed, and is alive in God, the earliest exaltation and resurrection traditions say nothing at all about the body of Jesus or any empty tomb.

Second, critical-historical enquiry shows that in proclaiming the resurrection, Jesus' earliest followers were articulating the theological conviction that there had been a revelatory act of God, the essential core of which was the location of intrinsic significance and necessity in the totality of Israel's history, Jesus' life and death, and God's intended future. The experience of perceiving and responding to the challenge of this significance could only be adequately articulated in terms of encounter with the divine.

This understanding is not a modern imposition on the historical data. On the contrary, it was almost certainly Paul's own understanding, and perhaps also that of the other individuals listed in the early 1 Corinthians 15:5–8 tradition. This may explain the absence of any reference to an empty-tomb tradition in Paul's writings. Although the appearance stories of the Gospels are in many respects problematic, critically interpreted they also testify to an early understanding of the resurrection of Jesus as an encounter with the divine, as manifested first in Israel's history and then reaching its climax in Jesus the crucified and risen Messiah.

Understood in this way, resurrection faith is not contrary to reason. *Pace* Lewis Carroll, no one is being asked to believe anything impossible or absurd, either before or after breakfast. Resurrection faith is coherent and consistent, and it has its own inner logic. Although formulated using concepts and terminology that are the particular property of a venerable faith community, it nevertheless affirms values and articulates religious experience in a way that is compatible with a commitment to a modern post-Enlightenment scientific world view. The statement that God raised Jesus from the dead should not be regarded—and never should have been regarded—as a proposition amenable to proof in the conventional historical sense. It articulates the conviction that the perception of intrinsic significance in certain specific historical events is one side of a coin, the other side of which is an act of divine self-disclosure. Responding to the challenge implicit in this understanding is an experience that can only be described as an encounter between selves. This experience of encounter, says Schillebeeckx, is like the human eye. Without the experience of faith-generating encounter, Jesus' disciples would have had no organ that could have afforded them "sight" of the risen, crucified one.

The wider intention of this book was to establish a platform of understanding upon which Christians and sceptics can engage in constructive dialogue. In the words of Albert Schweitzer, critical-historical enquiry assists by clearing away rubble. It also enables us to establish what can and cannot with reasonable certainty be known about Jesus of Nazareth. Knowing how theological language works, and understanding resurrection faith to be a theological interpretation of God's action in history, establishes a basis for constructive conversation.

The task now facing Christians is to explain to non-believers in what way, and up to what point, we can gain access to the Jesus of history, and how we may encounter the risen Jesus Christ of faith. Or, to put it another way, we have to consider how Christ is most appropriately to be proclaimed, and how historical scholarship should be used constructively to facilitate his mysterious emergence out of the traditions and texts of the Church into the minds and affections of modern men and women. Sceptics, for their part, are invited to set aside their prejudices and accept that religious belief, like science, seeks to engage with given reality, and that religious belief can be compatible with full commitment to a modern world view—and also to consider, with an open mind, the possibility that there is a specific voice to be heard, a voice speaking out of the past and into the present, an enticing voice demanding a hearing and deserving a response.

Suggested Further Reading

The sources listed below are not a formal bibliography. They are pointers to useful sources of further information, either generally or on topics and issues dealt with in particular chapters. With one exception, all the works referred to are available in English or in English translation. Full bibliographic details may be easily be obtained by online search.

Chapter 1

For an accessible overview of the changing relationship between faith and historical study from the Enlightenment to the present day, see James D. G. Dunn, *Jesus Remembered* (Eerdmans, 2003). On the impact of science on religion from the seventeenth century onwards, Ian G. Barbour, *Issues in Science and Religion* (SCM Press, 1966) remains valuable. Claude Welch, *Protestant Thought in the Nineteenth Century, Volume 1: 1799–1870* contains useful sections on Strauss and Baur (Yale University Press, 1985). On Reimarus, Strauss, and Baur, see also *Biblical Interpretation* by Robert Morgan with John Barton (Oxford University Press, 1988). The relevant sections of Reimarus's *Fragments* are available in English translation with an extended introduction by Charles H. Talbert (SCM Press, 1970 and 1971). David Friedrich Strauss's *Life of Jesus, Critically Examined* was translated into English by George Eliot in 1846 and edited by Peter C. Hodgson for Fortress and SCM Press in 1970.

Chapter 2

For an account of the development of Jewish thinking concerning life after death, resurrection, and the last judgement, see Emil Schürer's classic *The History of the Jewish People in the Age of Jesus Christ* (new English edition edited by Geza Vermes and Fergus Millar; T & T Clark, 1973). For accessible modern overviews, see Philip S. Johnston, *Shades of Sheol: Death and Afterlife in the Old Testament* (InterVarsity Press, 2002), Christopher Rowland, *Christian Origins* (SPCK, 1985), and N. T. Wright, *The Resurrection of the Son of God* (SPCK, 2003). *Life in the Face of Death: The Resurrection Message of the New Testament* (Eerdmans, 1998), a book of essays edited by Richard N. Longenecker, includes Edwin Yamauchi's "Life, Death and the Afterlife in the Ancient Near East" and Richard Bauckham's "Life, Death and Afterlife in Second Temple Judaism". On the Hellenization of Judaism, see Martin Hengel's *Judaism and Hellenism: Studies in Their Encounter in Palestine During the Early Hellenistic Period* (English translation; Wipf & Stock, 1974). In *Resurrection, Immortality, and Eternal Life in Intertestamental Judaism* (Harvard University Press, 1972), George W. E. Nickelsburg traces the development of themes which function as vectors for emergent resurrection belief, especially the motif of the vindication and exaltation of the unjustly persecuted righteous man, and an apocalyptic judgement scene in which a persecuted righteous man is vindicated by God. There are important essays by leading scholars in *Judaism in Late Antiquity, Part 4, Death, Life-After-Death, Resurrection and the World to Come in the Judaisms of Antiquity* (Brill, 2000), edited by Alan J. Avery-Peck and Jacob Neusner.

Chapter 3

In *Christian Origins*, Christopher Rowland provides an accessible account of Jewish angelology and intermediary figures. On the different conceptual backgrounds underlying the idea of angels and on the development of angel traditions in the Hebrew scriptures, Jewish apocalyptic texts, and the Qumran scrolls, see Andrew Chester's *Messiah and Exaltation: Jewish Messianic and Visionary Traditions and New*

Testament Christology (Mohr Siebeck, 2007). For a general discussion of the role of angels in Jewish and early Christian literature, see Volume 1 of George W. E. Nickelsburg's commentary, *1 Enoch* (Fortress Press, 2001). On the Divine Council and angels as heavenly counterparts of human priests, see Martha Himmelfarb, *Ascent to Heaven in Jewish and Christian Apocalypses* (Oxford University Press, 1993). See also Philip Alexander's essay, "Introduction to 3 Enoch" in Volume 1 of James H. Charlesworth's *The Old Testament Pseudepigrapha* (DLT, 1983). Specialist monographs by Charles A. Gieschen, Crispin Fletcher Lewis, and Margaret Barker take the discussion further.

Chapter 4

On the interpretation of the figure of the "one like a son of man" in Daniel 7:13, see the Hermeneia *Commentary on the Book of Daniel* by John J. Collins (Fortress Press, 1993). Maurice Casey, in *Son of Man: The Interpretation and Influence of Daniel 7* (SPCK, 1979), argues that the figure is symbolic. John J. Collins's view is that the figure is individual. See also Adela Yarbro Collins and John J. Collins's *King and Messiah as Son of God: Divine, Human and Angelic Messianic Figures in Biblical and Related Literature* (Eerdmans, 2008). On the Melchizedek text 11Q13, see Geza Vermes's *The Complete Dead Sea Scrolls in English* (Pelican, 1962/Allen Lane, 1997). On the Similitudes of Enoch, see George W. E. Nickelsburg's essay in *Enoch and the Messiah Son of Man: Revisiting the Book of Parables*, edited by Gabriele Boccaccini (Eerdmans, 2007), and also Volume 2 of Nickelsburg's and James C. VanderKam's *1 Enoch* commentary (Fortress Press, 2012). Additional information on 4 Ezra, Sibylline Oracle 5, and 2 Baruch may be found in J. H. Charlesworth, *The Old Testament Pseudepigrapha*. In addition to the books already mentioned, Michael E. Stone's Hermeneia Commentary *Fourth Ezra* (Fortress Press, 1990) is pertinent. On the question of a pre-Christian heavenly-redeemer tradition, see H. J. de Jonge's essay, "The Historical Jesus' View of Himself and His Mission" in *From Jesus to John*, edited by Martinus C. de Boer (Sheffield Academic Press, 1993).

Chapter 5

Among the numerous modern accounts of Jesus and his teaching concerning the kingdom of God, E. P. Sanders's *Jesus and Judaism* (SCM Press, 1985) and Gerd Theissen and Annette Merz's *The Historical Jesus: A Comprehensive Guide* (English translation: Fortress Press, 1998) stand out. John Dominic Crossan, in his *The Historical Jesus: The Life of a Mediterranean Jewish Peasant* (T & T Clark, 1992), argues that in Jesus' understanding the kingdom of God was not a future expectation but a "sapiential realm" or timeless ethical state. Dunn's *Jesus Remembered* has a clear analysis of the relevant data and addresses all the topics discussed in this chapter. Leander E. Keck's *Who is Jesus? History in Perfect Tense* (T & T Clark, 2001) is sharply focused on Jesus' kingdom teaching and on Jesus himself as the "embodied future". For a more theological approach to the historical data, see Edward Schillebeeckx's *Jesus: An Experiment in Christology* (English translation; Collins, 1979).

Chapter 6

For the historical setting, see E. P. Sanders (op. cit.), Theissen and Merz (op. cit.), and Richard A. Horsley, *Sociology and the Jesus Movement* (Crossroad, 1989). On revolutionary attitudes in Galilee and Jerusalem, see Sean Freyne's *Galilee from Alexander the Great to Hadrian* (Notre Dame, 1980). On the rebellions of Theudas, the Sicarii, and the movement led by Jonathan of Cyrene, see Josephus, *Jewish Antiquities* (XX) and *The Jewish War* (XI). On Jesus as Messiah, Lord, Son of God, eschatological prophet, and Son of Man, in addition to the standard works already mentioned see Nils Alstrup Dahl's *Jesus the Christ: The Historical Origins of Christological Doctrine*, edited by Donald H. Juel (Fortress Press, 1991). On Jesus as an anointed figure, see Marinus De Jonge, *Jesus, the Servant–Messiah* (Yale University Press, 1991) and *God's Final Envoy: Early Christology and Jesus' Own View of His Mission* (Eerdmans, 1998). On the Son of Man sayings, see Norman Perrin, *Rediscovering the Teaching of Jesus* (SCM, 1967), Geza Vermes, *Jesus the Jew: A Historian's Reading of the Gospels* (Collins, 1973), Maurice Casey, *Son of Man: The*

Interpretation and Influence of Daniel 7 (SPCK, 1979), and James D. G. Dunn, *Christology in the Making: An Inquiry into the Origins of the Doctrine of the Incarnation* (SCM Press, 1980). On the Son of Man as someone other than Jesus, see Adela Yarbro Collins in *King and Messiah as Son of God: Divine, Human, and Angelic Messianic Figures in Biblical and Related Literature*, by A. Y. Collins and J. J. Collins (Eerdmans, 2008), and H. J. De Jonge's essay, "The Historical Jesus' View of Himself and of his Mission" in *From Jesus to John*, edited by Martinus C. De Boer. On the Son of Man as Jesus' heavenly alter ego, see Bruce Chilton's own essay in *Authenticating the Words of Jesus*, edited by Bruce Chilton and Craig A. Evans (Brill, 1999), and Helmut Merklein's *Jesu Botschaft von der Gottesherrschaft* (1983/1989).

Chapter 7

On the earliest formulaic assertions of the resurrection, see *Christ, Lord, Son of God* by Werner Kramer (SCM Press, 1966) and *Resurrection: New Testament Witness and Contemporary Reflection* by Pheme Perkins (Doubleday, 1984). On the christological hymns and fragments, see also Martin Hengel's *Studies in Early Christology* (T & T Clark, 1995) and Ralph P. Martin's *Carmen Christi: Philippians ii.5–11 in Recent Scholarship* . . . (Cambridge University Press, 1967). The tradition in 1 Corinthians 15:3–8 is discussed by all the commentators. For an introduction, see Perkins, Theissen and Merz, or Dunn, *op. cit*. On the impossibility of harmonization, see C. F. Evans, *Resurrection and the New Testament* (SCM Press, 1970) and Gerd Lüdemann, *The Resurrection of Jesus: History, Experience, Theology* (Fortress Press, 1994). On Paul's conversion or experience of a call, see Krister Stendahl, *Paul among Jews and Gentiles, and Other Essays* (Fortress Press, 1976), Alan F. Segal, *Paul the Convert: The Apostolate and Apostasy of Saul the Pharisee* (Yale University Press, 1990), and Seyoon Kim, *Paul and the New Perspective: Second Thoughts on the Origin of Paul's Gospel* (Eerdmans, 2002). On heavenly ascent and divestiture/investiture, see Martha Himmelfarb (op. cit.). On the possible fluidity of the earliest understandings of the resurrection, see Gregory J. Riley's *Resurrection Reconsidered: Thomas and John in*

Controversy (Fortress Press, 1995). Ferdinand Hahn, in *The Titles of Jesus in Christology: Their History in Early Christianity* (English translation; Lutterworth, 1969), argues that the perception of Jesus as Lord lies at the root of all Christology and that belief in Jesus' heavenly exaltation and messianic enthronement are secondary developments. Donald Juel, in *Messianic Exegesis: Christological Interpretation of the Old Testament in Early Christianity* (Fortress Press, 1988), sees the historical starting point as the confession of Jesus as (crucified) Messiah. Eduard Schweizer, in *Lordship and Discipleship* (Allenson, 1960), suggests that the earliest form of resurrection belief was belief in Jesus' exaltation as the suffering righteous one. On the significance of the earliest Christians' invocation or acclamation of the risen Jesus as Lord, see Larry W. Hurtado, *Lord Jesus Christ: Devotion to Jesus in Earliest Christianity* (Eerdmans, 2003).

Chapter 8

On the influence of Psalm 110, see David M. Hay's *Glory at the Right Hand: Psalm 110 in Early Christianity* (Abingdon, 1973). For an account of the way in which resurrection faith directed the primitive community towards particular texts, see Barnabas Lindars, *New Testament Apologetic: The Doctrinal Significance of the Old Testament Quotations* (SCM Press, 1961). On the possibility that the "Name" awarded to Jesus in Philippians 2:10–11 is the Divine Name, see Charles A. Gieschen, *Angelomorphic Christology: Antecedents and Early Evidence* (Brill, 1998). For surveys of eschatological expectations in Second Temple Judaism, see Rowland, *Christian Origins*, and N. T. Wright, *The New Testament and the People of God* (SPCK, 1992). On the kingdom of God and the kingdom of the Messiah—and on the prevalence, variety, and coherence of the messianic hope in the Second Temple period—see William Horbury, *Jewish Messianism and the Cult of Christ* (SCM Press, 1998) and Frederick J. Murphy, *Apocalypticism in the Bible and its World* (Baker Academic, 2012). James D. G. Dunn discusses the resurrection, the gift of the Spirit, and mission in *Jesus and the Spirit* (SCM Press, 1975). For a discussion of resurrection and Jesus' redemptive death, see Hurtado's *Lord Jesus Christ*. On the understanding that the death of Jesus was "for us", see Martin

Hengel, *The Atonement: A Study of the Origins of the Doctrine in the New Testament* (English translation; SCM Press, 1981).

Chapter 9

On the historicity of the resurrection-appearance stories and the empty-tomb traditions, see Wright's *Resurrection of the Son of God* and Dunn's *Jesus Remembered*. For a different perspective, see Willi Marxsen, *The Resurrection of Jesus of Nazareth* (SCM Press, 1970). For other brief overviews, see the essays in *The Resurrection of Jesus Christ*, edited by Paul Avis (DLT, 1993). Perkins examines the evidence of the canonical Gospels in *Resurrection: New Testament Witness and Contemporary Reflection*. See also A. J. M. Wedderburn, *Beyond Resurrection* (SCM Press, 1999); Lüdemann, (*op. cit.*); Evans (op. cit.); and Norman Perrin, *The Resurrection according to Matthew, Mark and Luke* (Fortress Press, 1977). Hans von Campenhausen, in *Tradition and Life in the Church* (English translation; Collins, 1968), suggests that the empty-tomb tradition is reliable and that it was interpreted from the outset as a pledge that the resurrection had happened. John E. Alsup, in *The Post-Resurrection Appearance Stories of the Gospel Tradition* (SPCK, 1975), argues that the appearance stories of the Gospels constitute a separate stream of theologically significant tradition related to the OT angelomorphic theophany stories. In *The Historical Jesus: A Comprehensive Guide*, Theissen and Merz consider the different ways in which scholars have interpreted the Easter faith. Edward Schillebeeckx (op. cit.) maintains that the outcomes of critical historical investigation may be incorporated into the structure of belief, even though he holds the reality denoted by the "Easter experience" to be independent both of the empty-tomb traditions and the appearance stories.

Chapter 10

In *The Resurrection of Jesus of Nazareth*, Marxsen argues that exaltation and resurrection belief emerged as interpretations of the historical Jesus interacting with visionary experiences. Rowan Williams, in *Resurrection: Interpreting the Easter Gospel* (DLT, 1982), argues that the empty-tomb tradition provided the initial impetus for the emergence of resurrection faith. For modern conservative approaches to the resurrection, see Gary R. Habermas, *The Risen Jesus and Future Hope* (Rowman & Littlefield, 2003), and William Lane Craig in *Jesus' Resurrection, Fact or Figment*, edited by Paul Copan and Ronald Tacelli (IVP, 2000). N. T. Wright (*The Resurrection of the Son of God*) accepts the basic historicity of the empty-tomb tradition but stresses that resurrection involved the transformation rather than the resuscitation of Jesus' body. Dunn, in *Jesus Remembered*, argues that something perceived to have happened on the third day lies at the heart of the tradition; resurrection, although a metaphor, is saying some things that could not otherwise be said. Most authors stress the historical importance of the visions of the risen Jesus Christ. Schillebeeckx (op. cit.) suggests that the subjective and objective aspects of resurrection faith cannot be separated and that the resurrection "appearances" were faith-inspired experiences or perceptions of something real and given by God. In *The Resurrection of Jesus*, Lüdemann suggests that an initial vision in which Peter saw and heard Jesus initiated a chain reaction of further visions and interpretations. The role of visions in Judaism and early Christianity is examined by Andrew Chester in *Messiah and Exaltation: Jewish Messianic and Visionary Traditions and New Testament Christology* (Mohr Siebeck, 2007). For another overview, see Wedderburn's *Beyond Resurrection*.

Chapter 11

For an account of different interpretations of the resurrection, see Theissen and Merz (op. cit.). In *The Structure of Resurrection Belief* (Clarendon, 1987), Peter Carnley discusses historical and theological interpretations of the resurrection. On theological language and the way it works, see John Macquarrie, *God-Talk: An Examination of the Language and Logic of Theology* (SCM Press, 1967); Alasdair C. MacIntyre, *Whose Justice? Which Rationality?* (Duckworth, 1988); Roger Haight, *Jesus, Symbol of God* (Orbis Books, 1999); and Andrew T. Lincoln, *Born of a Virgin?* (SPCK, 2013). On the revelation of God in history, see H. Richard Niebuhr's *The Meaning of Revelation* (Macmillan, 1960). In *From Jesus to the New Testament* (English translation; Baylor University Press, 2013), Jens Schröter argues that the meaning of the reported events concerning Jesus is only revealed in the light of the history of Israel and of belief in God's action in the life of Jesus and everything that flowed from it. The possibility that modern science may be able to contribute to an understanding of the resurrection of Jesus is explored in essays in *Quantum Cosmology and The Laws of Nature: Scientific Perspectives on Divine Action* (University of Notre Dame Press, 1997), edited by Robert J. Russell, Nancey Murphy, and Christopher John Isham. See also *Resurrection: Theological and Scientific Assessments* (Eerdmans, 2002), edited by Ted Peters, Robert J. Russell, and Michael Welker.

Notes

1. David Hume, *Essays and Treatises on Several Subjects*, Part II: "An Enquiry Concerning Human Understanding", Section X: *Of Miracles* (London and Edinburgh: A. Millar, A. Kincaid, and A. Donaldson, 1758), p. 347.
2. Reimarus, *On the Intentions of Jesus and his Disciples*, section 32. See Talbert, Charles H. Talbert (ed. and tr.), *Reimarus: Fragments* (Eugene, OR: Wipf & Stock, 1970), p. 197.
3. Ferdinand Christian Baur, ed. Allan Menzies, *The Church History of the First Three Centuries*, Vol. 1 (English translation, 3rd edn; London: Williams and Norgate, 1878–1879), p. 42.
4. Albert Schweitzer, *The Quest of the Historical Jesus: A Critical Study of its Progress from Reimarus to Wrede* (English translation, 2nd edn; London: Adam & Charles Black, 1911), p. 396.
5. James H. Charlesworth (ed.), *The Old Testament Pseudepigrapha: Apocalyptic Literature and Testaments*, 2 volumes (Garden City, NY: Doubleday, 1983), Vol. 1, p. 89.
6. Charlesworth, *OT Pseudepigrapha*, Vol. 1, p. 15.
7. Charlesworth, *OT Pseudepigrapha*, Vol. 1, pp. 30–31.
8. George W. E. Nickelsburg and James C. VanderKam, *1 Enoch: A New Translation Based on the Hermeneia Commentary* (Minneapolis: Fortress Press, 2004), p. 53.
9. Charlesworth, *OT Pseudepigrapha*, Vol. 1, pp. 36–37.
10. Charlesworth, *OT Pseudepigrapha*, Vol. 1, p. 71.
11. Nickelsburg and VanderKam, *1 Enoch*, p. 159.
12. Nickelsburg and VanderKam, *1 Enoch*, p. 161.
13. Charlesworth, *OT Pseudepigrapha*, Vol. 1, pp. 24–25.
14. Louis H. Feldman (ed. and tr.), *Josephus: Jewish Antiquities: Books XVIII–XX* (Cambridge, MA: Harvard University Press, and London: Heinemann, 1969), p. 13.
15. Charlesworth, *OT Pseudepigrapha*, Vol. 1, p. 514.

16. Charlesworth, *OT Pseudepigrapha*, Vol. 1, p. 64.
17. Charlesworth, *OT Pseudepigrapha*, Vol. 1, p. 66.
18. Geza Vermes, *The Complete Dead Sea Scrolls in English* (New York: Allen Lane, Penguin Press 1997), p. 73.
19. Vermes, *Dead Sea Scrolls*, p. 261.
20. Vermes, *Dead Sea Scrolls*, p. 229.
21. Vermes, *Dead Sea Scrolls*, p. 185.
22. William Whiston (tr.), *Josephus: The Wars of the Jews* (London and New York: J. M. Dent and E. P. Dutton, 1936), p. 240.
23. *Josephus: The Life Against Apion*, tr. H. St J. Thackary (Cambridge, MA and London: Harvard University Press 1997), p. 381.
24. Vermes, *Dead Sea Scrolls*, pp. 500–502.
25. Charlesworth, *OT Pseudepigrapha*, Vol. 1, p. 268.
26. Vermes, *Dead Sea Scrolls*, p. 175.
27. Charlesworth, *OT Pseudepigrapha*, Vol. 2, pp. 339–340.
28. Charlesworth, *OT Pseudepigrapha*, Vol. 2, p. 374.
29. Charlesworth, *OT Pseudepigrapha*, Vol. 2, p. 238.
30. Charlesworth, *OT Pseudepigrapha*, Vol. 2, pp. 722–723.
31. Charlesworth, *OT Pseudepigrapha*, Vol. 1, p. 514.
32. Charlesworth, *OT Pseudepigrapha*, Vol. 2, pp. 167–170.
33. Charlesworth, *OT Pseudepigrapha*, Vol. 1, p. 791.
34. Charlesworth, *OT Pseudepigrapha*, Vol. 1, p. 44.
35. Charlesworth, *OT Pseudepigrapha*, Vol. 1, p. 638.
36. Vermes, *Dead Sea Scrolls*, p. 185.
37. Charlesworth, *OT Pseudepigrapha*, Vol. 1, p. 888.
38. Charlesworth, *OT Pseudepigrapha*, Vol. 1, pp. 889–890.
39. Charlesworth, *OT Pseudepigrapha*, Vol. 1, p. 64.
40. Charlesworth, *OT Pseudepigrapha*, Vol. 1, p. 86.
41. Charlesworth, *OT Pseudepigrapha*, Vol. 1, p. 66.
42. Charlesworth, *OT Pseudepigrapha*, Vol. 2, pp. 811–812.
43. Charlesworth, *OT Pseudepigrapha*, Vol. 2, p. 713.
44. Charlesworth, *OT Pseudepigrapha*, Vol. 1, pp. 30–31.
45. Nickelsburg and VanderKam, *1 Enoch*, pp. 93–94.
46. Charlesworth, *OT Pseudepigrapha*, Vol. 2, p. 139.
47. Charlesworth, *OT Pseudepigrapha*, Vol. 1, p. 267.
48. Nickelsburg and VanderKam, *1 Enoch*, pp. 94–95.

49 Vermes, *Dead Sea Scrolls*, p. 501.
50 Vermes, *Dead Sea Scroll*, p. 501.
51 Martinus C. de Boer (ed.), *From Jesus to John: Essays on Jesus and New Testament Christology in Honour of Marius De Jonge* (Sheffield: JSOT Press, 1993), p. 66.
52 Charlesworth, *OT Pseudepigrapha*, Vol. 1, p. 30.
53 Nickelsburg and VanderKam, *1 Enoch*, pp. 52–53.
54 Charlesworth, *OT Pseudepigrapha*, Vol. 1, p. 34.
55 Nickelsburg and VanderKam, *1 Enoch*, p. 61.
56 Charlesworth, *OT Pseudepigrapha*, Vol. 1, p. 35.
57 Nickelsburg and VanderKam, *1 Enoch*, pp. 80–81.
58 Nickelsburg and VanderKam, *1 Enoch*, p. 60.
59 Charlesworth, *OT Pseudepigrapha*, Vol. 1, p. 48.
60 Charlesworth, *OT Pseudepigrapha*, Vol. 1, p. 49.
61 Charlesworth, *OT Pseudepigrapha*, Vol. 1, p. 403.
62 Charlesworth, *OT Pseudepigrapha*, Vol. 1, p. 645.
63 Charlesworth, *OT Pseudepigrapha*, Vol. 1, pp. 630–631.
64 Vermes, *Dead Sea Scrolls*, p. 182.
65 Charlesworth, *OT Pseudepigrapha*, Vol. 1, pp. 809–810.
66 Wisdom of Solomon 2:13; 5:5.
67 Psalms of Solomon 13:9; Charlesworth, *OT Pseudepigrapha*, Vol. 2, p. 663.
68 2 Maccabees 7:34.
69 Vermes, *Dead Sea Scrolls*, pp. 576–577, 159.
70 Vermes, *Dead Sea Scrolls*, p. 392.
71 Vermes, *Dead Sea Scrolls*, p. 495.
72 Vermes, *Dead Sea Scrolls*, p. 110.
73 Jerome Murphy O'Connor, *Paul: A Critical Life* (Oxford and New York: Oxford University Press, 1996), p. 225.
74 Gospel of Peter, fragment 1, IX.35—X.42. *The Apocryphal New Testament*, ed. Montague Rhodes James (Oxford: Clarendon Press, 1924), pp. 92–93.
75 In addition to Jonah, other examples include Genesis 42:18 (Joseph's brothers released from prison on the third day); Exodus 19:16 (the Law of Moses given on the third day); Joshua 2:16 (the spies hiding for three days); 2 Kings 20:5 (the prediction of Hezekiah's going up to "the house of the Lord" on the third day).

76 *The Gospel According to Thomas: Coptic text established and translated by A. Guillaumont, H.-CH. Puech, G. Quispel, W. Till and Yassah 'abd al Masih* (Leiden: E. J. Brill and London: Collins, 1959), p. 57, lines 18–26.
77 E.g. 1 Corinthians 1:31, cf. Jeremiah 9:23–24; 1 Corinthians 10:26, cf. Psalm 24:1.
78 Nickelsburg and VanderKam, *1 Enoch*, pp. 91–92.
79 Charlesworth, *OT Pseudepigrapha*, Vol. 1, pp. 931–932.
80 Charlesworth, *OT Pseudepigrapha*, p. 37.
81 For example, Hebrews 2:17 and 1 John 2:1–2; 4:10.
82 Charlesworth, *OT Pseudepigrapha*, Vol. 1, pp. 882 ff.
83 C. F. Evans, *Resurrection and the New Testament* (London: SCM Press, 1970), p. 128.
84 Willi Marxsen, *The Resurrection of Jesus of Nazareth* (London: SCM Press, 1970).
85 Andrew Chester, *Messiah and Exaltation: Jewish Messianic and Visionary Traditions and New Testament Christology* (Tübingen: Mohr Siebeck, 2007).
86 See "Suggested Further Reading—Chapter 10".
87 Willi Marxsen, *The Resurrection of Jesus of Nazareth* (London, SCM Press, 1970) p. 188.
88 Hans Küng, *On Being a Christian* (London: Collins, 1977) p. 532.
89 Martin Kähler, *The So-called Historical Jesus and the Historic Biblical Christ*, English translation by Carl E. Braten (Philadelphia, Fortress Press 1964) p. 74.
90 John Macquarrie, *God-Talk: An Examination of the Language and Logic of Theology* (London: SCM Press, 1967).
91 Alasdair C. MacIntyre, *Whose Justice? Which Rationality?* (London: Duckworth, 1988).
92 H. Richard Niebuhr, *The Meaning of Revelation* (New York: Macmillan, 1960).

Lightning Source UK Ltd.
Milton Keynes UK
UKHW020948260221
379413UK00003B/330